Praise for Fatima Meer

"Fatima Meer is not only a witness to history but she has herself made personal contributions to this cause." – *Winnie Madikezela-Mandela*

"When we needed somewhere to stay or hide, Fatima was always first to mind. Both Madiba and I visited and used the Meer home as a hideout, both in Johannesburg and in Durban. And it was to her credit that even when there was a fallout between Madiba and I, she did not take the side of the most powerful man in the country. She remained loyal to both of us and this is an example of true friendship that is rare to find." – *Winnie Madikezela-Mandela*

"She has overcome race, class, gender and other barriers in a determined quest to contribute to the creation of a society based on social justice. The way Fatima has lived her life has served as an inspiration to a whole generation of South Africans." – *Dasarath Chetty*

"Driven by a caring and sweet spiritual temper, an instinctive capacity for moral passion, a gifted and prolific pen, and a consistent capacity to endure suffering with dignity and to turn adversity into triumph; she danced her way with a towering magnificence into our hearts and minds." – *Chief Justice I Mahomed*

"Fatima Meer is one of those rare persons who has been able to continue an extraordinary life of social and political activism with an outstanding academic career." – *Paul Maylam*

"Fatima Meer: a courageous, selfless, independent-minded scholar-activist, never afraid to speak out and always ready to act on her words." – *Paul Maylam*

"To me she was a sister, a friend and a comrade whom I have known for many years. I remember her as a courageous, forthright person who was committed to the cause." – *Ahmed Kathrada*

"She was always there for the less fortunate of our country and really one of the most amazing women I've ever met." – *Anant Singh*

"She is one of the last leaders of a generation that were so grand and strong and beautiful and principled in their day that it was almost impossible for us to imagine ourselves not consulting with them or not waiting for them to speak." – *Ashwin Desai*

"Her words, her work, her life has been as important for me as they have been for a generation of Southern Africans." – *Pumla Dineo Gqola*

"Fatima Meer was tough as she was compassionate and insistent as she was giving." – *Azad Essa*

"Not only was she a comrade, but a mother and a light for the oppressed." – *Desmond D'Sa*

"She was nothing less than iconic political royalty. Over the course of decades, Fatima Meer confronted apartheid with storied bravery: holding vigils outside brutal political prisons, organising marches of Indian and African women in defiance of protest bans; surviving assassination efforts after attempting to rally alongside Steve Biko." – *Dave Zirin*

"Fatima Meer's life was abound with good deeds." – *Dr Faisal Suliman*

"Your role in the struggles against apartheid and in the building of democracy is well documented, and should never be forgotten. On a personal note, I will never forget the support you and Ismail gave me and my family over many years." – *Nelson Mandela*

"My initial impression has since been confirmed by her sterling commitment and service to our country. As long as we have persons of her calibre, South Africa will shine." – *Nelson Mandela*

Judy David

FATIMA
MEER

Memories of
Love and Struggle

KWELA

Kwela Books,
an imprint of NB Publishers, a division of Media24 Boeke (Pty) Ltd
40 Heerengracht, Cape Town, South Africa
PO Box 879, Cape Town 8000, South Africa
www.kwela.com

Cover image: R. Bughwan and Sons, (Crown Studios) Durban
Cover design: Naadira Patel
Editor: Libby Lloyd
Proof reader: Sarah Koopman
Typography: Nazli Jacobs
Set in Minion
Printed and bound by CTP Printers, Cape Town

First published by Kwela Books 2017

ISBN: 978-0-7957- 0788-9
ISBN: 978-0-7957- 0789-6 (epub)
ISBN: 978-0-7957- 0790-2 (mobi)

When Time Leaves

When time leaves
it never returns
it takes with it
the people you have loved
and who have loved you
how sad is then the time left to you?

And so I spend that time writing
about those
whom I have loved
and who have loved me
and who are no longer here

I write about my parents
my aunts and uncles
about my husband
my son who pre-deceased me

I write
so that in the writing
they may live again
so that I may be loved
and so that I may love again

I write about my brothers and sisters
My daughters and grandchildren

Contents

SECTION 1V

Glimpses: 1970 to 2004   189

Foreword

Every time I land at Durban Airport, I am haunted by the memory of Fatima Meer – my dearest friend, sister and advisor whom I worshipped and treasured like my own possession. I have agonised for months about writing this foreword, wondering how anyone could do justice to this phenomenal woman's life. No words seem eloquent enough to describe her or capture the essence of that intellectual giant who epitomised the spirit of a totally liberated and emancipated soul.

Our relationship goes back many years to when I was a junior social work student and had just met and fallen in love with Nelson Mandela. From our first date on the 10 March 1956, Madiba spoke to me about his classmates from Wits University, Fatima and Ismail Meer. As we drove to a farm, known today as Orange Farm, he wanted to know if I would like to visit the Meers in Durban as they were newly married. I was puzzled and thought to myself what a strange man. I hardly knew him and he already took me so for granted. I sheepishly said it would be a good idea, believing that I would never go visiting strangers.

Madiba could be annoyingly persistent and he of course did send me to meet the Meers as our relationship developed. When I enquired later from him why I had to visit Fatima, he boldly told me that he wanted her to confirm whether he had "made the right choice of a woman". When I objected he just had a very good laugh.

On meeting them it soon became clear to me that the Meers were inextricably bound together ideologically. Both Fatima and Ismail were part of the core of the ANC that defied the segregationist ideology of the oppressive regime of the time that forced our organisation to be splintered into the Indian Congress, the Congress of Democrats, the Coloured People's Congress and the African Native Congress. They were very active in forming an inclusive organisation which finally gave birth to our present democracy, the African National Congress.

Fatima and I simply gravitated towards each other from when we first met. She became my friend, my sister and my confidant. She, like me, struggled within her community to be valued as an intellectual and activist – and more than just a housekeeper. Fatima was born before her time. She was passionate about human rights, she was a sociologist and a born social worker.

At times our friendship was at a great cost to her. During the 1976 uprising by school children in Soweto, the government looked to blame me. The regime knew the students could not have planned the uprising on their own as they had no money. I had assisted their leaders such as Tsietsi Mashinini and Dan Montsitsi and consulted with them almost daily. I was eventually detained in August 1976. While in detention at No 4 the Fort, which is today known as Constitutional Hill, I was horrified to learn I was joined by my dearest Fatima. Fatima and I had formed the Black Women's Federation in 1975 which was short-lived because of the brutality of the apartheid regime. Her detention with me in 1976 was partly connected to this.

Fatima was not only a loyal friend but suffered together with me the humiliating scorn of the Security Branch due to our fight against injustice and because of her loyalty to me. She made me a board member of the research institute she founded, the Institute of Black Research, when it was not fashionable to include me in any democratic formation as this attracted the attention of the vicious Security Branch. When, after my release from detention in 1977, I was banished to Brandfort, my first visitor was my friend Fatima. She bought me a load of groceries and everything one would need at camp. Fatima comforted me in that wilderness.

When Comrade Nelson Mandela was moved to Victor Verster Prison in Paarl after 1988, I received a message that he wanted to see me urgently. On that occasion he said he wanted to see Fatima to ask her to write his biography - *Higher Than Hope*. Fatima agreed, but this would have consequences for both her and me. We had to send every chapter to the ANC president in exile, Oliver Tambo (known as OR) for his approval. Fatima had followed Madiba's instructions to be brutally honest and had researched Madiba's private life and his numerous indiscretions. OR was furious and demanded that all the chapters dealing with this be expunged. Fatima and

I did just that, but she later told me she kept those pages somewhere in a vault in the bank.

Fatima and I had a mysterious bond, every time something happened to her, I would phone. My daughters would also visit for holidays. When her husband died, I phoned that very moment, knowing how she would feel. Fatima had actually never recovered from the death of her only son Rashid. She had known too much pain in her private life.

Fatima's dedication and commitment to the ANC was almost an obsession. I personally felt she deserved more recognition than she was given. But of course, ours is still a patriarchal society, in which men are more recognised than women. I hope that we will correct that situation with all our might as women. If Fatima was alive she would be contributing robustly to the current national debate about the grave problems we are faced with today such as the rumoured state capture, corruption and graft. I admired her open mind and the fact that she was a free spirit. Her biography makes fascinating reading!

Nomzamo Winnie Mandela
December 2016

Introduction

My mother started work on her autobiography in the year 2000 while putting together my father's autobiography – *A Fortunate Man*. While she read through the collection of his writings and transcribed the interviews he had recorded, her own life came into strong focus – since they shared family and political experiences. My parents were related to each other: My mother's father and my father were first cousins, and both my mother and father had been active in the liberation struggle in South Africa from the 1940s. As she reflected on my father's life, my mother began to record her own life in parallel.

My father's book was published in 2002. In August of that very year, my mother had a second stroke which changed our lives. She was paralysed on the left side, confined to a wheelchair and required 24-hour nursing care until her death in 2010. However, she did not let that deter her and she lived most of those eight years with her trademark feisty passion. The first year and a half were the most difficult as she and we adjusted – yet she journeyed to India some five months after the stroke to receive an award from India's president. She continued her engagement with the Concerned Citizens Group in Chatsworth, addressed gatherings, challenged injustice and went on marches throughout these years.

Reading and writing were made more difficult following her stroke, but in 2006 my mother resumed writing on her life, with the help of Ramesh Harcharan, who had worked with her at the Institute for Black Research, with great dedication, for two decades. She dictated her thoughts to two typists to assist with the writing process.

I first saw pages of my mother's autobiography around 2007 on one of my regular visits from Johannesburg to her home in Durban. I was charmed by the little girl who when asked by her mothers to bring three or four pieces of wood for the cooking fire, pondered on whether she should bring three or four, and then decided to bring seven, since three and four make seven! I was enchanted at her first memory of a patterned linoleum under a bed fringed with lace and moved by the strength of the young girl who, when run over by a car, did not tell her mothers for fear of their punishment. I was in awe of the schoolgirl who fundraised for flood victims and who gave her first political speech and led a march aged seventeen.

I said to my mother that there was sufficient material to publish. Even if the narrative was well developed only up to the end of the 1960s, other published autobiographies did not deal with the entire life of the person. Since Ramesh was now no longer working with her, I offered to help with revising her memories as she dictated these to me and to assist with the structure and reordering of her memories. I spent some weeks in 2007 and 2008 working with my mother. My niece Nadia spent a week reading pages to her and revising as she dictated. To help my mother to read the pages as we worked through the manuscript, we printed the text in a super-large font. By 2008, the narrative up to the 1960s was sufficiently well developed and I left this with my mother to look through and finalise.

While I felt this could be published, my mother still seemed uncertain. She agreed that I could make contact with a publisher, but she did not make any headway on finalising the script. Each time I asked she would say that Ramesh had some pages "in his computer" that he was to still to bring to her. It seemed to me she was not keen on finalising and I did not want to push her on this. Feeling her hesitation made me waver.

My mother passed away in 2010 after a final stroke that debilitated her so that she was unable to speak in the last two weeks of her life.

Many months after her death and up to October 2011, I returned to these pages and worked on them as time allowed in between my own work. I checked facts, edited, worked on family trees, a family glossary, on making the section on our ancestors more readable (the complicated family history being difficult even for a family member to get one's head around!). I stopped working on the manuscript in October 2011 as life and work intervened, and I resumed reviewing her notes in 2015.

The first part of the book recounts her family history and the arrival of the Meers in South Africa. The next two sections outline in beautiful de-tail the everyday experiences of a child growing into a young girl and into a woman within a large and mostly loving family, told against the backdrop of the political struggles of the times. The final part covers the period from the 1970s onwards and is somewhat sketchy as my mother did not write as detailed an account of these years. I have added to the fragments of her writings of this period by drawing from her book *Prison Diary One Hundred and Thirteen Days 1976* (Kwela, 2001).

Looking back, I think it was my mother's concern that her book was incomplete that led to her hesitation in finalising the manuscript. It was a concern she seemed to have felt when working on my father's auto-biography, for she writes in her introductory note to that autobiography, fitting words:

> *No biography or autobiography is a complete record. It is an abstract from the entirety, and so is this autobiography.*

This book paints a picture of my mother's life. It tells a coming-of-age story of a young girl and political activist in a significant time in our country's history and makes an important contribution to the memory of our country's collective past.

Shamim Meer
2016

I

A PART OF ME

The Family of My Birth

CHAPTER 1

India to South Africa

Ours was an unusual family – with two mothers, Ma and Amina Ma, and one father, our Papa. We were nine children, six brothers and three sisters – Ma's four (Ismail, Solly, Ahmed and Gorie) and Amina Ma's five (including me, Bhai, Siddiek, Farouk, and Razia). We children discovered that two mothers were better than one. They complemented each other.

The grandparents I knew were Ma's and Papa's parents. I never saw them, but we were told about them so often that they were in my memory – a part of me. I never knew anything at all about Amina Ma's parents or grandparents. The only person from Amina Ma's birth family I knew was her brother Cassim, and he was a floating presence, drifting in and out of our lives.

Ma and Papa were first cousins. They came from the lineage of Ahmed Asmaljee Meer, the grandfather they shared. The earliest Meer patriarch that can be traced is Ahmed Asmaljee Meer's great-grandfather Cassim Meer, who lived in the village of Garah in Gujarat in a time when the British East India Company had entrenched itself in India as a military–cum–political force.

The British imposition of taxes on farmers and produce had reduced peasants, including the Meers, to landlessness. Having lost their land and all their possessions to the local moneylender, Cassim's grandson, Asmaljee Meer (Ahmed Asmaljee Meer's father), was forced to migrate with his family from their village to the city of Surat. By 1860, Asmaljee Meer's two sons were established in Surat, eking out a living as telis (oil pressers).

It has never been explained why Asmaljee Meer named both his sons Ahmed. He differentiated between the two by adding the suffix 'jee', after the one son's name. Since 'jee' is a term of respect, one assumes that

Ahmedjee Asmaljee Meer was the elder and Ma and Papa's grandfather, Ahmed Asmaljee Meer, the younger.

Ahmed Asmaljee's first wife, Maryam Bana of Tadkeshwar (a town not far from the city of Surat), died when their son Suleiman was about seven years old. Following her death, Ahmed Asmaljee married Sarah Amin also originally from Garah. Sarah Amin was the mother of the three Meer patriarchs who would migrate to South Africa – Mohamed (Ma's father), Ismail (Papa's father) and Chota (my husband Ismail's father).

Suleiman, Ahmed Asmaljee's son from his first wife, never came to South Africa, though his son, Cassim, the father of YC Meer and MC Meer did. He became a successful businessman in Dundee and was close to his uncles. Suleiman married his first cousin, Maryam, the daughter of Ahmedjee Meer, and set up home next door to his father. It seems that Suleiman, or Halloo as he came to be known, and his new mother never got on. In fact, the hostility between the two was so intense that Sarah Amin is said to have left a testimony that her descendants should never marry in the line of Halloo Meer. Despite this, her granddaughter Ayesha and great granddaughter Zohra married grandsons of Halloo Meer – YC and MC respectively.

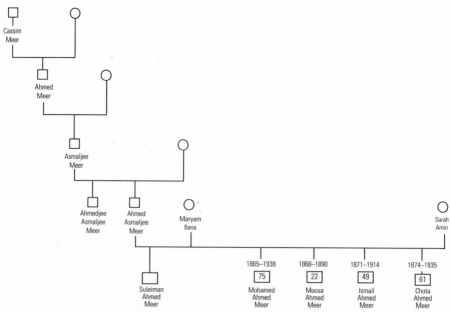

Ancestry of my grandfather (Ismail) and his brothers (Mohamed and Chota) who settled in South Africa.

Life for the Meers would have continued in a placid unambitious manner in Surat but for the Motalas who lived across the road.

Ebrahim Motala had emigrated from India and settled in the then British colony of Natal in South Africa, where he had established a lucrative business and was sending large sums of money to his elder brother in Surat, Ismail Motala. Ahmed Asmaljee Meer was influenced by Ismail Motala to send his eldest son, Mohamed, to Natal. He was further encouraged because Mohamed's uncles, Karodia and Saleh Mall, the husbands of Sarah's two sisters, were already in Natal. This was a time when the members of their community in Surat and surrounding villages were inspiring each other to migrate to Natal to improve their fortunes.

Ahmed Asmaljee Meer entrusted his son Mohamed to the care of a community member, Dawood Chuptie, who was returning to Natal, and they sailed steerage[1] on one of the ships owned by Durban-based shipping magnate Dada Abdulla[2], reaching Durban in 1882. As Ma told it, her father Mohamed was seventeen years old, the hair on his face not yet sprouted, when he arrived in Durban.

Ebrahim Motala met Mohamed at the Durban docks and took him under his care. They travelled to the town of Verulam, just north of Durban, where Ebrahim lived with his family and ran his business. Mohamed spent almost a year with the warm-hearted and helpful Motalas. Ebrahim had married a South Indian woman, the daughter of a sirdar who had come to the colony as an indentured labourer.

Ma often quoted an adage:

> *Seek a marriage partner in the family and if you can't find one there, then look in the neighbourhood, and if there is none there too, then look in the village. Heaven help you if you are forced to go beyond the village.*

Heaven, it seemed, did help Ebrahim Motala, for his wife Goriema was, by all accounts, a wonderful woman.

After spending just under a year with the Motalas, Mohamed began his journey into prosperity as a peddler– armed with a consignment of goods from Ebrahim Motala. Within a short time, he bought a horse and cart and set up his own little shop. Not long after that Mohamed went into partnership with Dada Abdulla, and together they expanded into the wholesale market, branching out to Johannesburg.

Their partnership ended, however, over the issue of canned beef. There was an excellent market for canned beef during the Anglo-Boer War but Mohamed refused to deal in haram meat and withdrew from the partnership. He folded up his business interests in Durban and Johannesburg and moved to Dundee where he opened a shop on the main street, McKenzie Street.

His business prospered, and he soon scouted the surrounding country on horseback to identify additional business spots. The justice of peace of the district, a Mr L. de Jager, had a massive farm in Waschbank – almost eighteen kilometres of the railway line from Glencoe ran through it. The region was rich in coal and thousands of indentured Indians worked in the nearby collieries in Burnside and Wesselsnek. There was no store to serve this vast population which had cash in hand. Mohamed leased land from De Jager, built a shop out of wood and iron in Waschbank, stocked it with groceries, and placed his maternal cousin, Ahmed Karodia, in charge as manager. The store came to be known as *Amos*, and it proved to be as lucrative as Mohamed had estimated.

In the late 1880s, De Jager cut up his farm and put up plots for sale. Mohamed Meer and Hajee Ebrahim Khan purchased the two highest priced plots at £200 each. These were record prices paid for land in the Colony, higher than prices of prime land even in Durban, but Meer and Khan knew what they were doing. New mines were being opened all the time and the cash-earning population exploded all around them. Their shops consequently became rich mines in themselves, and Mohamed sent handsome money orders to his parents in Surat.

Mohamed Meer is remembered as a softly spoken gentleman who dressed meticulously. He wore a woollen achkan (long coat) over a long silk shirt, fastened alternately with gold and diamond buttons arranged on a gold chain. His shoes in soft leather were Indian in style. He wore a red fez around which he wound a Kashmiri shawl to form a turban. Mohamed was reported to be fair of complexion, handsome and dignified, commanding enormous respect. He participated fully in the social, religious and political aspects of the community and was instrumental in building the Dundee Mosque and overseeing its typically Indian architecture.

By the time of Mahatma Gandhi's arrival in Natal in 1893, Mohamed was already a well-established businessman in Dundee. Gandhi relied on him to build up a membership for the Natal Indian Congress (NIC) in Northern Natal, and to report to him cases of maltreatment of Indian mineworkers. In a letter to his lifelong friend and confidant Herman Kallenbach, Gandhi makes mention of Mohamed Meer's assistance at the time of the 1913 strike of indentured mineworkers:

> *30 October 1913*
> *MY DEAR LOWER HOUSE*
> *I sent you a full message from Ingogo which I hope you received. Mr Mahomed Meer is at Waschbank. He has the 'phone. It was he who gave the information about the Ramsay Collieries assault. Please inquire further. You know that I telegraphed to the Protector at Durban and the Interior. You may now inquire further through Meer and if there (be) any workers send one to make local investigation.*
> *MK GANDHI*[3]

Mohamed's brother Moosa left India and joined him in Natal for a time. He was followed by his brother Ismail (my paternal grandfather) who arrived in 1890 to manage a second shop Mohamed had opened in the Talana area of Dundee. The following year Mohamed's youngest brother, Chota (my husband Ismail's father), arrived and was placed under the tutelage of the manager of Mohamed's Waschbank shop.

It is reported that Moosa arrived with a pair of fine bulls, which the brothers presented to the government in Pretoria. It is a family legend that the bulls, used for breeding, were classified genus Meer, but we have never found any evidence of this. Whatever Moosa's plans for his future, these were prematurely terminated when he drowned in a shipwreck off the coast of Mauritius while on his way back to India.

Mohamed made several trips to Surat and during one of these, in 1894, aged 29, he married Fatima Amin, from his mother's family in Garah. His brother, Ismail, aged 23, married Khatija Variawa, a granddaughter of Ahmedjee Asmaljee Meer.

Soon after their marriages the brothers returned to Natal. Their wives joined them later with their infant sons, born within months of each other, both named Moosa after their shipwrecked uncle. Fatima settled in Dundee with Mohamed. Khatija settled in Talana with Ismail.

*The shop in Waschbank that was established by
Mohamed and Chota Meer in 1893.*

Once his brother Chota had learnt the business, Mohamed went into partnership with him in the Waschbank shop on a 60/40 basis. Chota proved to be an able businessman. In 1893, two years after his arrival, they built a new shop on the same site – the largest in the area – under the name of *CA Meer*. The businesses flourished and the two brothers prospered.

My father's father, Ismail, however, was not suited to shop-keeping. He was miserable in the shop in Talana and soon abandoned it to move in with his brother Chota in Waschbank. He had a literary mind, a characteristic that would be evident in both his sons, my father Moosa and my uncle Ahmed. My grandfather was noted for his oratory skills, and it is said of him that he was the most concerned of all three brothers about the education of his children.

Chota returned to Surat only once – to marry Rasool Naroth originally from the village of Kohar. She was the daughter of Nawlakie Naroth, so named because it was believed that he had found a fortune of nine lakh rupees (nine hundred thousand) while digging on his land – nine being naw in Gujarati. They had seven children, all born in Waschbank. The youngest was Ismail Meer, my husband.

Mohamed had six children, three of whom, Khatija (my mother Ma), Ahmed and Essop, were born in Dundee. His two younger daughters, Amina and Ansoo, were born in Surat. Ismail had three children – Moosa, my father, born in Surat in 1897, and Fatima and Ahmed born in Talana in Natal. My grandmother, Khatija, was of failing health and returned to Surat. My grandfather, Ismail, made several trips to India to be with her, and Moosa and his brother Ahmed moved between Natal and Surat as children, while Fatima remained with her mother.

In 1906 at the age of 41, Mohamed decided to retire from active business. He felt the need to return to Surat so that his young children could be imbued with the culture and education of their motherland. So Ma and her siblings returned with their parents to India.

Mohamed sold a part of his Waschbank business for £25 000 to his brother Chota. In terms of the arrangement between the two brothers, Chota sent Mohamed a thousand pounds a year as his share of the profit. This amicable arrangement ended when distrust set in. Chota was influenced by his elder sons who began to resent having to send large profits to a sleeping partner. Mohamed was influenced by his elder sons, who questioned whether he was being sent his fair share of the profits.

In 1922, Mohamed returned to Waschbank to dissolve the partnership with his brother. Amid tense meetings, mediated by their respective advisors (their maternal cousins, the Amins and the Karodias), a bitter settlement was reached. Chota Meer bought over Mohamed Meer's interest in the business for £10 800. Of this, £6 000 was paid in cash and the balance paid in monthly bills of £100.

In Surat, Mohamed purchased a princely estate – *Raja Wadi* – part of the local Raja's estate. He pulled down the purana bangla (old bungalow) that had stood on it and replaced it with a palatial residence that cost 39 000 rupees – a fortune in those days – thereby changing the family's lifestyle.

Mohamed encouraged his sons to go to Burma (now Myanmar) and they set up businesses there. These businesses, however, did not prosper and within two years his youngest son, Essop, returned to Surat. Moosa, the eldest, however, remained and married a young Burmese woman, despite the fact that he had a wife and several children in Surat. Moosa's

Raja Wadi – the palatial residence built by Mohamed Meer in Surat.

descendants through his second wife continue to live in Burma, so there are Burmese Meers with whom we South African Meers have no contact.

Mohamed's wife, Fatima Amin, died in 1921, at the age of 52. He never remarried. He cared for his children personally, building close bonds with them. At the time of Fatima's death, Moosa, the eldest, was 23 years old and the youngest, Ansoo, was six. Fatima had lived to see the marriage of only her eldest son, Moosa.

Mohamed Meer died in Surat in 1938 at the age of 73 when I was about ten years old. I recall my mother's grief when she learnt of her father's death. It was my first experience of death and the grief death evokes. Ma's heart had hankered for her father and for her childhood. We knew her father and her Surat home, *Raja Wadi*, from the stories she told us. Ever since her return to South Africa as a young married woman, she had hoped to visit her father, but she had never returned to Surat.

Chota Meer's businesses were hit hard by the depression and by 1930 he was forced to sell. His two eldest sons had left the failing business some time before and his daughters were by then married and living in their marital homes. It was their youngest child, twelve-year-old Ismail, who was left with his parents, trying to make ends meet. As Ismail, who was to become my husband, related, he was born a prince but he left Waschbank a pauper.

The family's last possession was a rooster and Ismail took the fowl from house to house to try fruitlessly to sell it. He took a job in the shop previously owned by his father, but left this to work in a bakery in Waschbank so he could be closer to his parents. Until the day in 1931 when his brother AC arrived to take Ismail and his parents to live with him in Durban. AC was living with his in-laws and had started a cut-make-and-trim shirt-making home 'factory'. He wanted Ismail to help in the business, sewing button holes, and so Ismail and his parents moved to Durban.

Chota Meer and his two youngest children – Ismail and Ayesha.

Chota Meer died in Durban around 1935, aged around 61 years old. I have dim recollections of visiting AC's flat in Pine Street as a child. Chota Meer comes to view the clearest, lying on his bed, parting the segments of a peeled orange and giving this to me with a mischievous look in his eyes. Ismail treasured this image of his father when I recalled it during our marriage.

CHAPTER 2

My Parents

My father's greatest admirer was his younger brother Ahmed. Ahmed's adoration of his big brother is quite clear from his testimony about their early life together. Growing up, I was witness to the wonderful bond that existed between the brothers. Ahmed (who I called Gora Papa) related some of their early experiences to me after my father's death and it is from his handwritten record that I draw this picture of my father's early life.

My father, Moosa Meer, was born in Surat in 1897 at a time when the citizens of the town were returning to their homes after having been evacuated due to an outbreak of plague. His birth date was considered auspicious because it coincided with the day water came through the city taps for the first time. My father's father, Ismail Meer, was in Natal at the time of my father's birth and my grandmother, Khatija, joined him in Natal when my father was an infant. Since she was of failing health, my grandmother returned to Surat, and my father and his younger brother Ahmed spent their early years moving between their father in Natal and their mother in Surat.

As children in Surat, Moosa and Ahmed played cricket, soccer and participated in jujitsu and wrestling. My father was a very good wrestler and accepted challenges from professionals, at times even beating them. Ahmed boasted that his big brother could take on five men at a time. He also boasted that my father was a champion kite flyer. Once a year there was an annual kite festival in Surat. Competing teams of kite flyers vied to bring the others' kites down. My father's kite was never brought down. Ahmed recalled one competition in which my father's team emerged victorious, rousing the anger of a vanquished team, whose members tried to rough his brother up. They were real toughies but my father had them running.

My father often talked about his enjoyment of the tranquil life on the banks of the river Tapti that flowed through Surat. He reminisced about watching the fishermen, each with a bamboo across his shoulder, with baskets at either end of the bamboo in which the fish were carried.

Around 1909, when my father was about twelve years old, my grand-mother Khatija died in Surat. A few months before her death, my grand-father and my father had both left Surat for South Africa. While in South Africa they received word that my grandmother was very ill. They im-mediately left for India by boat. From Bombay, father and son took the train, arriving at their house in Surat at midnight. My grandfather told my father to call out to his mother – it would surprise her and make her very happy he said, since he was her favourite. But it was my father's grandmother who came to the door to inform them of his mother's death. She had passed away when they were midway on their journey, on the first day of Ramadan.

This event remained firmly marked in the memory of both my father and Ahmed. The young Ahmed said he never felt as alone in his life as when his mother died in the absence of his father and elder brother.

A few months after his mother's death, my father left again for Natal in the company of family friends while my grandfather and Ahmed re-mained in Surat. In Durban my father lived with a family friend, AC An-galia, and was enrolled at school but a few months later, at age thirteen, he left school to take up work as a shop assistant in Pietermaritzburg.

From Pietermaritzburg, my father moved to Thornhill Junction at the invitation of a shopkeeper known only as Vanker in Ahmed's testament. He was paid £3 a month to assist in the shop. According to Ahmed, my father was happy at Thornhill Junction. He worked there for about eight months, leaving to join his maternal uncle Ahmed Mohamed Variawa in one of his shops in Kimberley. My father spent somewhere between one to two years in Kimberley. Ahmed Mohamed Variawa, a remarkable per-sonality, was something of a leading figure in Indian politics and sport, and he had a positive influence on my father.

For a short while in early 1914, my father, grandfather and Ahmed moved to Winters Rush, an area in the Barclay West district of the Cape inhabited by Afrikaner diamond diggers. They subsequently returned to

Waschbank and later that year (in July 1914) my grandfather died, leaving twelve-year-old Ahmed in the care of their Uncle Chota Meer.

My father, seventeen years old at the time, started working in Chota Meer's shop. He worked there for a number of years under harsh conditions, thirteen hours a day – from 6 am to 7 pm – seven days a week. He did all the manual work and, even though he had only passed standard two at school, he was able to keep the books, and tutor his cousins and young brother. One of his duties was to read the English language newspaper, the *Natal Witness*, to his Uncle Chota Meer each morning as his uncle could not read English. My father, though, angered his uncle since he not only read the news but also analysed it. Chota Meer did not tolerate anyone else's views and he ordered Moosa to read only the news to do with business and prices.

Chota Meer had a short temper and my father was often the butt of it. They clashed over many things. When the First World War broke out, my father applied to be enlisted in the Turkish army to liberate the caliphate held captive by the British. His letter of application fell in the hands of his uncle who forbade him from pursuing such nonsense.

My father was unhappy in this restricted environment but was particularly concerned that Ahmed was growing up without any education. He decided to leave his uncle's home and he asked Ahmed to go with him and be educated. Ahmed enthusiastically opted to accompany my father, but wanted to say goodbye to his Uncle Chota Meer and to fetch his clothes. My father told him that the train was leaving for Dundee in an hour and there was no time so they boarded the train and arrived at the house of another uncle, Cassim Meer (the son of Suleiman, the only Meer brother who remained in Surat). My father enrolled Ahmed at the only school in Dundee, a Coloured school which went up to standard six. Ahmed continued at this school to standard six, while my father worked.

In 1916 my father found employment at the *AM Kharwa & Son Car Wash* in Ladysmith at a salary of £60 per annum. Working conditions were less restrictive than at Waschbank. My father had weekends off, his daily routine was much shorter, and he and Ahmed were able to spend more time together. They played soccer and cricket, and once a month they went to the cinema – my father apparently knew all about the films. During this time my father developed his love of books and reading and

he started building a library of books, ordering them by mail – his favourite authors being Charles Dickens, Walter Scott, Victor Hugo and
Alexander Dumas.

Around 1921 my father, then 24 years old, went back to Surat to marry
his Uncle Mohamed's thirteen-year-old daughter Khatija. Their first child,
Ismail, was born in Surat in 1922. My father spent some three years in
Surat as a gentleman journalist. He enjoyed the company of Monadi, the
editor of the *Muslim Gujarat,* and he wrote a few columns for him, so
discovering his talent in journalism. To Monadi, my father was an intellectual and to young Ahmed he was a physical giant – in different ways
quite a romantic hero to each of them.

Mohamed Meer, a keen businessman, whose business sense had taken
him from a peasant to a nawaab (prince), decided that my father, his new
son-in-law, should either join his businesses in Burma or return to South
Africa. My father chose the latter. So, bidding goodbye to his young wife
whom he loved very much and his young son, the apple of his eye, he set
off for South Africa to join his maternal uncle, Ahmed Mohamed Variawa, in Kimberley. His wife and son were to join him once he had established himself. His younger brother, Ahmed, already living and working
with the Variawas had sent good reports of life there.

Khatija (our mother, Ma) described *Raja Wadi*, the palatial home her father had built in Surat, and the joys of her childhood to me:
   "The bungalow is large, double storey, with porticoes embellished with
flowers and leaves etched in gold. There are palm trees and fruit trees-
bor, custard apple and annoos. On Eid day, swings were tied on their
branches and we would paddle through the wind to reach the sky, and
when the vendors came, we ran to Utawala Pir's shrine and spent our Eid
money on ice cream and sweets. In the afternoons when the sun was low
and no longer beating on our heads, our coach would draw up at the entrance of our bungalow and we would go riding into the city."
   Oh how many tales Ma wove.
   About Fatima Chachee, who came to teach them to embroider in gold
thread. About the jewellers summoned by her father to fashion jewellery

of their choice and how he would weigh the jewellery on completion to ensure that the gold was intact. About how her eldest brother had sat sobbing at the foot of the stairway on his wedding night because of his disappointment with his bride (they subsequently had five children) and about cream so thick that one could lift it up. About green wheat or ponk, and neera – the juice tapped from palm trees in the early morning before it fermented into toddy.

While we grew up on stories of Surat and *Raja Wadi* and of Ma's early years, my mother, Amina Ma was a mystery in the Meer clan. Amina Ma never talked about her parents and siblings. It was as if she had no family. She just was.

All the other elders in the clan in which I grew up had parents and brothers and sisters. They were all rooted in the past. Amina Ma appeared to have nothing and perhaps I rejected her because I did not want to have nothing.

Had I known Amina Ma's life prior to her marriage, I may well have had a closer, more positive relationship with her, but I did not know that life. It remained a family secret to me until after she died. The only person I knew from that life was her brother Lionel, who came to be known as Cassim, and who, after my mother died, sketched out the bare bones about her life. I tell what I remember from his account.

Amina Ma was of European descent. She was born in Kimberley in 1912 to Hannah Farrel, the eldest daughter of Charlie Farrel and Amelia van Vollenhoven. She was named Rachael Farrel.

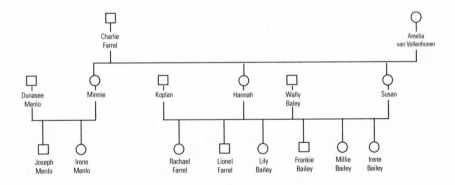

The family tree of my mother, Amina Ma, born Rachael Farrel in 1912.

Charlie Farrel was originally a farmer who emigrated from Longford in Ireland to the United States of America and from there to South Africa. He had a sister (whose name is not known to me) and a brother, John Farrel. Amelia Van Vollenhoven's family had emigrated from Holland and settled in the Cape.

Amina Ma's father is known to us only as Koplan, a Russian Jew who was a tailor by profession. Koplan probably promised Hannah marriage but kept procrastinating. She bore him two children – Rachael and Lionel. Hannah apparently eventually discovered that Koplan was already married and had another family in Russia. She then left him and married Wally Bailey. Bailey was at the time working for Ahmed Mohamed Variawa, my father's maternal uncle, in the small town of Douglas near Kimberley. He and Hannah set up home next to the Variawas in a semi-detached cottage, where Hannah bore Bailey a daughter, Lily.

In 1918, when Rachael was about six years old, and Lionel about three, Hannah died in the influenza epidemic. After Hannah's death, Wally Bailey married Hannah's sister, Susan, and she bore him three children – Irene, Millie and Frankie.

Bailey was prepared to accept Rachael but was not interested in Lionel – partly because Lionel had inherited his biological father's dark looks.

Rachael with her mother, Hannah, and stepfather, Bailey.

Rachael (the tallest) and Lionel (second from left) with cousins.

Bailey would tell Lionel to keep out of sight when the family had visitors. Lionel was later palmed off to their grandparents, the Farrels, who lived at 4 Ross Street, Kimberley, in very poor circumstances. Later, two more grandchildren, Amelia and Joseph, came to live with the Farrels. These were the children of the Farrels third daughter Minnie, who died in 1922.

Rachael was unhappy with her aunt Susan and her stepfather Bailey who beat her. She wrote to Granny Farrel asking to be taken into her home, but Granny Farrel, not wanting to upset Bailey, was reluctant to take her in.

In 1926, when Rachael was about fourteen, my father Moosa Meer entered her life. He had returned to South Africa to work in his maternal uncle's shop where he was placed as shop assistant under the management of Bailey. My father soon learnt about Rachael and how miserable she was. When she came to the shop he saw how petrified she was of Bailey.

Perhaps Rachael confided in my father and soon the two became drawn to each other. Practically all the adults in Rachael's life had rejected her – her father Koplan, her aunt/stepmother Susan, her stepfather Bailey and Granny Farrel. Rachael perhaps saw in my father a kindly person, offering to protect her. My father was outraged by Rachael's plight and decided to rescue her and her eleven-year-old brother Lionel.

Bailey discovered the growing relationship between Rachael and my father. He was incensed, and as my father's boss, he reported the affair to Ahmed Mohammed Variawa and prevailed on him to dismiss my father. Bailey sent Rachael off to her grandparents, the Farrels, in Kimberley.

One may conjecture that my father used all his powers of persuasion to win over the Farrels, and that they, in their overburdened poverty, saw a solution in my father's offer to take over the two children – Rachael and Lionel. So it was with their grandparents' agreement that my father left Kimberley with Rachael and Lionel at 4 am one morning by taxi for the nearby town of Christiana.

The local white community was enraged when they discovered the children missing, and the local church deacon, a Mr Basson, intervened. The police set out to rescue the children, but failed to find them. The story circulated that Charlie Farrel had sold Rachael for a Scotch cart.

My father took Rachael and Lionel to the home of a Muslim family in Christiana. From there they took a train to Leslie, a small town on the outskirts of Johannesburg. It was probably here in Leslie that Rachael was converted to Islam, given the name Amina, and my parents were married by Muslim rites. For a while Lionel and Amina lived with my father's friends in Leslie.

My father went to Waschbank to seek the assistance of his cousin AC, the son of his uncle Chota Meer. AC arranged with a friend, Ismail Master, to fetch Amina and Lionel from Leslie and he prevailed upon his father to accept Amina into the family. Chota Meer made clear that my father had to bring his wife, Khatija, and his son, Ismail, from Surat and commit to caring for both his wives equally. Khatija –

My mother Rachael Farrel and my father Moosa Meer.

Ma was informed in Surat that her husband had taken another wife. My father wrote to her and asked her to join him. Her family advised her against doing so, but Ma, as she was to tell me many, many years later, told her family that she loved my father and that her place was with him. She immediately left for Natal with her five-year-old son Ismail.

For a time, my father and two mothers lived in Waschbank. Ma told me that Chota Ba (as she referred to Chota Meer) took them in on her account. She was Mohamed Meer's daughter. Mohamed was not only Chota's elder brother but also his former business partner.

And so it was in Waschbank that Rachael's Indianisation began. There is a photograph of the young Rachael, in a plaid skirt and white blouse. But in Waschbank, under Chota Ba's severe authority, her plaid skirt disappeared and she was put into trousers, long dress and head scarf like Ma and Ma's cousins, the daughters and daughters-in-law of Chota Ba.

Rachael was a quick learner and her transformation to Amina appears to have been rapid. She was soon indistinguishable from Ma and the other aunts in my clan in her Indianness. She spoke Gujarati exactly like the

My mothers Amina Ma and Ma in Waschbank.
Left to right: Chota Meer's daughters-in-law, Gori Ba and Gori Apa,
Chota Meer's daughter Badi Motala, Ma, Amina Ma and Chota Meer's daughter
Ayesha who we called Choti Khala.

others did. Amina struck roots in the Meer family. She was integrated into the Meer clan and nobody asked any questions. It was sufficient that Chota Meer had accepted her. She related as sister-in-law to every one of my father's generation and was respected by all as their own.

My father sent Lionel to work for his relatives, the Malls, in Howick. However, Lionel found conditions so miserable that he wrote to my father that he would commit suicide if he were not rescued. My father then asked his cousin Cassim Meer of Dundee to take Lionel on. Cassim Meer took Lionel in and it was around this time that Lionel converted to Islam and was named Cassim.

My father, unemployed with dependants, and an uncle whose displeasure he could sense, was offered a job as editor of the weekly English-Gujarati newspaper *Indian Views* by the owner, Ebrahim Jeewa. He left for Durban and found accommodation at 137 Grey Street close to the newspaper's offices and printing press.

The Jeewas had immigrated to Natal from the same neighbourhood as the Meers in Surat, and had bought the newspaper and printing press from its founder MC Angalia in the 1920s. My father had by then established a reputation as something of a writer both in English and Gujarati, having written for a newspaper in Surat. Although he had to this point in his life earned a living as a shop assistant, he now found his vocation in *Indian Views*. In 1927 my father became the manager of the Indian Views and by 1934 he became the proprietor of both the press and the paper, and its highly regarded editor.

When my father arrived in Durban, the police caught up with him. A charge was laid against him for kidnapping Rachael and Lionel, but due to the intervention of A.I. Kajee and Sorabjee Rustomjee, the case was dropped. My father had by then achieved sufficient status to be patronised by these leaders of the premier Indian political organisation, the Natal Indian Congress.

My father sent for his family from Waschbank and they began their life together in the home of my earliest memories. Papa, Ma, Amina Ma and my brother Ismail were soon joined by two additions to the family: I was born to Amina Ma on 12 August 1928 and a few months later Solly was born to Ma. I was a pleasant, healthy baby. Solly was sickly, and forever crying. Ma did not have sufficient milk for him so Amina Ma breastfed both Solly and me.

Amina Ma at fifteen was perhaps not yet ready to be a mother, perhaps not even really a wife yet, since Ma was the dominant wife, and she an intrusion. Amina Ma, younger than Ma by four years, did most of the household chores. She was probably accustomed to hard work, and to being ordered about.

One can but conjecture that she was vulnerable to exploitation since early childhood. Ma, on the other hand, had been brought up in relative luxury by her father. She had done very little work, and was used to being waited on. But this is speculation on my part – to place myself in the vortex of my clan and to understand my relationship with my mothers.

II

BLUER THAN THE BLUE SKY

My Childhood

CHAPTER 3

Jeewa's Building: 1928–1931

My early childhood sweeps through a number of houses. My earliest memories are of our flat in Jeewa's Building at 137 Grey Street[4] where my consciousness of self began. My first recollection of physical space is not of a house but of a floor, lino-covered in green with red roses under a bed screened off from the room by the crocheted edge of a quilt.

Jeewa's building still stands today, little changed, thanks to the 1950 Groups Areas Act which froze all development for three decades in Durban's Indian business area. There are shops on the ground floor and residences on the upper floor along a passage protected by a black cast iron railing.

One entered the residences through a large quadrangle and up a flight of steps. Our flat comprised of a small covered courtyard, at the entrance of which was the kitchen, the washroom and toilet. The entrance led to a front reception room and two bedrooms. All the rooms led to a wrap-around veranda which overlooked Victoria Street, named for the Empress of the British Empire, Grey Street, named after one of Her Majesty's colonial governors, and Queen Street[5]. The British royal family thus encircled our quarters, but we remained oblivious of that family.

We lived in this accommodation for a number of years – our unusual family with two mothers, Ma and Amina Ma, and one father, our Papa.

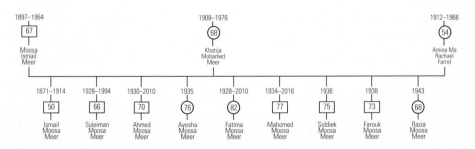

My family: Our Papa Moosa, our two mothers Khatija (Ma) and Amina Ma and their nine children.

In my earliest memories there were my three brothers (Ismail, Solly, Ahmed) and myself. Ultimately there would be nine children – six brothers and three sisters. Ma's Ismail, Solly, Ahmed and Gorie and Amina Ma's which included me, Mahomed, Siddiek, Farouk and Razia. My family called me "Behn" meaning sister.

As the years went by and the children multiplied, Ma and Amina Ma grew very close. Ma organised the household, which included extended family members – our aunts, uncles and their children. She also sewed all the clothes for the family. Amina Ma did most of the daily household chores and attended to the raising of the babies. Our mothers never went out onto the street, never walked on the pavements or crossed the road. If they stepped out of the flat and went down the stairway, it was into an enclosed rickshaw. My brother Ismail, six years older than me, did the small shopping, our father the big. Most of the shopping was small and so Ismail did the bulk of it, purchasing lentils and the small quantities of meat almost daily from the grocer and butcher downstairs. He was also sent on errands to my father at his work at the printing press across the road in Grey Street.

My early images are of Amina Ma forever punishing me and Ma and Papa rescuing me from her anger. While most times I did not know why I was being punished, the first time Amina Ma raised her hand on me I knew exactly why.

My two younger brothers – Solly, a few months younger than me, and Ahmed, two years younger – had been newly bathed, powdered, fed and left in their pram outside the kitchen door. I found the wheels and the anticipation of mobility too tempting to resist. I reached out to the handles and began pushing the pram. I had almost reached the landing when I was stopped by Amina Ma's angry voice and soon she was upon me, snatching the handles from my hands and slapping me. I was crying, fully aware of my misconduct and overcome by the sense of the imminent danger my mother had stopped. I had learnt my lesson and knew that my punishment was fully deserved.

Our mothers were very good disciples of the dictum 'spare the rod and spoil the child'. The rod though came down all that harder on Ismail who often got slapped and cuffed. I think our mothers had the impression he was already spoiling. When Solly and I were about two and Ahmed not yet one, Ismail, then about eight, had made a castle of matchsticks and set it ablaze in a darkened room for our entertainment. His fingers were smacked. "Can't you see how dangerous that is? You could have set the house alight!"

I remember, Ismail as a very good older brother. He went to school close by. I think it was the Surat Hindu School. On special school days he took me with him and I felt his pride in me.

The ultimate authority in our home was Papa. He was always just and fair, rarely punishing us – either physically or with words. We loved him unreservedly. I was safe with Papa. When he returned from work, he rested in bed on the veranda and I cuddled up next to him. Probably all three of us did, but I recall just myself. It was Papa and I as we lay on that double bed on the veranda in Victoria Street, with its bustle intruding into our privacy. At night the aroma of freshly cooking food from a mobile café parked below our

Ma, Papa and Amina Ma.

balcony tantalised our taste buds. Papa would tell me many things about the world we lived in, in the form of stories.

I never heard or saw Papa raise his voice or his hand to any one of us children. We thought the world of him and we believed everything he said. We regarded him as the dearest man in the world, and a veritable genius. I was indifferent to my mothers, but my father was as God and the thought of his disapproval and disappointment numbed me into a silence from which I could not be withdrawn.

Consciously, I always saw Ma as my mother. I was Ma's baby. When I could talk, I reacted with great hurt and anger when the odd person would ask Ma, "Is this your daughter or Amina's?" Ma would be obliged to admit I was Amina's daughter. I recall clearly even today, some 79 years later, that on one occasion I screamed and ran out of the room because Ma had said I was Amina's.

Ma indulged me. She took me everywhere with her. She developed an image of me that I took on. "Our Behn will not eat dhall and rice and she won't eat fish," she declared. So I did not eat these foods and when they were cooked she would produce something special for me.

Ma was most attentive to all my moods. She somehow knew when I had bad nightmares just after sehri during Ramadan (the meal before dawn during the fast). Going back to bed immediately after eating a full meal brought the nightmares on and I would feel as if somebody was throttling me. I would try to call out, but there would be no voice. Ma would come running to me, awaken me and put me out of my nightmarish misery. As far as Ma was concerned, I could do no wrong and if anyone dared say anything against me, she would shout them out of order. It was Ma who would save me from Amina Ma's beatings. "Are you gone mad?" she would say and take me into her arms and console me and still my sobbing.

My first great thrill came when my uncles AC (Ma and Papa's cousin) and Cas (Amina Ma's brother) presented me with two dolls, one dressed in pink, the other in blue. They had collected coupons from tea packets and got the dolls in exchange. I had not seen such beautiful dolls before.

My friend, Fatima Jeewa, came to see the dolls and she enticed me to take them for a 'walk', which we did while my mothers' backs were turned. We went down the forbidden stairs and out of the entrance, and then our courage failed us. We stopped in the foyer of the first shop, sat down on the floor, and began playing with the dolls. But one doll was dropped, cracking its china face. Fatima was scared and ready to run. She wanted no part of the broken doll, but my crying stopped her. She couldn't very well leave me in the foyer, and she did not know whether I would find my way home. She did the decent thing, helped me with the doll and left me at our flat door. There her courage failed and she fled to her home no doubt pretending all innocence for it was she who had dropped the doll.

My mother found me weeping with a cracked doll in my hand. She retrieved the doll and began shaking me at which I cried all the louder. My uncles rushed in and rescued and consoled me. They took my doll and stuck its face together. But she was no longer as pretty as before and I did not care to play with her.

Random fleeting images remain of that time and that flat. A white man lying flat on his back in our courtyard "dead drunk and disgraceful" as our mothers observed and children taunted him. I did not know what it was, but there it was, my first sight of a flying machine, zooming in the sky as I watched transfixed from the landing of our stairway. I saw my first movie – a soundless Mickey Mouse movie – at the Kharwas who lived in a building adjoining ours. I sat in silent awe as the pictures moved on the small screen, and accepted the half banana that our host provided as our interval fare.

I remember our move from the flat. One night – I must have been around three years old – I suddenly found myself standing in an empty kitchen, the fire still flickering in the stove, but the house empty, and suddenly it dawned on me that I was alone, that they had all gone and left me. I became gripped with fear and then convulsed with loud sobbing at my fate. Our neighbour, Ahmed Jeewa, rescued me. "Aw! Bibi! Bibi! Bibi!" he consoled me as he picked me up. I buried my face in his shoulder and believed at that moment that I would never let him go. He delivered me to my family in the car which was all packed and ready to leave for our new house.

We were leaving for faraway Wentworth, some fifteen kilometres from Victoria Street. People did not live beyond a few yards from their work-place. Not our kind of people – Gujaratis both Hindu and Muslim. They were shopkeepers or shop assistants. Now my father, who was neither shopkeeper nor shop assistant, though he had been promoted from the latter, was editor and proprietor of a newspaper and as exceptional as that was, he was also exceptional in moving out of town.

CHAPTER 4

Wentworth Days: 1931–1932

Each Wentworth day was adventurous, some more so than others and it is the latter that I remember.

The sum total of our family when we moved to Wentworth was my father, my two mothers, my three brothers and I, my uncle AC (Ma and Papa's cousin, the son of their Uncle Chota Meer) and his family and my uncle Cas (Amina Ma's brother). Uncle AC though soon left with his wife, Gorie Ba, and his son, Haroon, to establish his own household in Pine Street[6] in Durban. From time to time family members from Dundee, Waschbank and Kimberley, would join our household.

My early recollections of Wentworth are hazy. In my mind's eye I can locate three bedrooms, a sitting room, a kitchen, and washroom with a tap and a crude outlet for water. A veranda led to the house and to the shop adjoining the house. Papa had rented the house and shop. My mother Amina Ma was going to be the shopkeeper, her brother, Cas, and when possible my Uncle AC would also help. The idea of a shop was exciting to us children. We identified it with sweets, but there was very little of that delicacy, or any delicacy for that matter, in our shop.

I became conscious of trees and birds in Wentworth. Grey Street had been all concrete, not a tree or flower in sight. Now I awakened each morning to the sound of birds. I would lie in bed looking out of the window to see the birds flying and twittering about in the branches. In my imagination they had human experiences, forever preparing for weddings, parties, or for school or work.

Papa would help embellish my fantasies, but Amina Ma would snatch me out of such musings. 'Brush your teeth and wash your face!' was her morning call, as she readied me for my first madressa lessons and the lift I had to take with Papa. We were each given a bowl of warm water. We brushed our teeth with our fingers, with powder ground from embers collected from the grate. Amina Ma then settled us down with bowls of porridge and coffee and bread.

Every morning when Papa went to the printing press, he took me with him and dropped me off at the madressa in Clairwood. He had a car and a driver, a man called Billah. After work Papa lay in bed reading and writing. Sometimes he pottered about the house and made medicines. I thought of him as a genius inventor.

Amina Ma and Ma.

Amina Ma was nineteen or twenty years old at that time, and judging by her photographs, very pretty. But I did not think of her in those terms. I only thought of her in terms of her authority and the fire of that authority. Amina Ma made very cautious purchases for the shop from a man who openly admired her, but she barely gave him a look beyond ordering and paying for her purchases. As part of his attention-seeking, he gave us children a sweetie now and again.

Her brother, my Uncle Cas, the only family of Amina Ma we knew, loved me very much and he paid me special attention. Uncle Cas made no secret of the fact that I was his favourite child.

While living in Wentworth Uncle Cas married Baby Idries. Amina Ma seemed upset about this. Perhaps she felt that he ought to have consulted her and included her in his marriage arrangements since she was his older sister. He took me to see Aunty Baby and while I was eager to go meet this new aunty, Amina Ma wasn't at all pleased that I went with him.

Once Uncle Cas took me for a holiday to his house in Clairwood. I enjoyed myself there. We would get up in the morning and feed the fowls. He seemed to have hundreds of them. Aunty Baby was a very good dressmaker. She took me to a very special hairdresser. There was magic in his fingers, she said. If he trimmed your hair at the edges it would grow very long. My hair did grow very long. Amina Ma was very pleased.

I was conscious of being pampered, not only because I was the only girl in the family, but also because I was deemed to be pretty. I had golden brown hair, hazel eyes and an almost European complexion, inherited from my blue-eyed, near-blonde mother.

Sometimes Papa would go away for several months on trips to collect payments from the subscribers to his newspaper. I missed him greatly and his homecoming, when he returned laden with presents, was sheer happiness.

I remember on one of his homecomings though he went straight to bed, without picking me up or hugging me. Instead he lay in his bed weak and shivering, and our mothers piled him with blankets. From where I stood in the corner of the room, afraid and isolated, I heard Papa say: "Behn too is not coming near me. I must be very frightening." That hurt me. I wanted to run to his bed and crawl under his blanket, but I dared not. I fretted all day. How could Papa think I did not wish to be with him?

Often Papa told us stories, and he allowed us to jump on his stomach. I found the soft white flesh of his belly most attractive. I never saw my mothers' bellies. They were always discretely covered up. In fact I do not even remember seeing their arms, even when they bathed and washed us.

We did not have electricity in the Wentworth house – we used candles. Papa would place a lighted candle on each of the wooden posts of his double bed. In retrospect I think how dangerous that was, and then the thought comes to me that my father was somewhat reckless, and that I have acquired that streak from him, through example, because such things are not genetically inherited, however much one may think they are.

At the back of our house, on a higher ridge was my friend Sissie's house. Sissie was an Afrikaner girl and I enjoyed her company. She was my age, but more important, she was a girl. Her mother was a large woman, with a great big sore on her leg.

Our favourite pastime was playing house. My mothers had bought me a small grass and cane table and two chairs from a vendor who had come by the house. With just those three items of furniture, Sissie and I constructed a whole house in our minds and on the ground on which we played. We could be anything we desired, and we had all sorts of domestic adventures.

One day we were dining on onions on my little grass table when a snake came slithering by. We were shocked into total silence. We saw the snake snap up and swallow a frog, and we watched mesmerised as the frog disappeared and the snake's thin body became bloated with the frog. We never said a word to each other, nor to anyone else. It was as if that snake had cast a spell over us. We moved only after the snake disappeared to wherever it had come from. Then we went rather hurriedly into our respective houses.

Ma would sew together fabric samples and I would have patchwork dresses of sorts. Maybe I only had one such dress, but then I also had one dress that was a little girl's dream, or rather nearly had it. Ma had sewn a sleeveless, frilly dress for me of a gossamer, fairy-like fabric, bluer than the blue sky and yet not quite blue. It was turquoise, the sky mixed with green of the land around me. I imagined myself in it, but it was snatched away from me before I ever wore it.

Someone in the neighbourhood, someone important to my mother, had a baby and the dress was presented to that baby. I was very disappointed, but I did not complain. I have never in my life seen a comparable dress and yet I suppose it must have been pretty ordinary. What could have come off a hand sewing machine in Wentworth in 1932?

Then came Ramadan and my first fast. I had just turned four. Ma had cut up one of her trousseau long scarves – chocolate-coloured and heavily embroidered in gold and made me a dress with matching trousers. To help me while away the last hours of the fast which can become trying, I was dressed in this finery and taken for a drive to the second Meer home in Durban – Uncle AC's flat in Pine Street.

Uncle AC's parents made a huge fuss of me and my mother Ma sent for flowers and made me a garland. I have never felt so decorated and honoured in my life. Even my reception in Surat in 1995 – when I was presented with an award and draped with so many garlands that the photographer had to ask me to remove the garlands so that he could see my face which was lost in the roses – did not compare with the thrill I experienced on that day. The fast was more than worth it. I felt so grown-up, so important.

Eid followed Ramadan and was very special. We got new clothes and were taken to Durban to be fitted with new shoes. I set my heart on a black patent leather pair with white bows. The shoes were displayed in the window of the shop at the entrance of the passage that led to my father's printing press. I could not have known greater joy than when Papa bought the pair for me.

On Eid day we woke to the aroma of frying samoosas and boiling cardamom milk, to our mothers' distant voices from the kitchen, and the hazy memory of pillowcases put up the night before at the end of our beds for presents that would be brought by the angels – the faristas. We cast aside the clinging sleep and jumped out of bed to look at our presents.

In my pillowcase I found a large celluloid doll in a blue dress. I shouted for my parents, "Ma! Papa! The faristas came!", and I ran to show them my doll. My brothers came after me with their motor cars. Our confidence in our parents was strengthened. They said the faristas would come, and they had, and they cared sufficiently for us to bring us toys.

My new Eid dress was pretty and Amina Ma put an apron over it. Papa gave us Eid money and Ismail was allowed to take us for a train ride to nearby Jacobs where we spent some of this money on ice creams. I wished Eid would go on forever, but our Papa said that all things come to an end and so did Eid.

Other charmed days followed. Papa brought Allah Pak into my life. Solly, Ahmed and I sat in a circle on Papa's bed and he said, "Close your eyes tight so that everything is black and no light can enter." And we did just that. "Keep them closed", he said, "until I say open."

We opened our eyes to a feast before us. Each of us had a plate of sweets and fruit. We looked in wide-eyed wonder at Papa, Ma and Amina Ma. We asked, "Where did all this come from?" Papa said: "It all comes from Allah Pak." I asked, "Where is he?" and my father said he is far, far away in the heavens. "He sent us these things from all that distance?" I asked. My father confirmed that he had. And my mothers smiled approvingly as my father added, "Allah Pak can do anything. He is all-powerful. He looks after you. He looks after all of us."

I constructed my own image of Allah Pak. I identified him with my father and he took on his gender, but I saw him in a red dress, reclining above me in levitation. I did not share this image of Allah Pak with anyone. It was a secret in my mind, a secret between Allah Pak and me. One day I was walking with my uncle Gora Papa, my father's brother. I saw something red levitated far above me in the sky, and I called in great excitement, "Allah Pak!" and Gora Papa said, "That is a kite".

Ma told us about the Prophet Muhammad and we listened in rapt attention as she told of the time he was dying.

"The Angel Jibreel comes to take away our souls and we die," she said. "He comes at his will, and he takes our soul at his will. We are all helpless before Jibreel, but in the case of Prophet Muhammad, Jibreel knocked on the door, and Bibi Fatima the Prophet's daughter asked, 'Who is it?' and Jibreel said 'It is I, the angel of death'. Bibi Fatima said, 'I will not allow you in, go away'.

"The Angel knocked again. This time Prophet Muhammad asked his daughter who was at the door and she told him it was Jibreel. 'Then why did you not let him in?' She said 'He wants to take your soul. I won't let him in.' Then the Prophet told her she had to open the door. 'It is a courtesy that he asks to come in. He can come in without opening the door. He is paying his respect and you must respond with respect.' Then with tears streaming and sobbing, she opened the door. Jibreel entered and asked Prophet Muhammad if he was ready and could he take his soul and Prophet Muhammad said 'Yes', and then with great gentleness, Jibreel took the Prophet's soul and bore it away to Allah."

I was deeply impressed by this story and by another Ma told us about the Prophet.

"It was the custom in those days among the wealthy to bring in a wet nurse to nurse a baby and she would take the baby to the countryside and nurse him there where the air was clean and fresh. So the baby Muhammad was sent to spend the first few years of his life with Dai Halima, his wet nurse. Dai Halima had her own baby and the two babies suckled at her breasts. When the two boys were about three years old and were playing together, two angels came and took Muhammad away, and opened his heart. The little friend ran in consternation to his mother, screaming that two men were attacking Muhammad. Halima ran to rescue him. She found a laughing Muhammad and no sign of the two men. Muhammad told her not to be alarmed. It was only the angels, 'they opened my heart and cleaned it!'"

Ma added that Muhammad was thus without sin. He was pure. He is the model for us all to follow.

One of the earliest stories my father told us which left a lasting impression on me was about King Solomon's justice:

"Two women came to King Solomon with a baby and each claimed the baby belonged to her. To prise out the truth King Solomon said to the two women 'Since you are both claiming the baby, why don't we settle this by cutting up the baby and giving each of you half?' The false mother accepted the solution but the true mother said she would give up her claim as she could not allow her baby to be cut up. She wanted her baby to grow up and have a good life, and if the other woman could give him that life, she could have the baby. So King Solomon satisfied himself as to who was the real mother. The people marvelled at his justice and that has remained recorded for all time."

I could not have been more than four years old when my father told us this story, but I remained troubled for days that the false mother could have opted for half a baby. I could have asked my father to explain how any human being would want another human being cut up, only it wasn't done to ask questions, and therefore it never occurred to me to ask. The thing was to listen and if there were questions, to hope that they would be answered somehow in the course of telling the story. So my questions remained unasked, and therefore unanswered.

The madressa I went to was at the Motala's home in neighbouring Clairwood. The father and son ran a shop. The mother and daughter-in-law ran the house – two rooms at the back of the shop. There were no children in the house so the daughter-in-law, who gave me my first lessons in Arabic, welcomed me most warmly. The book I was to learn from was one Papa had made for me. He had written the Arabic alphabet at the back of an advertisement which had a picture of a girl drinking a popular cold drink called Sun Crush from a bottle with a straw. Daughter-in-law and mother-in-law were critical of this human image on the back of Allah's alphabet. They were a simple and gentle couple but they made me critical of Papa, and Papa was someone only to be admired. I wished he had bought me a proper book instead of making me one, and that too on the wrong paper. It seemed that he could not afford to buy a book.

The most interesting thing in the Motala home was a basket hung at the entrance from a rafter. The Motala's kept mithai – sweetmeats – in it. I discovered this on my first day. Lonely and upset, tongue-tied and weepy at being left with strangers, I did not respond to my first lesson. To entice me, the older Mrs Motala brought down the basket and withdrew from it delectable portions of mithai. I was sufficiently comforted to start my first lesson. The next day I kept looking at the basket. The daughter-in-law saw this and inquired if I wanted mithai. I nodded vigorously. She gave me some and as I guzzled it, she gave me a lesson apart from Arabic. Very gently she explained that I came there to learn Arabic and she was there to teach me. I did not come to eat mithai and that was the last mithai I would get because there was no more.

The next morning I was reluctant to go to madressa. "Yesterday you were so keen, what is the matter today?" Ma asked. I said there was no more mithai today. They were horrified when they learnt I had asked for mithai. Ma told me how wrong it was to ask anything of anybody outside of the family. Amina Ma gave me a slap and sent me off with Papa making it quite clear that I went there to learn, not to eat mithai. I got down to my lessons after that. I was left at the Motalas all day. Papa usually fetched me on his return home.

CHAPTER 5

A Growing Family: 1933–1934

The family I grew up in was never confined to my parents and siblings. It extended to many uncles and aunts and dozens of cousins living in a kutum, a constellation of nuclear families who could trace their origin to a common progenitor. My father was the recognised head of our kutum. As such he was not only highly respected but also held responsible for all members of this extended family. He was also the first member to establish himself in Durban and thus our home became the reception point for relatives who migrated to the city from northern Natal and Kimberley.

In Wentworth our family soon almost doubled in size. First came Papa's brother, Gora Papa (Ahmed Meer) and his wife and two children from Kimberley. Gora Papa worked with Papa in the press and he and his family lived with us. Later Papa and Ma's cousin, Gora Mamoo (Hoosen Meer, son of their Uncle Chota Meer), and his wife and daughter came from Dundee to live with us also. Some months later Papa and Ma's cousin, Choti Khala (Ayesha, daughter of their Uncle Chota Meer), joined our Wentworth household.

Our uncles brought with them three cousins – Gora Papa's sons, Unus and Abassi, and Gora Mamoo's daughter, Zohra. We had three bedrooms and we lived a family to a room, the older children sleeping on mattresses on the floor or with the parents on the beds, as space permitted.

The day Gora Papa came into my life, the family was in celebration. I was four or five years old and there was love between us at first sight. Well my sight was somewhat dim, for I had been awakened early that morning to travel from Wentworth to the Durban station and had promptly continued my sleep in the car. When we arrived at the station, Uncle Cas (Amina Ma's brother), had draped me on his shoulder and I lay there, a dead weight, while he carried me all the way from the car. I was roused from my sleep when the train steamed in, in time to welcome my new uncle, my father's brother.

I saw my new uncle and aunt and my two boy cousins, Unus and Abbasi, through sleepy eyes. In fact, I think my sleepy eyes saw only my uncle. I more than saw him, I felt him, for he immediately took me from my Uncle Cas. I snuggled against him, spontaneously claiming him as my own as he claimed me his own.

My cousin Unus was the elder of Gora Papa's two sons. My first recollection of Unus was that he spoke words that were foreign to us – he spoke Afrikaans. My eldest brother Ismail led the way in laughing at him and we all followed. Abbasi, the younger of Gora Papa's sons, was a Down syndrome baby. He lay inert in his cot or pram, unable to move. There were few things that made him laugh. He was helpless, harmless and always pleasant.

I had always complained that I had no one to play with since I had no sister. When Gora Mamoo's family came to stay with us I expected his daughter, Zohra, to fill that vacuum, but she, like my cousin Unus, was eight years old, and closer in age to my brother Ismail than to me. Zohra, Unus and Ismail went to school together. They were the big children and I was in a hurry to be part of their bigness. They were our older siblings and we, the younger lot, who were not yet at school, my two younger brothers Solly and Ahmed and I followed them whenever allowed to do so. When they returned from school we particularly enjoyed eating their leftover sandwiches. It was most fortunate for us that we had our elder siblings for they made it possible for us to go places we would never have ventured on our own.

The clearest memory I have of Zohra at Wentworth is going to the toilet with her at night. The toilet, a bucket enclosed in a tin shed, was some distance from the house in the bush. We had to take a hurricane lamp to light our way, and we kept each other very good company as we took turns on the bucket and chatted away. We were never in a hurry to leave the toilet.

I also remember spending some nights at Uncle AC's flat with Zohra. Her father, Gora Mamoo, would make shadow animals on the wall and tell us stories about Shaka and Dingaan and how a seer predicted that once they quarrelled and lost their unity a white man would take over and they would be enslaved. It was from him that I heard my first political statement. I was sufficiently impressed by it to remember it as an adult.

I met Choti Khala (Ayesha), when I was five years old and I fell instantly in love with her. She was much older, in her late teens. I had never known anyone like her. She was so vivacious, so pretty and so fashionable. Choti Khala wore her long headscarf as a decoration piece, as part of her dress. She swirled her scarf under her arm, brought it across her breast and pinned it on her shoulder with a glittering brooch. With my mothers, scarves were a sort of nuisance cloth that got in the way when they worked, something they respectfully and hurriedly draped over their heads when visitors came. I had the impression that they would be rid of most of them if they could, save the going-out long scarves that were trimmed with gold braids.

Choti Khala was a gifted reciter of the life of the Prophet and she was invited to recite at public mouloods (celebrations of the birth of the Prophet Muhammad). Ma would take me to these and Choti Khala would sit with the other reciters, three or four young women like herself, in front of a row of pillows, beautifully embroidered with gold beads, alongside vases of flowers and incense sticks. At the end of the event the reciters would be given presents. I was so proud of Choti Khala on these occasions.

Choti Khala spellbound me. I followed her around like a little puppy. I slept with her at night. I was mesmerised by her dainty movements as she applied her creams and powders, and when she settled down to tell me stories, I was sold to her forever. Yet all the while I got this insidious message from my mothers and from Gorie Apa, married to Choti Khala's eldest brother Gora Mamoo, that she was "bad". They frowned on her use of cosmetics: Who was she preening herself for? They did not say it in words, it was implied in their attitudes.

Ma spoke disparagingly of people who were too free. Could one be too free? Was Choti Khala too free? Such questions began forming in my mind and I answered them by drawing unreservedly closer to Choti Khala. My mothers could really do nothing about it, for their disapproval of her remained unspoken. What was there to speak about? As I was to learn much, much later Choti Khala was, at the end of it all, guilty of no more than escaping her unhappiness which began with her marriage at the age of seven.

When she joined our household Choti Khala must have been seventeen, but she had already been married ten years. Although married at seven years old, she had joined her husband's home when she was thirteen. She had not taken to her equally youthful husband. She had found him clumsy and crude and rumour had it that she did not allow him in her bed. Her mother-in-law did not stand for that and so the little girl's life became hell. Choti Khala would not knuckle down to her marriage and there was continual friction between her and her husband and between her and her mother-in-law.

As my mothers and the women of the family saw it, the mother-in-law, Bhabie, was a terror, but then which mother-in-law was not? It was the lot of daughters-in-law to be punched and slapped. In their eyes Bhabie's treatment of Choti Khala was not exceptional, but Choti Khala's treatment of her husband YC, was shocking to them.

"How could a wife behave like that towards her husband?" they said. "She did not want her husband. So who did she want? She is a loose cannon."

As far as they were concerned, she was the worst kind of role model a young impressionable girl could have, and my mothers were afraid for me. Choti Khala was a free soul who had taken charge of her life by leaving her husband, and it was this freedom that my mothers and her cousins resented. It was this freedom that they sought to stifle. Choti Khala had no right to that freedom since *they* had no right to it.

We children were far more mobile in Wentworth than we ever were in Grey Street, largely because we were older, the environment outside the house was safer and because there were more of us in Wentworth than there had been at Grey Street. Our parents felt more comfortable when we went around together, conscious of both safety and pleasure in numbers.

We would go on errands together. The butcher shop was at quite some distance and we broke our journey midway, sitting on the grassy bank, dawdling. Sometimes my brother Ismail produced a sausage or two which we shared, eating them raw, relishing the meat squeezed out of the membrane. My mothers never bought sausages – that was too much of a luxury. Dried beans and lentils cooked in a substantial soup was our usual fare. What with sixteen mouths to feed, they never bought more than a pound or so of the cheaper cuts of meat and this had to go a long way. Ismail said the butcher had given him the sausages, but in retrospect I suspect he had just helped himself to a few. However, he came by them though, we enjoyed them.

We went into the bushes, gathering berries and sweet-sour (khati mithie) herbs and weeds. There was a kind of unproclaimed competition over who would collect the most herbs. On one occasion I displayed a huge pile, outstripping all. "Look at Behn, she's got the most," my big brother Ismail called out in praise. I was inflated with pride, but was as quickly deflated when Zohra examined my pile and said, "That's not khatie mithie. That's just weeds!"

I had no idea what I was picking. It was all the same to me. The praise had come as a surprise, the disappointment was an unbearable shame. I had let myself down; I had let the others down. I felt so ashamed and wondered whether I would ever be admired again, for to me, at that age, praise and love was one and the same thing. To be loved, one had to be praised and to be praised, one had to be loved. That was my understanding of a good child.

Our herbs and blackberries gathered, we stored them away for after supper when we put them out on a white sheet, danced around them, and then sat down and relished them. Our parents came nowhere near us and appeared to be quite oblivious to our goings-on. It was our great luck that we didn't collect any poisonous herbs.

When mango season arrived, our parents bought the ripe juicy round sugar mangoes in large dishfuls and left them under the bed to take on that rosy red colour that brought out all their sweetness. I walked on the veranda ledge, precariously, and for that reason all the more joyously, sucking one sugar mango after another, until I fell off and bruised my knee and arm and got a scolding from Amina Ma for doing so.

The excitement of us children heightened when visitors arrived to stay. They usually had leftovers from their padkos which we found delicious. Our usual fare was curries with a lot of watery gravy. The padkos were rare treats such as fried or grilled meats, fried fish, samoosas and so on. We children made a party of it, orchestrated by the oldest of us. We placed the 'offerings' in the centre and danced round and round them. There was a joyousness about it that came not simply from the delicacies we were about to relish, but from being together, the younger children with the older, and most important of all, the younger accepted by the older as having the same rights, the same claims, though dependant on them for protection if it came to that.

One morning I awoke to Ismail's screams. He and our cousin Unus were caught smoking cigarettes in the toilet. Their sin though was suspected to be more than smoking. What that suspicion was, we couldn't imagine and never came to know. Years later Unus confided to us: "All we were doing there was smoking. They wanted us to confess to something else and we never knew what that something else was." They were both punished severely.

On summer evenings, the whole family, all the elders and their children, walked up the heavily forested hill to the lighthouse. We made quite a group, three sets of parents and their children. We watched the light circle the sea, illuminating the path of ships and far beyond we could see the lights of Durban. It was also an occasion for our parents to tell us about shipwrecks and sea rescues. Some days we would be taken to nearby Salisbury Island into the mangrove swamps, where the forest warded off the light. We lost each other in the sinister darkness and our hearts pounding, we called out to each other.

Our greatest pleasure though was Sunday picnics at Brighton Beach. This was our beach, since no one else appeared to use it. We would all pack into our car, parents, uncles, aunts and children, and spend the whole day on the beach. We would run down the dunes to the sea and run up again at the end of the day, and if a child could not make the climb, a father would sweep him or her up onto his robust shoulders.

Our uncles would lie on the sand and encourage us to bury them until only their heads could be seen. We would struggle to bury them and then dig them out again, and they would erupt out of their graves, and stand up, giant-like, shaking off the sand.

We didn't have bathing suits. We children swam in our briefs and vests, our mothers fully dressed. They would stand at the water's edge, allowing the waves to do their will and the waves would soon lash them and fling them and pull them down and they would be thoroughly wet from head to toe.

I would run from Choti Khala for she was invariably after me and I knew why, and I trembled in delicious suspense of being caught and hurled into the sea, and then frightened to death as the waves whirled around my ears and into my nose and I gasped for breath, and panicked at the feeling of being washed out to sea, of never seeing the shore again and then come up spluttering and crying from the shock of it all. But Choti Khala would be laughing, and Amina Ma would chide me for being such a crybaby, and I would realise that what had seemed to me to be an eternity of being lost in the waves was only a moment in time.

We were not often taken to town, so I remember clearly one Sunday when we were all put into our best clothes and Papa took us. For some inexplicable reason I was dressed like a boy in my brother's clothes. We were taken to Mitchell Park to ride on Nellie the elephant. That was the first time I realised that we belonged to a group called non-Europeans[7]. I sat on a bench and the park ranger was promptly on to me, shooing me off the bench. My father came as quickly to my rescue. He whisked me off the bench and distracted my attention away from something he resented deeply, but did not think I was ready to understand. He was determined not to have our day spoilt. He bought us ice creams and settled us on the grass to enjoy these and then we had our rides on Nellie. A year later I visited Nellie's birthday with my brothers and cousins and we received gifts of handkerchiefs and balloons and buns.

I was a little more than five years old. Sleep had not quite left me when Ma, excited to give me the news, awakened me and told me I had a little brother.

"Brother!", I cried, "I don't want a brother. I want a sister. Where did the brother come from? Let him go away."

My curiosity was however roused and I followed Ma. I saw Amina Ma lying on the floor. Dai Ma, the traditional midwife, was beside her and there was blood. It was a fearful sight and I retreated into my bed and lay there quietly until Papa came and picked me up and took me to see my little brother who was lying in Ma's lap. Ma smiled at me and said, "Come and see your beautiful brother". I looked at him but remained pouting. If they had to bring a new baby to our home, why could they not have brought a girl? There were so many boys in our house and I was the only girl. I needed a girl to play with. What would I do with the boy?

The new brother was laid to sleep in the jhorie, a cradle made of cloth suspended from a red and green cradle stand. Dai Ma looked after him, sitting nearby, getting on with other chores like cleaning the vegetables for cooking while she rocked the jhorie by pulling the twine attached to the cradle with her big toe. I have an image of myself bending into the jhorie in an attempt to see my baby brother and nearly falling on top of him as Dai Ma screamed and Amina Ma rushed in to arrest an imminent catastrophe.

As baby Mahomed, who we called Bhai, grew, I came to love him and showered him with kisses. Ma could not restrain herself from teasing me.

"You didn't want this brother, now why do you smother him with kisses?"

I protested, "He is my brother!"

CHAPTER 6

Convent Lane: 1934–1937

The Wentworth days ended. The shop had failed. My father's daily trips to Durban were tiring and expensive. There was no point living so far from town, so we moved to a house my father rented in Convent Lane in the centre of Durban. The lane was so called because a convent took up half of it. One never saw the convent since a very high concrete wall barricaded it, but it came alive once each year, when a colourful procession left it for some mysterious place. We all came out to watch because it was so pretty. Little girls in blue cloaks, bearing baskets of flowers, scattered handfuls of petals as they led the procession. The procession went past our house to the end of the lane, where it turned and disappeared into Broad Street[8].

Our home was a semi-detached cottage, with three bedrooms upstairs and a sitting room, dining room, breakfast room, and kitchen on the ground floor. A veranda bordered the sitting and dining rooms, and the kitchen led to an outside yard.

Our mothers cooked on a coal stove and the wood was stored in the bathroom. My mothers would say to me, "Behn, go and fetch three or four pieces of wood," and in my mind I would wonder if I should take three or four and I would end up adding three and four and taking seven.

It was at Convent Lane, when I was seven years old, that the sister I hankered for, Gorie, was born. A year later my brother Siddiek followed, and two years after him my brother Farouk. By the time we left Convent Lane my parents had eight children, four born to Amina Ma and four to Ma, six brothers and two sisters. Though our household consisted of many more people than that.

My father's brother Gora Papa and his family moved with us to Convent Lane from Wentworth, as did Zohra and her parents. We were also joined by two older cousins from Dundee, Chota Motala and MC Meer, who came to live with us while they studied at Sastri College, a high school for Indian boys. From time to time other family members joined us, some for shorter periods, others for longer – cousins Kader Motala from Dundee and Gorie from Pietermaritzburg and Ma's brother, Chota Mamoo from Surat, among them. A young girl, Amina Essop, also came to live with us for a time. She had written to our father to say that she wanted to study but there was no school in her home town of Lady Selborne in the then Transvaal, so he solved her problem by bringing her to live with us.

Thus at any one time, there were eighteen to twenty people at meal-times and bedtimes in that three-bedroom house. Somehow there was enough food and sleeping space for all.

I remember Ma bargaining with sari-clad women vendors. The women would come into our yard, carrying large baskets of fruit and vegetables. They would lift their baskets off their heads and place them on the floor, faltering a bit as they did so. When Ma thought the price right, she made her purchase. Because of the size of the family Ma bought the whole basket, pleasing the vendors.

Our Victorian dining room table of solid oak was purchased from Khan Saab's second-hand shop; a shop which furnished much of our house. The table could be extended – with the turning of a handle the sides moved creating space for a third piece which was stored away when not in use. The table came with a green velvet cloth, fringed with tassels. I do not re-member eating off that table. We ate in the breakfast room, off a pine deal table. We sat around the dining room table during Ramadan and read the Quran. Papa worked at the dining room table and once he brought two ostrich egg shells and he painted them. On the one he painted the map of the world, making it into a globe, on the other he painted flowers. I thought my Papa so clever.

Ma embroidered scarves, with badla, a metallic gold thread, and this earned the family some money. Amina Ma baked our daily bread. While her home-baked bread contributed significantly to the household saving, I thought that miserliness. I preferred bread bought from the shop at seven pence a loaf, to her bread. To my mind, at that time, the things my mothers did were not clever things.

However, I was proud of Amina Ma's looks. She had lovely golden brown hair and blue eyes. I was glad I looked like her and not like Ma or Papa, who were darker complexioned.

We had a gramophone and a radio. Papa would play his qawaalis – Urdu songs in praise of the Prophet and Allah. I didn't like the qawaalis very much. Uncle Cas, Amina Ma's brother, had a very different taste in music from my father. He brought dance music – fox trots and waltzes. I recall one tune, *Faint Harmony*. He must have loved it a lot for he played it often and the tune still echoes in my mind. At times Amina Ma joined him, and brother and sister listened to tunes that I imagine took them to the life they had left behind.

It was unheard of in our household to entertain children with special children's records, but the Children's Corner, a programme on the radio at 4 pm, made up for the absence of children's records. Amina Ma and I listened to this daily.

Our mothers never went shopping in the Indian commercial area; they maintained their purdah from the Muslim shopkeepers and their assistants. They wouldn't be seen dead there. They preferred shopping in the European West Street[9] for despite the snooty European women condescending to serve them, they felt free there since they did not have to maintain purdah. When they visited anyone in the predominantly Indian Grey Street complex, they went in an enclosed rickshaw. Ma usually took me with her and I would sit alongside her. My brother Ismail came as a 'mascot' and ran alongside the rickshaw.

One day I was on the veranda when I saw my mothers come back from shopping, very angry and swearing at a group of young men who had been following them. Then my mothers were throwing their shoes at the young hooligans. I thought this was getting serious for they would surely lose their shoes, but at that point the hooligans decided to retreat. "Moowa!" my mothers swore after them in Gujarati – meaning 'dead ones' – and then their anger turned to me. "You are sitting, watching and doing nothing about it!" I thought they meant getting help, but there was no one at home on whom I could have called for help.

When we moved house, from Wentworth to Convent Lane, I and my brothers, Solly and Ahmed, were enrolled at a madressa in Pine Street. It was only one street away from our house but to get there we had to cross West Street, a big busy street. Papa arranged with the caretaker of a cycle shop at the corner of West and Saville Streets to help us cross this road each morning and each afternoon on our return.

At madressa, which was the first formal educational institution I attended, I was enrolled as Fatimabibi bin Moosa Meer, the daughter of Moosa Meer. I had to wear a headscarf and my cotton georgette headscarf was a nuisance but I found a use for it as a sort of pacifier. I chewed on it the whole day and by the time I reached home it was full of wet holes.

Gender separation was firmly entrenched in our minds. The girls' madressa was upstairs, the boys' downstairs. The girls and the boys had separate play times under the trees in the small yard. Neither gender would dream of being in

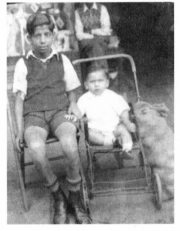

Right: Ismail and Bhai.

Top: Amina Ma, Ma and Solly.

the playground during the time of the other, so the teachers had no problems in keeping us apart. Our teachers were all men.

We sat on long benches with attached desks and cubicles. The cubicles were our play areas. My friend, Hazra Randeree, and I furnished our adjacent cubicles with paper furniture and played house when the Molvi Sahab, our madressa teacher, fell asleep in his chair. We would be startled by his cane stinging us sharply on our backs when he got up and took a walk to see all was well, and found that with us it wasn't.

Hazra's family was rich and had a cook and she brought delicacies to school. Ma was very interested in these, especially in varkhi samoosa, a flaky pastry filled with coconut. Hazra told me stories and I believed all of them. Practically every morning she came with the news that her sister had given birth to a baby and each time the baby was just a few inches in length. I imagined her house full of little elves. I begged her to take me home so I could see them, but she always came up with some excuse. Then one day Hazra didn't come to school and in shocked silence we heard that she was dead. We were not told how she had died and it didn't matter. Hazra who had fussed around setting up her furniture in her cubicle next to mine never came to Madressa again.

I turned my attention to another Hazra, Hazra Jeewa. I took her home one day and Amina Ma set us down on the table in the yard overlooking the kitchen window and gave us a plate of beans to share. I was cross with Amina Ma. I had just brought Hazra home. I hadn't brought her to share my beans. What was Amina Ma up to, paying her all that attention? I drew a line through the centre of the beans and instructed Hazra to eat from the one side and not intrude into my side. But the line soon disappeared and Hazra did not know which was her side. Amina Ma seeing all the fuss I was making came over and gave me a tight slap filling me with such shame that I could no longer face Hazra. So that friendship ended.

But my days were lapped up by the madressa. When I had a penny I snatched time off to go across the road to buy the sour dried fruit kokam, small and black but deliciously tangy – seven for a penny.

When I was about seven years old my world widened. I was allowed to move around on my own unattended. Children, in those days, had their different uses depending on their size. I was sent on errands to Grey Street to our printing press and visited Uncle AC's family in Pine Street.

Before I entered the streets of Indian commerce and residence, I had to turn into Broad Street from Convent Lane where the European world began. It was opulent, fashionable and neatly ordered, quite different from ours. There was a block of flats on the corner of Broad Street and Convent Lane. A wide passage with mirrored walls led to the lift and stairway. I wondered what sort of apartments white people lived in. Across the road was a jewellery shop with a window that displayed sparkling earrings and bracelets and exquisite china figurines. If I turned right at the corner, I entered what was then West Street with its smart shops and even smarter windows.

Turning from Grey Street into Pine Street and then into Cathedral Road was the Haqqani Building. Papa's friend, Chota Jeewa lived there with his wife in a flat overlooking the cemetery. They had no children but they had a fridge. Papa liked his watermelon chilled. He had no fridge but a house full of children. His choice fell on me to take the watermelon to the Jeewa fridge. Ma said Mrs Jeewa was fond of me. She used to borrow me when I was a baby, and though I was now no longer borrowable, I was always welcome. The Jeewa's called me Bibi and whenever I went there, I was sure to be given sweets or fruit, something nice to eat.

I was happy to go during the day to leave the watermelon in the fridge. In fact, I liked doing so and receiving Mrs Jeewa's hospitality, but it was a chilling experience when I collected the watermelon in the evening. On my left was the cemetery of the Europeans, all of them candidates for hell since they were selfishly celebrating their heaven in this world. I knew this from the standard reply our mothers gave when we asked why we were excluded from the pool at the beach where European children played. "This world is for Europeans only, heaven in the next world is for non-Europeans only," they comforted. "Where will the Europeans go?" we would ask, and they would say "to hell!"

My imagination ran wild, especially when it came to dead Europeans. I had to pass all those European corpses waiting to be sent to hell on the Day of Judgement, when, as I was told, we would have to walk across a hair-thin bridge over the fires of hell – fires forty times hotter than the fires of earth, which had been washed forty times before being sent to us.

Gora Mamoo had also told us the most frightening stories about the Boer War and the dead European soldiers buried near their house in Waschbank, saying their ghosts would suddenly appear in the most grotesque forms. I shuddered with all these thoughts, but conquered them with prayers to ward off the sin-burdened spirits of the European corpses. As I undertook my nocturnal trip to Chota Jeewa's fridge, I repeated the first kalimah '*La ilaha illalla Muhummedur rasoolallah/There is no God, but God and Muhammad is His Prophet*'.

During Ramadan we stood against the convent wall at sunset, for from that position we could see the light on the minaret of the mosque in West

Street. We waited for the light to go on as did all Muslims within sight of it, for that marked the exact moment of sunset and the signal for us to open our fast. We never said "break" our fast. If the fast was broken, it was never completed. So at sunrise, we began our fast or closed our eating and at sunset we "opened" our eating. As soon as the light went on, we ran the short distance to our home, chanting at the top of our voices, '*Buthie hargie, roza kholaw*' – meaning 'the light is on, open your fast'.

From the time we moved to Convent Lane I kept all thirty of the fasts during Ramadan until the new moon announced Eid and the beginning of the new month.

It was the housewives on whose shoulders the entire cooking fell who suffered during this time. Those were not the days when one could keep meats in freezers. Our mothers waited anxiously for news of the Eid moon sighting and once this was confirmed they would begin a frenzy of shopping, slaughtering of fowls and an equal frenzy of cooking.

Papa was modern and moved with the times. Many years later, Papa introduced the moon issue in his newspaper, resulting in a raging controversy in the community and rousing such passions as to threaten its peace.

He had dared to write that in this age when there are calendars, it was antediluvian to insist on sighting the moon to celebrate Ramadan and Eid. The calendar clearly showed their dates. However, the moulanas insisted on sighting the first moon before they accepted that Ramadan had begun or ended. If the moon was sighted in one area and not in another, Eid would be celebrated on different days in different areas. Papa argued that the Muslims were one community and that there should be unity in celebrating Eid. The moulanas contended that the Prophet measured the months by the moon, that was the tradition and tradition should be preserved.

Things got so hot that Papa had to have bodyguards. Meetings were held between him and his followers in our sitting room. My father was an intellectual Muslim, not a ritualistic one. I never knew him to perform namaaz. Although he went to mosque during the two Eids, I do not recollect him going to the mosque on Fridays. As a firm believer in Islam he saw it as fitting into a logical framework that gave him logical guidance in living his life. He could be impassioned about that framework and was prepared to defend its truth to death. He knew his theology. He knew the

Quran and the Hadis, the teachings of the Prophet Muhammad, and he knew the Shariah. He had to be armed against the ignorance the Moulanas purveyed.

Ma described heaven to us. It was a place of eternal joy, of cool streams and fountains, and tall houries or damsels for the pleasure of men. Her younger cousin, Choti Khala, wanted to know if there would be male hoors for the women. Ma's elder cousins were shocked and amused in turn. Choti Khala's older sister, Apa Ma, said this was very silly, but Choti Khala was adamant. She believed in the equality of the genders. If men were rewarded with houries, then women had to be equally rewarded. Gorie Apa their sister-in-law said a man could have more than one wife. "You know that," she said. "A woman can only have one husband, so how would women have hoors in heaven?" Choti Khala however insisted on equal rewards for men and women.

I often went to Papa's printing press to play there. The press was a world of its own. It had very high ceilings. Papa had walled in a small section as part of his office. The walls went halfway up to the ceiling and a ladder led up to the roof. The roof was a dumping ground and one could pick up all sorts of things, useless and useful, neither having much meaning for a seven-year-old.

I enjoyed climbing the ladder and losing myself in all the trash that was deposited there. I would see below me the printing machine that filled practically the whole of the press. Mohan, the machine operator, fed paper from the one end and I watched the huge rollers of the Heidelberg machine pushing out the printed sheets, the newest edition of *Indian Views* at the opposite end. I was mesmerised by the rhythm and sound of it all. When the forms were not locked in for printing, the wheels on which they were driven lay about and I skated on them from one end of the press to the other. One of my father's colleagues, the English language edition compositor, Chamberlain Nakasa[10], distracted from his typesetting, paid me some attention. Some days I went to the press during the lunch break and Papa would send for a saucer of dhall and a slice of bread from the vegetarian restaurant nearby.

Thursday was the day on which the paper was posted to subscribers and it was therefore a very busy day for the press. The entire staff assembled. Flour and water was mixed and boiled into glue on a Primus stove and spread on the addressed wrappers into which the papers were folded. The staff appeared to be having a party, working together and I loved joining them. On Friday, the paper hit the streets.

Once when I visited the press, Big Ismail (as we called Uncle AC's and Choti Khala's brother) took me for a treat to Peter's Lounge. That was very special. We climbed the stairs and took a seat at a table and Big Ismail ordered doughnuts and milkshakes. I felt very grown up and special and I had never eaten anything as wonderful as that doughnut. The next day I went to the press and asked Big Ismail if he could take me again for that doughnut treat, but he was not as friendly as the day before and said he had no money. After being refused, I felt quite ashamed of myself. Somehow Amina Ma came to hear of this incident and she reprimanded me severely.

I was only vaguely aware of Big Ismail at the time. Little could I know that some seventeen years later we would fall in love and marry! At seven years of age I had seen Big Ismail only once or twice at Convent Lane watching me draw and saying that I could draw very well. Once I remember him reprimanding me because I was condescending to one of the other children. "That's not nice," he had said. I had felt very ashamed of myself.

Big Ismail was seventeen years old and working at the press while completing high school. He had worked for his brother AC, sewing buttonholes in the home-based shirt factory, but that business had failed and he was considering returning to Waschbank to work as a shop assistant when my father, who was his cousin, had offered him a job at the press.

During one of his trips away, my father bought a box full of ladies' nighties and undies. He thought my mothers could sell them and make some money, but I am sure we lost on that deal. They sold some stuff to the ladies next door. The young ladies were working, earning money, and smartly dressed. They were paying for their purchases in weekly instalments, and at the end of each week I was sent to collect the money. I usually went through the back gate and stood in the yard. They knew I had come for the money and resented me. I thought it made for bad neighbours.

Better not to get your neighbours and friends indebted to you, but where would my mothers go to get customers?

Kunwar Singh, agent for the Government of India in South Africa and of royal descent, was friendly with my father and often called on him at the *Indian Views* office. His wife, the Kunwarani, expressed a wish to visit our mothers. There was great anxiety about the visit and my mothers wondered what they would talk about and what they would serve. They eventually decided to let her conduct the conversation and to serve her ice cream. I was sent to the local tearoom with a glass bowl to purchase a tickey's[11] worth of ice cream. That was a great luxury.

Later we discovered that one could buy half-a-gallon of ice cream at Model Dairy for five shillings and that could serve the whole family, so once in a while we had a big treat, though it was cheaper to make your own ice cream at home. We had an ice cream tub and we bought ice from a factory opposite the cemetery. Our elders took turns churning the milk mixture while applying coarse salt on the ice to preserve it. The tub was filled several times until everyone was served. Another delicacy reserved for special occasions was samoosas. Ma was the expert fryer – she fried them slowly to get the right colour and crispness.

Chota Mamoo, Ma's youngest brother, came to Durban to stake his claim to South African citizenship. Born in South Africa, he and Ma had left as children with their father and siblings. After some years of running a business in Burma, Chota Mamoo now came to establish himself in the land of his birth. His wife Choti Mamie and his children were in Surat and were to join him once he was established.

Chota Mamoo was living with us in Convent Lane when he was informed by letter of the birth of their last child, Mohamed Gora. He came excitedly to Ma and said, "I have very good news for you. It calls for a vadamrie." Good news, according to tradition, had to be welcomed with a gift referred to as a vadamrie. I do not recall whether Ma gave him a gift, it is more likely that she told him to get on with whatever he had to say or to get lost. But I took the cue.

That afternoon I was sent on an errand to Dawood Rajah, who was married to my parents' cousin. They were in the midst of preparing for their eldest son's wedding. We went out with them daily, all dressed in our finery to invite potential guests personally, for that was how it was done traditionally. I loved to accompany them, visiting dozens of families for it was a big wedding.

On that afternoon, I sat on the low stool in the kitchen and watched the women cut pineapples into small pieces for the jam they were preparing for the wedding. I came up with what was upper most in my mind.

"I will give you some good news if you give me a vadamrie," I said. Mrs. Rajah gave me a shilling, a fortune then, and I gave my great news in exchange. "Chota Mamoo has a new son, Mohamed Gora." All the ladies smiled down at me and I left very pleased with myself.

Ma and Amina Ma were appalled when I showed them my shiny new shilling.

"Of what value is a Meer baby to the Rajahs? How could you have done such a thing, taking a shilling from them? That is not a child born into their family. You were very silly asking for money like that. You have put us all to shame."

I was very confused. I had been told the whole month that the Rajahs were our relatives and now all of a sudden it seemed they weren't.

I repeated the forbidden one day. I must have been eight years old. I took Siddiek and Gorie for a ride in their pram. I wheeled the pram up into Russell Street.[12] With much difficulty, I got the wheels over the kerb, then pushed the pram along the pavement and turned into West Street. As I did so, the pram unbalanced, and fortunately or unfortunately for me, a European lady got hold of the pram and brought it right. Siddiek and Gorie fell onto each other and began to cry. The European lady looked at me angrily and demanded to know where I lived. In utter shock and fear and quite wordlessly I walked towards home, the lady following and pushing the pram.

The European lady knocked soundly on the door and Amina Ma came out and looked at us in surprise. Gorie held out her arms to be picked up. Siddiek had not stopped his bawling. Amina Ma was all flustered. The European lady scolded Amina Ma, "Are these your children? Why don't you look after them? How can you send them off with this young child?"

Amina Ma didn't even attempt to explain that she had not done so. She just thanked the lady for bringing the children and apologised adequately. When the lady had gone, she caught hold of me and gave me the spanking of my life. Ma attended to the babies, whilst simultaneously shouting to Amina Ma to stop, she had beaten me enough. I think that cured me of pushing prams and taking babies out for rides.

The prize-giving ceremony at madressa was a wonderful affair. It happened at night and that in itself gave it a special lustre. I was given as first prize a glass sugar bowl and I presented it to my mothers in great disappointment, but when Amina Ma opened the bowl, there was, to my great delight, a wrist watch inside. Papa's friend, Molvi Munshi, who was at the ceremony as a learned Islamic scholar, received a bouquet sprinkled with tinsel. He gave that to me and I presented that to my mothers as an additional prize.

I was among those chosen from our madressa for a ride in the small aeroplane flown by a pilot, Manmohan Singh, who had come from India and was giving free rides. Billah, our family driver drove me to the airport, and when it was my turn I was ordered to run to the plane. It was a very unpleasant run, for the elastic of my panty was loose and my panty kept threatening to fall off and I kept pulling it up from outside my dress, while pretending not to be doing so. I climbed into the plane, holding onto my panty. I remember very little of that ride for my mind was on my panty. I was in fact relieved when the ride was over and I was safely in the car. Back home I was asked a hundred questions about the plane ride, what I had seen below and how I had felt and so on, since I was the only member of the family who had flown in a plane. I, however, could not report much and disappointed them.

I remember being herded one day from madressa with my class and taken to West Street where we joined hundreds of other school children in a procession to celebrate the coronation of the new king. I was around nine years old. I was bemused and didn't know what was going on neither did any of my companions.

We were in a jumble and the head of the madressa, Molvi Saheb, kept shouting at us to do what we did not know. Then some teachers came and they sorted us out according to size. Some of my companions and I were

led to the front. We marched down West Street with the children from all
the schools in the city. We marched, waving little flags, I in a white dress
Ma had sewn for me. I was surprised to hear that our mothers had
watched the procession with great pride and they told me I was right up
front leading it. I had been totally unaware of that. All I knew was that I
was in the procession. We received mugs at madressa and brought them
home jubilantly. Amina Ma, who was a great admirer of the royal family,
arranged the mugs neatly on a shelf.

Our visit to the Empire Exhibition[13] in Johannesburg in 1936 when I was
eight years old was a memorable event. We travelled by car, Papa in the
front seat with our new driver Omar Khan, known to us as Khan. We
had left Durban very early in the morning, leaving one passenger, Unus,
behind because his father Gora Papa would not allow him to accompany us.

Us children took turns to sit on Papa's lap. Ma, Amina Ma and Choti
Khala occupied the back seat with the babies on their laps – Choti Khala's
son Bubbles, and our Bhai, Gorie and Siddiek. Solly and I, prone to vomiting, were placed at their feet opposite each other with a tin can each,
which, much to our distress, had to be emptied repeatedly throughout the
journey. On the way we stopped at the homes of Papa's subscribers and
they offered us sliced mangoes, sliced pineapples, and cooldrinks. Solly
and I were hungry, our stomachs having been emptied and we ate and we
ate and drank despite our parents warning, so the vomiting started all
over again. After a while we were too ill to eat.

We reached Johannesburg in the evening. We were most excited when
Papa pointed out the lights of Johannesburg in the distance. We stayed
with Papa's friends the Jazbhais the first night. Ma drew Amina Ma's
attention to the Jazbhais opulent living standards and there was much
discussion about this. They had a cook who did all the cooking. The rich
and the gracious kept cooks, their women relieved of the drudgery of
cooking. Of all the women in our clan, Ma alone knew something of such
high living, for after all she had been brought up in *Raja Wadi* in Surat
and had touched royalty.

The next morning we were up early, excited about going to the exhibition. I felt absolutely beautiful in one of my new dresses especially sewn
by Ma for the trip. The exhibition was a bustle of people and – wonder of
wonders – Unus was suddenly there before us as if by magic. We looked at

him in utter amazement. How did he get here? We had travelled a whole day before we could get to Johannesburg and Unus was there ahead of us. After we had left for Johannesburg, Gora Papa had regretted that he had not allowed him to go with us. Big Ismail had suggested he could catch up with us if he flew up to Johannesburg and so Unus made his first aeroplane trip.

On the second day we moved to Gora Ba Karodia's in Commissioner Street in the centre of Johannesburg. Papa had gone there to pay his respects and Gora Ba Karodia and his spinster daughters had taken great exception that we were staying with non-kinsmen when we had our kinsmen in Johannesburg. Gora Ba Karodia was a thin old man in a long coat. Only one of his five children, his eldest daughter, was married. He had not allowed his other children to marry, so there were two middle-aged spinsters and two middle-aged bachelors in the house. They were glad we were there and fussed over us.

The old patriarch never allowed his daughters out of the house. The world outside was totally strange to them, though they were as old as our mothers or even older. They lived in the heart of Johannesburg, but their door was locked on life outside and they remained imprisoned in the rooms inside. Gora Ba Karodia didn't approve of us leaving the house each morning and having our lunch and dinner elsewhere. The daughters awaited our return each evening and asked us about all we had seen and done, details of the food we had eaten and how it was served. They were loath to let us go, but we thought old Gora Ba Karodia didn't like us bringing the outside into his little inside in case this might make his daughters conscious of their oppression.

We enjoyed the Exhibition and visited every hall. One of my most vivid memories is of the train. I was watching the miniature electric train; Bhai my little brother, two years old to my eight, racquet in hand, watched with me as the train wound its way through the tunnel and stations and forests and buildings. It was heading towards us when I saw the racquet in its path. A few seconds and the coaches would be piling up one on top of the other. I watched, waiting for the accident, but Amina Ma saw the impending collision and quickly snatched the racquet out of the way. The train continued its journey.

CHAPTER 7

School Days: 1937–1939

The days of madressa ended. I completed my Quran and my parents distributed packets of dry fruit in celebration. I could read and write Urdu. I was sufficiently schooled in Islamic education and I could now go to school.

Our immediate neighbours were the Aysons, a Malay family.[14] Mrs Ayson urged that I should be enrolled at the Albert Street School within walking distance from our house in Convent Lane. I could go with their daughter Maryam who was older than me. I was fond of Maryam. We sat on the veranda for hours talking while she made buttonholes. The Aysons were tailors and specialised in making men's suits. My cousin Zohra and I competed for Maryam's attention. Each of us saw her as our special friend. Zohra went to school in Winterton Road, in the opposite direction and a good walk from Convent Lane. I was happy at the thought of going to school with Maryam

However, the Albert Street School was a Coloured school.[15] My father could not take me there to be enrolled since he was Indian. They would surely throw out father and daughter, so Amina Ma, blue-eyed and blondish, took off her ijar and took me to school in her dress. It worked.

I was enrolled in class two, skipping the first grade, due to the good work of Miss Naidoo, the sister of another family friend, Dr Goonam. She had given all the children in Convent Lane private lessons in English each afternoon after our return from madressa. I was registered as Fatima Moosa Meer, and Moosa was taken as my second name.

"This is not my second name!" I protested. "How can I have a boy's name for a second name? Moosa is my father".

"What is your father's name doing here?" I was asked.

The question left me confused. I knew my father's name was rightly where it was, but I did not know how to explain it.

A few years later when I changed schools, I dropped my father's name and gave my name as just Fatima Meer. That is how I have come to be known. My sisters lug around Moosa and so they have two names and one of them a male name. "Why do you carry this incongruity around you?" I ask. "Our father an incongruity?" they respond, pointing a finger at me and I left it at that.

I liked my school. It was co-educational but I was totally unaware of sex differences until one of the boys in my class, Ronnie, drew the attention of us girls to his penis and pushed it into a hole that he in all probability had especially made in his desk. We were so shocked that we looked at each other aghast, fearful for Ronnie if the teacher caught him. Ronnie just grinned.

Our mornings at the Albert Street School began with musical games on the ground facing the pavement. *'This is the way we clap our hands, clap our hands, clap our hands . . . early in the morning'* and so on to other stanzas. Choir singing was another favourite. We went into the big room with the piano. The walls of the room were adorned with pictures of the blue-eyed blonde Christ in a long white robe tending his flock, holding out his arms to children to come to him, and the baby Jesus in a manger with the three wise men. I loved the pictures and loved the hymns we learned to sing – '*Away in a manger, no crib for a bed'*, '*Onward Christian soldiers marching as to war'*. There were songs other than hymns also – '*On yonder hill there stands a maiden, who she is I do not know'*, '*Gin a body meet a body coming through the rye . . .'*

The songs, the religion, my friends, my teachers all took me into a completely different world, strange and new and attractive. I was eager to be of it. My parents and uncles encouraged my enthusiasm for it. There was no apprehension whatsoever that I might leave the world they had inculcated in me, that I might be lost to them in my new world. In my mind, the two worlds converged easily as one and there was no conflict.

In my second year of school, in standard one,[16] I had a wonderful teacher, Miss Norman. She read us *Little Women*. I loved it – especially the outspoken tomboy Jo who was clearly also Miss Norman's favourite. Miss Norman taught us gardening. Each one of us had our gardening plots and each one of us had our beans and saw them germinate as if by magic.

My standard two teacher, though, was horrible – Miss Kornby, or corned beef as we called her. She seemed to have an intense dislike for us Coloured children.

The government education department distributed free milk. It came cold in half-litre bottles. I hated the milk but we were forced to drink it. There were those of us who could not hold our milk and soon after drinking it wet our panties.

I made many friends at school. The fact that I was Indian in a Coloured school never bothered me and never bothered anyone else. There were three Fatimas in my class–Fatima Jacob, Fatima Edries and me, Fatima Meer. The other two were Malay. Fatima Edries was closely related to Aunty Baby who was married to Uncle Cas. I didn't care for her, she was too chatty and somewhat callous, but Fatima Jacob and I became great friends. Her sister Rita was also a good friend.

The health nurse on a visit to school inspected our teeth, our ears and our hair. The two other Fatimas had lice in their hair and were sent off home to have their hair cleaned. Fatima Jacob, who had long hair, was ordered to cut it short. I was spared that ignominy.

I hated my mother oiling and combing my hair. Amina Ma tied it into two tight plaits and fussed over my hair. When I was about four or five years old, my head had been shaven bald, because Amina Ma thought my hair was too thin. I suppose her care despite all my protests paid off as I had very long hair for most of my life, though I think that was because she had beautiful long hair and my hair was just like hers, brown and thick.

A favourite game I played with Fatima Jacob and her sister at their house in Avondale Road, was bouncing a tennis ball on the wall and chanting what sounded like '*Ahm lay duck, wags his tail and touches the ground*'. We would turn around quickly enough to catch the ball and if we failed to do so we were out. The Mall children, Behn and Bhai Gora, played with us on occasions.

'Give-us-support' was the game that gave me most pleasure. All the children from the Meer and Ayson houses, the big children and the small children, played it together on the road in Convent Lane. A 'court' – three sets of parallel lines which the challengers had to get through to win – was marked out with chalk right across the road. The defending team took their positions in the parallel lines and the attacking team shouted, '*Give us!*' The defending team would mobilise its members and shout '*Support!*' The attackers tried to get through without being caught; the defenders tried to stop them and there was great screaming when an attacker was caught. It was a robust and very noisy game.

'Policemen and robbers' was another favourite game. The robbers fled to West Street; the policemen followed in hot pursuit and if the robbers were caught, they were imprisoned in any large cardboard box dumped by one of the shops in West Street. Meanwhile on Cathedral Road and in Madressa Arcade, my brother, Ismail, and Hassan Mall, played cricket. They also played cricket in Convent Lane when we were not playing 'Give-us-support'.

The backyards of the shops in West Street, the main shopping street in Durban, were in Convent Lane. We rummaged in the bins and the boxes dumped in these and often came up with what we considered treasures – broken toys, scraps of material, electrical parts. We were particularly happy when our parents found use for any of these. We also played 'Hide-and-seek' with the Aysons in the empty boxes that were dumped in Convent Lane.

We sat on the pavement and heard our mothers' insinuations as they commented on the traffic that passed through the dark passage in the building opposite our home. They whispered knowingly to each other about the suspected activities in the rooms upstairs with their coloured windows.

Solly, Gorie, me, Bhai, a cousin, Ahmed   *Solly, Bhai, Ahmed, me*

We younger children went to Albert Park, a public park near the harbour, and collected Dutch apples, red and somewhat tangy in taste. We sat on the swing and vied with each other to swing the highest. We went to the harbour area and looked for guppies.

All of us children enjoyed the delicious pleasure of smoking on one occasion or another. These episodes of cigarette smoking were sometimes discovered, sometimes secret. One day Papa was lying on his bed when he saw smoke spiralling from below. Papa pulled out the dumbstruck Solly, gave him a terrible hiding and, for good measure, made him eat a packet of cigarettes. If my father thought that would clear him of smoking, it never did.

One Christmas Eve we were a ragamuffin gang walking down West Street, collecting discarded butts and puffing away on these. Somebody produced pieces of cheese for us to nibble on so that the pungent flavour would camouflage the tell-tale odour of smoke. In fact, we did not like smoking, but illicit puffing was the closest we got to sinning and we found it utterly delicious, like the apple shared by Adam and Eve.

We had our world and our parents theirs and we hoped the two would never meet for we believed our parents would not like our world. We had no power to censure their world but they had all the power to censure ours and us. We were expected to keep ourselves safe and secure and if we defaulted, we could expect severe admonitions and even a slap or two. So if we fell and hurt ourselves, we were scolded and attended to but not consoled for the pain we had suffered. The result was that we hid our accidents from our parents as far as we could.

One day I had a road accident and even this I kept secret, locked in my heart, for fear of the scolding or even spanking I would get. I was on my way to Uncle AC's flat and crossing West Street when a car knocked me. The driver probably applied his brakes in time, but I fell in a state of shock. The driver came to attend to me but I insisted I was all right, trying desperately to escape from him, for my only concern was that Amina Ma should not come to know about it. I did manage to get away and reached home and fell asleep in the safety of my bed.

A miserly old man, Karodia Chacha, settled in with us at Convent Lane for a time. My brother Ismail was full of pranks and Chacha became the object of them as Ismail forever plotted how to upset our visitor.

Chacha made up his bed very neatly with not a crease in it. He forbade us all to go anywhere near his bed. He was a namazi, praying five times a day, and we would pollute his bed and break his wuzoo so that he would have to perform his ablutions again before prayer.

Chacha collected biscuits and fruit from the people he visited in the course of the day and hoarded these at his bedside. His hoard though would often disappear. One day he found what he thought was a man sleeping in his bed. Flustered and frightened he alerted my father to the stranger making his bed napak or impure. Papa ripped away the bed-clothes to remove the stranger – a dummy placed there by our brother Ismail. On another occasion, my brother placed a bucket of water on top of the door so that when Chacha opened it he got drenched in dirty water.

He complained bitterly to our father about all these pranks and our father rebuked the older boys, but rather mildly.

One day, the school health nurse on examining me said I had tonsillitis. She wrote a letter to my father and another to Addington Hospital to have them removed. My father took me to the outpatients' section at Addington. The doctor was quite curt: Addington was for Europeans and Coloureds, we were Indians and so we had to go to King Edward Hospital. My father was put out but he did not say a word. He simply started walk-ing the roughly four kilometres to King Edward Hospital, with me in tow for there were no trains or buses between the two hospitals.

We walked in silence and I didn't quite know what was going on. I think this was a time when my father had stopped playing with me and spoke to me only when necessary. My father left me at King Edward Hospital where I was admitted as a patient and taken upstairs and put to bed.

I was given food to eat and told to cup my hands so that custard could be dished out in them. I declined the custard, not understanding how I would eat it. My mothers came to see me with my uncle Gora Papa in the afternoon. I said I didn't like the place and I wanted to go home with them, but they said they would remove my tonsils and I should stay. They left and the nurse brought me a cup of milk so I threw it out of the window and gave the nurse an empty cup.

The next morning I was taken down a lift in a stretcher to another room where a doctor pressed a hat to my nose. I could not breathe. I was terrified. I tried to push away the hat, but the doctor's hands were too strong. I relaxed and found myself descending through circles of coloured light and then I remembered nothing.

When I came to, I found I was back on the bed in the ward, my throat was sore and I was spitting blood. An operation, I realised, happens when you are well and then you get sick. My mothers and Gora Papa came to see me again. I said I wanted to go home. They cajoled me into staying and said they would take me when my operation healed. They bought me a Donald Duck book and I was very pleased with that. I loved Donald Duck and his nephews and Daisy.

Two days later I was back home, being fed ice cream and made a fuss of. My brothers gave me a whole lot of chocolates. I told our mothers that I couldn't eat the chocolates. "Of course you can't!" Amina Ma said in alarm and took them away.

Then began the inquiry. My brother Ismail was called in and asked where the chocolates had come from. The story came out that he and Unus had stolen them from a shop in West Street. Gora Papa marched the two of them to the shop where they were made to apologise and my father paid for the chocolates. Unus and my brother Ismail returned from their ordeal and looked at me accusingly.

Gora Papa opened his own printing press, The Express Printing Works, close to Papa's in about 1938, and soon after this he and his family moved away from us. He bought a wood and iron house with furniture in Ritson Road for £600. Ritson Road was about two kilometres away from our home in Convent Lane. The properties there belonged to whites. Many white properties in those days had an anti-Asiatic clause built into their deed of sale[17]. The Ritson Road properties did not. A year or so later Papa also bought a house in Ritson Road.

Gora Papa came to fetch me and I went with him proudly and happily holding onto his hand, and – joy of joys – stepped into a tram and excitedly walked up the stairs to the top deck and looked out onto the street below. I visited Gora Papa's family often. On the one occasion, Gora Papa, as usual sitting at the head of the table awaiting his dinner, invited me to join him. I declined.

"Why won't you eat?" he asked. "Is the food not to your liking? Aren't you hungry? There is a very nice dessert."

"The food looks very good," I said.

Gora Papa persisted: "Then aren't you hungry?" I said I was *quite* hungry (in fact I was *very* hungry).

"Then why won't you eat?" he asked again. I responded: "You must ask me three times. Only then can I accept your invitation."

Gora Papa said he had already asked me once and he proceeded to ask me two more times and I settled down promptly next to him to be served my dinner. He and his family thought I was very funny and they laughed at my expense for months to come and I was teased about it by them forever.

Papa had told me that it was impolite to eat at other people's houses.

"They invite you out of politeness. They don't expect you to accept their invitation," he said.

"How many times should they invite you?" I asked.

"Three or so times," my father said.

These words had stuck in my mind and I explained my reasoning to Gora Papa. "That applies to strangers," Gora Papa explained. "You have rights here. You don't stand on ceremony."

Our brother Ismail believed that it was all very well being stuffed with lessons, but we also had to have fun. He used to take us out with him in the afternoons. Usually he took us to Albert Park, but sometimes he took us to the bioscope. We would be thrilled to bits when he mentioned the bioscope, but a rehearsal would follow.

"I've only got money for my ticket," Ismail would school us. "You walk low and that man in the ticket booth will think you are young and not charge for you." Sometimes we got by, sometimes the man scolded our brother Ismail and said he was cheating.

I loved going to the bioscope. Victoria Street was where the bioscopes were, the Victoria Picture Palace and the Royal Picture Palace. These were bug houses but that never bothered me. My eyes were on the screen. I saw *How Green was My Valley* at Victoria Picture Palace. We queued and waited for what seemed like hours before we got in to see *Snow White and the Seven Dwarfs* at the Royal Picture Palace. I identified completely with Snow White's fear when night descended on her in the forest and I closed my eyes petrified. It was at the Royal that I met the swashbuckling Errol Flynn as Robin Hood and Olivia de Havilland as Maid Marian. It was at the Royal too that I fell in love with Ashok Kumar and equally in love with Devika Rani and the dancer Mumtaz Ali. The tune, '*Gôre gôre hatho mê kalie kalie choorya/Black bangles on white arms*' played in my mind for the rest of my life as did '*Mein ban kie chidya ban ban bollo re/I am a forest bird, I chirp around in the forest*'.

At the Avalon I met Tyrone Power and Joan Bennet, Carmen Miranda, Don Ameche, and Spencer Tracy. And there was Judy Garland in the *Wizard of Oz. The Jungle Princess* was showing at the Royal Picture Palace with Dorothy Lamour and we wanted to see that above all else in our world. We begged our parents to allow us to see it. We promised that we would not ask to go to the cinema for three months. Our parents relented. I entered into a romance with Dorothy Lamour and whether I had a singing voice or not, I sang *Moonlight and Shadows* around the house '*and you in my heart in the Jungle Night my sweet . . .*' or words to that effect.

Shirley Temple was my idol. I collected Shirley Temple pictures from my penny chocolates. I saved up my Eid money and bought a Shirley Temple doll. I bought a yard of pink satin for six pence, and walked all by myself across the bridge into Cathedral Road near the market to Warwick Avenue and to Gorie Bai, Uncle AC's wife, who had promised to make my doll a dress. But tragedy of tragedies! When I reached her house I discovered that the packet was empty, the precious pink satin had fallen out on the way and was lost forever. My doll never had her new dress.

At night in my room I worried about my heroes and heroines the film stars, whose pictures I collected and whose every new film I saw. They were all non-Muslims and therefore they would go to hell. I prayed fervently to Allah each night to make them into Muslims.

I was ten years old and totally unprepared for it. I had no idea that such a thing happened to girls or to anyone. I found blood in my panty and wondered at it. My mind went wild with thoughts. I had noticed the blood at school. I thought somebody may have killed a man and put him in the toilet pan and his blood must have dropped into my panty. The next morning I was sitting on the bed, putting on my socks and Amina Ma noticed the blood and she was shocked. She obviously had not expected me to start menstruating so soon. She transferred her shock to me in anger and made me feel as though I had done something wrong.

I was bustled off with no explanation. Some rags were found, a cord tied around my waist, a folded rag placed in between my thighs and a long cloth passing through the cord and pinned at the top to keep the folded rag in position. I was to tie the rags securely so that the blood did not leak out. It was most uncomfortable – the rags were hard and chaffed my skin. I was given another set of rags and taught to wash them on the rough cement toilet floor and hang them to dry on a special line.

I was sworn to secrecy about my condition. Amina Ma didn't want anyone to know I had started menstruating. I tried my best, but my dress got soiled and Choti Khala saw it and asked me what was on my dress. I was deeply embarrassed but Amina Ma quickly took me aside and scolded me for my carelessness. It was difficult keeping the blood from soiling my dress. It was difficult with all those rags around me.

I was beginning to be a woman and the process was painful. Ma warned me that I should have nothing to do with boys. I should not have them near me. I should not laugh with boys. I should not smile at them. My breasts began to grow and I wished I could cut them off. An aunt made me bras out of some grey cotton cloth. I felt ugly and gawky and I bottled up all these bad feelings about myself. I confided in no-one, not even my close friends at school. My play with brothers and sisters and my cousins became inhibited.

I saw some hair on my upper lip and I began to remove this secretly with a blade. Nobody remarked on it. My mother never saw it, never stopped me. It was not observable. My mothers were remarkably unhelpful during this crisis period in my life. Why did they not see what was going on with their daughter?

CHAPTER 8

Ritson Road: 1939–1944

I was probably eleven years old when we moved from Convent Lane to 84 Ritson Road, the first house Papa owned. Our house had three bedrooms, a sitting room, a dining room, a breakfast room, a bathroom, kitchen, pantry and a veranda which we later enclosed with windows and a canvas blind over the doorway.

Our parents occupied the front bedroom with its bay window. Papa and Ma's cousin Gora Mamoo and his wife Gorie Apa occupied a second bedroom, and us children filled the beds in the third bedroom. A studio couch in the enclosed veranda was used for any extra people sleeping over. Our driver, Omar Khan, used it often. The toilet was in the garden, and behind the toilet were the servants' quarters where our housekeeper, Landeni, her son, Ginger Pop, and daughter, Bukusa, lived.

While most properties in the area still belonged to whites, there were six Indian families already living in Ritson Road when we arrived there. In the house next door to ours were the Naidoos, two very fat brothers. The one brother was married to a very petite lady. Rumour had it that she slept on the floor while the brothers occupied the bed. The other brother married after we moved in and theirs was the first South Indian wedding we attended. The marigolds and jewels decorating the bride's thick plait charmed us. I thought the Naidoo house better than ours for the veranda went right around the house. A golden creeper grew luxuriously between our two houses and I painted this, I thought rather well.

Across from the Naidoo house, on the corner of Ritson Road and Youngs Avenue, was another Naidoo house. That Mr Naidoo, a kind hospitable man, was a herbalist with a shop in Victoria Street. His daughter, Madraj, was very athletic and a keen cyclist. We became good friends. She had a younger brother, Das. Their dining room was very sombre, filled with heavy mahogany furniture.

Next to the Naidoos were the Budhoos. They seemed to forever have prayer meetings and weddings, and the main attraction during these celebrations, the religious dramas performed by the Riverside Natak Mandal, went on all night. Not obliged to sit from start to finish, we children would walk in and out of the Natak performances as we pleased. We enjoyed the vegetarian feasts they served. The adults in our family never attended. There was no formal invitation, we children just felt free to attend.

Then there were the Meer houses on Ritson Road. My father's brother Gora Papa's house at 62 Ritson Road on the corner of Waynes Avenue stood close to ours. The local tearoom to which we made numerous trips during the course of a day stood at the opposite corner. Ma's brother, Chota Mamoo, bought a house next to the tearoom, concluding the Meer houses in Ritson Road.

Gora Papa and Apa Ma's family had expanded. Apa Ma and Gora Papa had taken in Apa Ma's invalid mother, their sister, Choti Khala, and their brother, Big Ismail, when Apa Ma's brother Uncle AC could no longer care of them. Big Ismail had a small room leading off the breakfast room and on the wall he had a large framed photograph of his sister Gorie Bai who was in India. I went there sometimes and he told me about the stars and the light years they were away from the earth while I listened fascinated.

To make ends meet, Apa Ma and Gora Papa also took in boarders. At meal times Gora Papa sat at the head of the table, presiding over the boarders. Nobody spoke while Gora Papa was there. The boarders called him Willy behind his back, I never knew why.

Apa Ma served her boarders and her family hot rotis with every meal. She would make a kind of fudge – gor paprie – and always saved some for me. I liked Apa Ma and flattered myself that I was her favourite. She cooked at the end of the breakfast room, close to the door leading out to a back yard dominated by an avocado tree which produced the best avocados in the district – very large and very tasty. She preferred cooking there than in the kitchen, because she could look out into the backyard where her invalid mother and invalid son, Abbasi, would sit. Apa Ma could also look out at the passers-by on Waynes Avenue, and spot us when we returned from town or school.

Soon I had an additional house to visit. Papa and Ma's cousins, Gora Mamoo and Gorie Apa, and their daughter Zohra moved to a double-storey house at 10 Lanyon Grove about five minutes' walk away from our house. It was an exciting house with a basement and an attic comprised of a room and balcony. Zohra, her cousin Bibi and I spent a great deal of time there. We sang and we ate green mangoes with salt and chilli powder, or red tamarind – all very sour and very delicious. Choti Khala soon left Ritson Road to rent a room with Gora Mamoo's family in Lanyon Grove.

Gorie Apa later moved from Lanyon Road to Madras Road opposite the racecourse. While the horses raced, other petty gambling activities went on outside. We children were attracted to that gambling. I crouched beside the feet of the grownups who eagerly awaited the results of the races. I placed my pennies on the checkerboard, thrilled when they doubled and greatly disappointed when I lost.

Of all these homes, however, it was our veranda in Ritson Road that became the favourite meeting place for our mothers and aunts. They would sit on the veranda, gossip and watch the passing traffic, and I would find them there when I returned from school.

Ma's authority was decisive among the women in the family who did everything together – shopping, attending weddings and funerals. My father's car, driven by Khan, was the only car among all the Meers. My mothers' mobility depended on Khan's convenience and he had to be persuaded to drive them. He grumbled when there were too many of us, but Ma packed all the women cousins and the children into the back seat, even though its capacity was for three passengers. We sat one back, one forward, each occupying half a space, with us children somehow fitting on the half laps.

My mothers went to the bioscope once a week. They attended the special matinee for women, and sometimes I went with them. Occasionally my mothers sent me to the bioscope with my father and his friend though the men saw this as an imposition, not liking female intrusion in their male company.

There were by now several rungs of children in the family. The highest rung included my brother Ismail, cousins Chota Motala and MC Meer, and the Mall brothers, Hassan and Mahmood, whose family moved next door to us when the Naidoo family moved out. The second rung consisted of myself, my brothers Solly and Ahmed, and my cousins Zohra, Haroon and Unus. My sister Gorie, my brothers Bhai, Siddiek and Farouk, cousin Rasheeda and the Mall girls Behn, Gorie and Choti made up the lowest rung.

The numbers living at Ritson Road diminished as the older boys, Ismail, Unus, Chota and MC left to study in India. MC and Chota went to study medicine while Ismail and Unus went to attend Aligarh College in Uttar Pradesh. Unus was then just fourteen years old and many years later he recalled how his maternal grandmother chided his mother Apa Ma for her cruelty in sending a 14-year-old away from her.

I loved putting on plays with the younger children. Our front veranda was our auditorium, and we marked out a stage at the one end and raked up a curtain. The grown-ups obliged by making up the audience. I was invariably the master of ceremony, but was brought up sharply at the end of our first performance for giggling.

We went on picnics together, just the children, the older children looking after the younger ones. We also played at the Botanic Gardens, just across the road from us. We were particularly afraid of Parky, the park ranger, whose eyes were always on the children. There was a bamboo grove and many names had been carved on the bamboo trunks but we did not add ours. There was a large greenhouse where we liked walking among the ferns. As focused as Parky was on us, we managed to steal a plant or two, and we wreaked revenge on those Europeans who had labelled us criminals before we had committed a criminal act.

On Eid day we combined to do naughty things, like smoking cigarettes in secrecy, crawling into the large underground pipes lying around and making our home there.

We gathered on afternoons to play cards – a game we called 'Seven Hands' was our favourite. Every now and again, our elders, especially Gora Papa would express their distaste for what they called the 'evil' game, for they linked cards with gambling. There was a word Ma used incessantly, 'soomyathie', which I suppose would translate into abiding evil. It was 'soomyathie' to be outside the house in the hours between sunset and nightfall, when evil spirits abounded. It was 'soomyathie' to play music or read an English novel during the times of namaaz. Playing cards was very 'soomyathie' indeed, at all times.

Choti Khala ran a mini-madressa at her home in Lanyon Grove. She conducted lessons in Urdu, Arabic and Gujarati and I was one of her pupils. If we made a mistake, down came her ruler. One afternoon I became so infuriated with the caning, that I grabbed the ruler from her, broke it in two, threw away the two pieces and ran away. I could only go home though and Choti Khala followed me, with the two pieces of ruler and an inflamed temper. She confronted Amina Ma with my outrageous behaviour. I got a thrashing which I thought would never end until Papa retrieved me and put me beside him on his bed and I fell asleep sobbing.

"You shouldn't console a naughty child. She was punished as an example to the other children," Amina Ma chastised Papa.

There were times when our housekeeper, Landeni, took me with her when she went to visit her friends at the Bantu Women's Hostel, as it was called then, in Carlisle Street. I liked going with her, though all I did was sit quietly while they talked. In winter, Landeni and her friends sat around an mbawula (a paraffin tin with holes which she filled with coal) in our backyard and sometimes I joined them and watched the glowing red coals.

One day our backyard teemed with police and it seemed that no one could do anything about it. They raided Landeni's room and found a drum of home brewed beer[18]. They spilled it in the yard and my only thought was of Landeni's loss. The police then slapped her. I was angry with the police but also frightened and stood by helplessly while her dignity was assailed. I wondered whether I should be angry with myself too for being so helpless. My parents appeared to be able to do nothing for Landeni and I wondered at that too. She was then pushed into a police van only to return some seven days later.

When we first moved from Convent Lane, I continued to go to the Albert Street School until that school year was completed. Each morning I walked up Youngs Avenue and into Botanic Gardens Road to catch the tram. The tram stop was opposite a block of flats and I saw European men and women come out of it. I wondered about them and about their lives inside the flats. When the tram arrived I would take my place in the back three seats reserved for non-Europeans. The Europeans sat wherever they wished – downstairs or upstairs.

When the new school year began, I left the Albert Street School and was enrolled at Dartnell Crescent which was closer to Ritson Road. I skipped a year and went into standard four instead of three. Dartnell Crescent was a primary school for girls started by the wife of the High Commissioner of India, Lady Kunwar Singh.

At Dartnell Crescent I was referred to by my fellow students as 'the white girl', but it was said in Tamil, 'vellaikara' and I didn't know what it meant at that time.

My class at Dartnell Crescent. I am in the top row, third from right.

Up to standard four, our teachers were Indian but thereafter they were whites. There was one white teacher who made us feel she did not want to teach us because we were "non-whites". One day we were at the City Hall and I went into the 'Whites Only' toilet and she was also using it. She didn't say a word to me. It was as if she didn't recognise me, yet she communicated without words her displeasure at my being in her toilet.

In moving from Albert Street School to Dartnell Crescent, I had moved from a Coloured school to an Indian school. My friends were now Hindus and Christians. It was an adventure to visit their homes which were very different from the one in which I lived. During those visits I existed in my own world, apart from my family. I wonder now if my family did not miss me and worry about my whereabouts. I have no recollection that they did.

Naomi was a Tamil-speaking Christian who lived in Magazine Barracks, built by the Durban municipality for their workers. I liked going home with her; it was altogether a new world. There was a temple and rows of flats. The people were poor, the men all employees of the municipality.

Vatsala lived close to the school and I visited her home during school breaks. She played lovely Tamil songs on her gramophone. She lived in a small ground floor flat with her parents and elder sisters. As the youngest in the family she was pampered. Vatsala was older than me and had a secret boyfriend. Her parents would have killed her if they knew, or so she said.

We were once at the Avalon Theatre and she persuaded me to go with her to Albert Park to meet her boyfriend. "They won't miss us," she said. "We'll just be away a short while and return before the movie ends." She was right. We were not missed. Vatsala had older sisters who were supposed to keep an eye on her but they obviously did not do a good job.

Once I accompanied her and her boyfriend Freddy to the beach and we took photographs in the amphitheatre next to the stone basket with real flowers. For days thereafter I was petrified that somehow those photos would appear and my parents would see them.

Vatsala became a popular ghazal and qawali singer who performed regularly at the Avalon Theatre. She married Ramachandra, also an accomplished musician, and their son became a great tabla player.

I loved Doreen Samuels who lived in Agnes Road, not far from Ritson Road. I never quite knew whether she was Indian or Coloured. She was just Doreen, older than me and very feisty. My father found a note I had written to her in one of my notebooks and I think in retrospect he saw some strain of lesbianism in it. It was not what he said, it was what he did not say, his attitude, his coldness, his withdrawal from me. I suffered terribly.

Jessie Waghmarae and Ivy Bunsee became my best friends. We called ourselves 'The Three Ps' like the group of best friends in one of our prescribed books, *The History of Mr Polly* by HG Wells.

Jessie was tomboyish, hailing from the only Marathi family in South Africa. When I started at Dartnell Crescent, she was away in India, but the girls talked a lot about her. She was some sort of a leader and I was determined to outdo her so when she returned I picked a fight with her. The famous child star actress at the time was Vasanti who starred in a film called *Sant Tulsidas*. Jessie claimed Vasanti was her friend and that they had lived in the same block of flats in Bombay. I didn't believe her and accused her of boasting and lying. After that initial clash though, we became firm friends. Jessie's family lived on the ground floor of a flat in Beatrice Street[19] that her father had inherited from his father.

Ivy on the other hand was a devout Roman Catholic who knew the different types of sins you could commit and firmly believed in the punishment that would follow. She was very good and very pretty. She lived at the end of Wills Road. Her mother was a beautiful Coloured lady, a devout Catholic whose purpose in life was to keep her family on the straight and narrow. Her father was Indian. He was less strict and had an interest in Indian music. I was surprised one day to discover Ivy singing with Abdul Rahman's group at a celebration in Uncle AC's block of flats. I thought she sang most beautifully. This part of herself contrasted with her Catholicism.

Big Ismail was close to his sister, Choti Khala, and to Zohra who was his brother's daughter. One day he brought two beautiful European ladies, Leslie de Villiers and Pauline Podbury, who were both members of the Liberal Study Group and the South African Communist Party, to give Zohra and Choti Khala lessons. I felt excluded. Choti Khala spoke very admiringly of the two ladies to my mothers and Apa Ma, and I had the feeling that they were not too enthralled with her talk. Everyone though respected the fact that Big Ismail had brought them to Ritson Road. The European ladies talked about putting on a play in which Big Ismail would be the hero and Zohra the heroine. The play never materialised, but the prettier of the two ladies, Leslie, gave me her album of film stars. I was mad about Hollywood and its stars and I kept that album for a long time.

When Indira Gandhi came to Durban, Big Ismail took Zohra and Choti Khala to meet her. I wasn't taken as I was considered too young, though at age thirteen I didn't feel it. I just felt excluded and it was not a nice feeling.

When I was fourteen I started attending the Durban Indian Girls' High School. In my first year there, my baby sister Razia was born. I came home from school one day to find, to my joy and excitement, this new baby girl, who had arrived as inexplicably as all the other babies.

In my high school years, my Gora Papa took me to what were considered intellectual meetings, symposiums and lectures by eminent scholars. He had just joined the university as a part-time student, the University of Natal[20] having started classes for non-Europeans at Sastri College (the only high school for Indian boys). These classes were started on the initiative of the educationist and academic Mabel Palmer with support from two of the other female lecturers, Elizabeth Sneddon and Florence McDonald. Gora Papa took great pride in presenting me to these fine ladies, his tutors. He arranged for Professor Sneddon to give me elocution lessons in her studio in one of the tall buildings in West Street.

Me with my brother Farouk,
Ma's brother Chota Mamoo holding my
baby sister Razia and Papa's brother,
Gora Papa, beside us.

When I look back on my time spent with Gora Papa, I have the sense that he was cultivating me. This cultivation was continuous until I passed matric and went to university. Then I think he saw his mission as accomplished and he relaxed. He never gave as much of his attention to any of the other children, and this I think included his son Unus.

It was Gora Papa who put the idea in my head that I could get up and speak to people. The 'people' in those days were the family. He would make me stand on a log of wood give me a staff and say I was on the nimbar and I could give a lecture like the Molvi Saheb. To him, it was probably a game to see his cute little niece mimicking a Molvi Sahib. Perhaps he was also deriding the Molvis. I learnt later that both he and my father had a hearty disdain for Molvis whom they considered ignoramuses,

Above: Dartnell Crescent School, 1939. I am seated third from right.

Top: With high school friends Jessie Waghmarae and Ivy Bunsee in 1940s.

Above: Photo by Dennis Govender, 1948.

Opposite top: Walking in West Street – captured by a street photographer in 1940s.

Opposite bottom left and right: Portraits from the 1940s.

*My engagement day
in 1949.
Photos by
Dennis Govender.*

Street photo – West Street, Durban 1940s.

Above: With Shamim, Shehnaz and Rashid during the Treason Trial in 1957.
Photo by Ranjith Kally.

Top: With Myna Mangal, Ismail and Violaine Junod, Pinetown, 1950s.
Photo by Dennis Govender.

With Ismail, Rashid, Shehnaz and Shamim, 1959.

With Shamim, Rashid and Shehnaz in our
Burnwood Road garden.

Opposite top: With Shamim, Shehnaz and Rashid in 1960 –
Photo taken by Ranjith Kally while Ismail was in prison.
Ismail put this picture up on his cell wall
during his detention.

Opposite bottom: With Ismail, Shamim, Rashid and Shehnaz in
Burnwood Road, 1960s.

Above: With Ismail, my siblings and their spouses in 1977. Standing from left to right – Bhai, Farouk, Ismail, Ahmed and my brothers-in-law Hoosen Seedat and Ebrahim Goga. Seated left to right: sisters-in-law Marie, Zubeda, Rasheeda, Gorie and my sisters Gorie and Baby.

Top: On a panel of speakers at the 1971 Conference of the Association of Sociologists of Southern Africa in then Lourenco Marques.

Opposite: My Masters graduation.
Top: With Professors Hansie Pollack (second from left) and Hamish Dickie Clarke (fifth from left).

Bottom: With my children.

Above: Photo taken by R Bughwan & Sons (Crown Studios), Durban in the 1960s –
Ismail had this photograph on his desk in his office in Verulam.

Opposite top left: With Monty Naicker.

Opposite top right: With Rose Catchings of the Global Ministries of the United
Methodist Church (standing) and Zanele Mbeki during my visit to the USA in 1972.

Opposite bottom: With Ismail Mahomed.

Above: With Sushila Behn Gandhi, daughter-in-law of Mahatma Gandhi, at Phoenix Settlement.

Top: With Ismail, Monty Naicker, MN Pather and George Singh at the opening of Alan Paton's Umkhumbane at Durban City Hall. The following morning the post-Sharpville State of Emergency was declared and Ismail, Monty and George were arrested.

Above: With Ethel Payne renowned African American journalist (next to me), and the staff of Ebony Magazine during my visit to the USA in 1972.

Top: Guest speaker at the prize giving ceremony at the Charles Johnson Memorial Hospital in Nqutu 1971.

Taken around the 1980s.

misleading people with their ignorance. I took my role very seriously and
Gora Papa showed me off. Sometimes I would giggle and then he disciplined me, but most times I was a hit.

In 1944 in my second year of high school, I became involved in my first
fundraising venture. Terrible famine had broken out in Bengal. My brother Ismail was at the time a student in India and we wrote to each other
regularly. He sent me his published short stories and I poured my heart
out to him about all the things that touched and moved me.

When he wrote to me about the famine in Bengal and that his close
friends were going there on relief work, I decided to raise funds in Durban. Armed with a notebook and facts about the famine, I went from
shop to shop after school. I started with the tailors in Field Street[21] and
collected ten shillings from each of them. I also went to the well-known
cartoonist and music director, Yusuf Kat, and negotiated with him to
produce a concert at the Avalon Theatre. My classmates and Yusuf Kat
helped sell the tickets at a pound each. The concert was a great success
and we had people clamouring to get in.

I found myself in a pleasant situation where people approached me, to
'please, please sell them a ticket'. I wanted to do everyone a favour but I
could not. We raised over a thousand pounds for the Bengal Relief and Papa
made arrangements to have it sent to the correct official source in India.

That year I wrote my Junior Certificate (JC) examinations. It was my
second public examination, the first being the standard six exam. When
the JC results had been released, I had not got mine as my school was
closed and no one was there. I was anxious, as was my family and Hassan
Mall, the eldest son in the Mall family and a first year Fort Hare student.
Hassan was convinced that the results were in the principal's office, but her
ladyship was on holiday and there would be no results until she returned.
He felt I had a right to my results, so this future judge, the first among
non-whites, broke into the principal's office discreetly and got my results.
I had gained a first class pass!

Life was full of fun at high school. I excelled in literature and history.
Miss Hammond was our teacher in both subjects. She was over-nervous,

so much so that there was a constant shaking or shivering about her. She wore very pretty dresses, more in the style of a teenager than that of a spinster lady past forty. She was an inspiring history and literature teacher and she had a high moral sense which she imparted to me.

Miss Hammond taught us South African history with an understanding of its colonial implications, something quite amazing for those times. She had a friend who headed one of the legal firms in Durban and who had a beautiful cottage on Brighton Beach in the Bluff area. She took the class to that cottage for a picnic.

I became quite close to Miss Hammond. She lived not far from Ritson Road and I often walked with her from school to the end of Botanic Gardens Road where she turned into Berea Road[22] to her flat in Berea Court. I walked on from there, cutting into Youngs Avenue and then on to Ritson Road. On one occasion Miss Hammond invited me to her home to work on the school magazine. Miss Hammond lived with her old mother who had once been a skilful painter and their flat was adorned with many of her paintings. Miss Hammond asked me to prepare scrambled eggs for our lunch. I really did not know how to do it but would not admit my ignorance. I turned out a rubbery mess which horrified Miss Hammond.

Miss Hammond encouraged me to open my mind and heart to her. She did not treat me as a child. We discussed history, literature, religion, Indian culture and civilisation. We discussed Islam and Christianity and I probably told her a great deal about my family, but strangely never invited her home to meet my parents.

Miss Hammond though did get to meet my father and my Gora Papa. She was lecturing us on the history of printing and I reported that my father had a printing press. The class thought it would be a good idea to visit the press. I felt very proud and told my father, who appeared pleased but also a little apprehensive: "Your class will be visiting us. We will have to extend our hospitality. Do you think it will be alright to serve your class ice cream?" I was overjoyed.

The visit was a great success and I went up a notch in the estimation of my fellow pupils.

Soon after this event, Miss Hammond arranged for all the standard nines to go to a performance of *Richard of Bordeaux* at the YMCA enacted by a Black high school. I asked Gora Papa to take Miss Hammond and me to the performance in the small French car he had recently acquired. My class girls were very amused that Gora Papa had given Miss Hammond a lift, and they manufactured a romance where none could have existed, Miss Hammond being a confirmed spinster and by our reckoning over the hill, and my uncle, a very married man.

CHAPTER 9

Pinetown: 1944–1946

I think Papa for years had nurtured a desire to buy a property in the country and move his printing press there. He needed more room, besides the rental did not make operating in town economical. I do not know what other thoughts went through his mind, but this, as far as I know, was his reason for purchasing our house *Ocean View* in Pinetown, in my sixteenth year.

When I first saw the Pinetown house, I fell in love with it. For the first time I had the sense of having a home that suited my family. In practically all the English literature I read, families were known by their houses. Now we could be known by our house, and *Ocean View* would be to me what *Raja Wadi*, Ma's house in Surat, was to her.

Ocean View, our family home in Pinetown.

Ocean View was a large rambling house with a wrap-around veranda, four bedrooms and two large living rooms, one of them used as a library.

Our parents occupied the two front rooms. My younger siblings occupied the middle room, where they crowded together, two to a bed. For the first time, I had a room to myself and I dressed it up as prettily as I could.

I also decorated the walls of the library – in blue wallpaper sprinkled with white lilies of the valley, and I framed photographs and prints cut out of books and mounted these on the walls. A bookcase took up one wall of the library, and a studio couch slept members of the extended family who came on weekends. We now had two cars, and Khan was still our driver.

One approached the house through a poinsettia-lined driveway. A stream meandered across the southernmost boundary. A small portion of the 25-acre property was thickly forested. I loved retreating into its darkness and going on adventures – with Robin Hood and his men, with Tarzan, with real hard-core bandits, or lost princesses waiting to be rescued by princes.

Pinetown was sunny and warm and altogether splendid. I cannot recall a rainy day, though there must have been enough of these. The land was dotted with pecan nut trees. We picked the nuts in season and took them to our mothers who made presents of these to the different households in our clan. We had a bull, Badsha, and a cow, Najma. Badsha seemed a useless, parasitic fellow, but Najma was full of milk and kept us in good supply. My mothers churned butter and separated the cream.

The families from Ritson Road came over weekends. They liked visiting us in Pinetown and we loved entertaining them. We took our cousins on picnics to the nearby stream in Sarnia. Our mothers would prepare a delicious picnic lunch, which would include jelly and custard for dessert.

As always our family kept expanding – the house seeming to shrink in relation to the people living in it. My father enclosed a part of the veranda and made room for six beds. My young brothers, Siddiek, Farouk and Bhai, and our male cousins and uncles slept in these beds. Our cousin, YC Meer, bought a house next door to ours in Pinetown and my cousin Zohra's family and her widowed aunt and three children lived there but spent most of their time in our home.

Our mothers, especially Amina Ma, had enough on their hands. Each morning they prepared their own nine children for school, helped the younger children dress, and prepared breakfast for them all. The younger children of school going age were enrolled at the local primary school. A hot meal was prepared for their lunch each day and Jim, who worked for us, delivered it each lunch time on his bicycle.

Soon there were more additions. My father's cousin, Dawood Variawa, who lived in Kimberley, had marital problems and his five children, the youngest about four years old and the eldest around twelve, came to live with us. We were excited by these additions. The two girls Minnie and Fareeda stayed with us until they married, but the three boys left for boarding school.

I now travelled to the Durban Indian Girls' High School by train. My life was conditioned by the train timetable and I seemed forever to be running to make it. If I missed the train in the morning there wasn't another for at least an hour and I would lose half the school day. There was a way around this. If I missed the train in Pinetown, I would run down the back slope of our land to the stream and across it onto the railway line, jumping from sleeper to sleeper, until I reached Sarnia Station. If lucky, I would get the train there and be on my way.

Missing the train in the afternoon meant meeting Amina Ma on her way to the station as mad as hell, and ready to thrash me there and then. Her mind, I think, went in the direction of my keeping a tryst with a boyfriend.

One afternoon, I found myself alone in the second-class coach. The European train conductor came in and began making sexual advances to me. I resisted as strongly as I could and when I saw that he would overcome me, I opened the compartment door and threatened to jump off. That frightened him and he let off and I walked into the third-class compartment where I was safe with the other passengers.

At school we standard nines were a group of twelve strongly bonded friends. My closest friends then were Ivy Bunsee, Jessie Waghmarae, Perin Randeree and Dhun Rustomjee. We visited each other's homes and we learnt about each other's cultures – Parsee and Christian, South Indian, Hindustani, and Marathie – seeing each as our own since we belonged to each other.

Dhun lived in central Durban with her cousin, Deena Ma. I often visited their home and when Deena Ma had a baby girl, Amina Ma knitted her a pretty pink jacket and bonnet. We attended Dhun's birthday at her uncle Jalbhay's house in Ninth Avenue, and her sister's navjot ceremony for which Dhun's father, the powerful community leader Sorabjee Rustomjee, brought out a Parsee priest from India since there were none in South Africa.

We were all invited to Perin's brother's wedding at the Avalon Theatre. Later her family invited the class to a special Parsee lunch of dhansak – the fish, steamed in wrapped leaves was a speciality.

One of our class girls was Binnie Ballaram. Her father ran buses from Hillary, a suburb north of the city centre. One day the bus driver was drunk and Binnie took over the bus, bringing the passengers safely to their destination. Binnie's father was most charming and gave us a donation for our school magazine.

Our friend Minnie Ramawtar's father was the hearty, hospitable Ben Ramawtar, a keen fisherman who had his own rowing boat. He organised a picnic for our whole class on Salisbury Island. My parents wouldn't allow me to go alone and sent my sister Gorie with me. I resented Gorie's presence and poor Gorie had to suffer an elder sister who practically ignored her and a picnic where she had no friends.

We standard nines formed a social club and invited speakers to address us. Our social club organised an end of year 'thank you' celebration for our teachers. We collected money and bought each of our teachers a present. They were very pleased with our effort. I was the director of ceremonies, and I could not understand why each time I made a presentation I was met with peals of laughter. It was later pointed out to me that each time I made a presentation I said, "This prize is for Miss Hammond", and "This prize for Miss Perrins", and "This prize for Miss O'Del". Instead of distributing presents, I was distributing prizes! I had remained totally innocent of my faux pas but was pleased I had caused so much mirth.

We had a school magazine which was always run by the English teacher, and in standard nine I was given the task of editing the magazine. That year I did not only edit and write for the magazine but also organised the printing of it and collected advertisements to pay for the cost of publication.

It was in standard nine also that Miss Hammond produced *Macbeth*. I was Lady Macbeth and I think Jessie was Macbeth.

Our class held many debates and challenged the Sastri College boys and the Ohlange School, in Inanda township. Jessie, Ivy and I formed the school debating team. I usually both introduced the subject and summed it up so I had a lot of thinking to do on my feet.

The small front garden of the school had a large bed of nasturtiums. My mother, Amina Ma, loved flowers so one afternoon I picked a bunch for her. The next morning at assembly the principal announced that somebody had picked flowers from the school garden. It was embarrassing for me and painful but I put up my hand and confessed that I was the culprit. My reputation was suddenly born as a truthful and brave girl. I glowed in this new reputation.

At one stage our class took on the fashion of wearing cheap gold beads which we threaded into jewellery. One of the girls had discovered these beads and had come to school wearing them in bracelets and a necklace. A few days later the teachers found the whole class wearing identical gold-beaded jewellery and they laughed.

It was not an occasion for laughter when we began reading in our prescribed textbook an essay by Thomas Babington Macaulay on Warren Hastings, the first Governor General of Bengal. His utterly insulting essay on Indians devastated us and we listened to the reading by Miss Hammond with glowering faces as if she were responsible for that so-called literature at the expense of the Indian people. She was actually very sympathetic to our feelings, and her approach in teaching history was remarkably radical.

While the education planners inflicted on us prescribed works we could not bear to read, we privately, in between lessons, focused on our own syllabus. We read and discussed Gandhi, Nehru and Sarojini Naidu and we followed the Anti-Imperial Freedom Movement[23] which was reaching its climax. Nearer home, in our matric year, we were inspired by the revolutionary climate in our community. We focused on the Passive Resistance Campaign launched by the Transvaal and Natal Indian Congresses against racist laws[24]. We focused on the leaders of the Passive Resistance – Dr Yusuf Dadoo, Monty Naicker and Dr Goonam[25]. I was one of the regular hangers-on at the Resistance Plot in Gale Street where resisters pitched tents on a vacant plot and were arrested by police, only to have a new batch of resisters take over, these too arrested.

My family bubbled with the energy of the Passive Resistance Campaign. Gora Papa, then Joint Secretary of the Natal Indian Congress[26], was involved in organising meetings and resisters. Big Ismail had suspended his legal studies and was devoting all his time to the Natal and Transvaal Indian Congresses and to recruiting batches of resisters from Johannesburg. Both my mothers and Choti Khala had become members of the Women's Action Committee, which focused on raising funds. My mothers also provided refreshments for resisters. Our home had become a virtual "halfway station" where resisters travelling by car from Johannesburg to Durban, would stop to rest and refresh themselves before going on to offer their resistance in Gale Street.

Passive Resistance Students Committee 1946. Among the Committee members were my close friends Ivy Bunsee, and Dhun Rustomjee (extreme left and centre in the second row), Minnie Ramawtar, Jessie Waghmarae and myself (seated from left to right).

I took off from school, usually with Jessie or Dhun, and we gave moral support to the resisters. MD Naidoo, Joint Secretary of the Natal Indian Congress (NIC), was our heartthrob. We thought him so handsome, so commanding and such a wonderful orator. We met him at the Resistance Plot and were flattered by his attention. Though he tended to order us around somewhat, we didn't mind at all.

We matrics threw in our lot to support the Passive Resistance Campaign and in doing so we took a revolutionary step. At a time when a girl could be expelled if seen talking to a boy, and when the very idea of co-education was taboo, our matric class reached out to the boys at Sastri College and invited them to join us in forming the Passive Resistance Students' Council. After school and at weekends, we were absorbed in our organising, planning ways and means to raise money.

We decided to stage two plays, *King Henry V* and *Catherine of Aragon* as part of our fundraising. I played Catherine and Dhun King Henry. We went to see the chairman of the Surat Hindu Association and requested the use of the hall for our meetings and rehearsals. He respected our intention to raise funds for the Passive Resistance Campaign and was sufficiently broadminded to give the hall to a co-educational group. For the public performance we hired the Avalon Theatre. With tickets selling at £5 each, we would raise £5 000 if we filled the hall.

We went to Stanger, Umzinto, Port Shepstone and Pietermaritzburg to sell tickets. A Sastri boy, Bhamjee Manjee, was able to get a friendly taxi owner to place his taxi service at our disposal. Papa also gave us his car and my brother Solly drove us so we had two groups on the road. One of us invariably had contacts in the towns we visited and he or she arranged for our reception, a sumptuous lunch, and introductions to prospective donors.

These excursions were great fun. We enjoyed each other's company and we deported ourselves in a manner that earned us a great deal of respect. There were some budding romances from these associations, but only one resulted in marriage, that of my friend Ivy Bunsee and her love, a boy called Ved Meharchand.

We tried to prank Binnie (our classmate who had saved her father's bus passengers) and were left with the highest respect for her following her response. We sent her letters purporting to be written by one of the boys, Awath Beharie. She, the practical upright person she was, replied that she could not accept his love. Love would come after marriage and she left these matters in the hands of her family. We were thoroughly ashamed of ourselves.

Our Passive Resistance Committee participated in the very successful Freedom Fair organised by the Natal Indian Congress. We had a stall where we sold milkshakes and sandwiches. Uncle AC had a stand close to ours, and the glamorous Dr Ansuya Singh, recently returned from the UK, ran a very popular stall nearby. In the centre was a dance floor for speeches and performances. I was besotted by PR Singh's rendition of *Raas Lila* (the dance of Krishna and the Gopis). He was a charming Krishna and with his equally graceful and agile Radha worked magic.

The big event of the Freedom Fair was the crowning of the queen and princesses. Our beautification and dressing took practically the whole afternoon. Radhamonie Padayachee who was secretary of the Women's Action Committee was crowned queen and Perin and I her princesses.

That year, 1946, I made my first public speech at a mass meeting at Red Square (now Nicol Square) on the 31 March, speaking after Dr Monty Naicker and Dr Goonam. A group of women resisters led by fearless activist Zainab Asvat[27] from Johannesburg was there all garlanded and ready to occupy the plot and court arrest. Gora Papa, as secretary on the Passive Resistance Council had influenced the executive to allow me to speak at that meeting. My father had written my speech and I had memorised it. I was a great success. As a young girl, standing up on that lorry which was our platform, I caught the people's imagination. Monty Naicker then asked me to join him and Dr Goonam in leading the 6 000 strong march that followed the speeches. Days later Monty gave me a photograph of myself making the speech which he had signed. I was very proud of myself.

When next I attended a meeting at the Gandhi Library, I was called on to speak alongside Western Cape activist, Cissie Gool[28]. I was in my school uniform, but before I spoke, I took off my tie with a sense of bravado so that my principal, Miss Guy, could not accuse me of defaming her school. She had rebuked me for speaking at the rally, and while I was

Right: My first public speech, 1946.

*Top: Leading the march with
Monty Naicker and Dr Goonam.*

prepared to concede that she had control over me and the school uniform, when I was out of school and out of uniform, I was my own free
person. Cissie Gool complimented me on my speech and gave me tips on
public speaking.

Miss Hammond's great stage production that year was to be *Richard of Bordeaux*. This never came off however because Miss Guy, who we thought was the worst principal we had ever had, decided to punish us for our involvement in the Passive Resistance Campaign. In her eyes I was the main culprit. We had our costumes ready. I had the role of king and I had made a red cloak with gold painted borders but Miss Guy cancelled the performance. We were most disappointed because we had looked forward to showing off our dramatic skills.

The British royal family's visit to South Africa coincided with the Passive Resistance Campaign. The Natal Indian Congress called on the highly politicised Indian community to boycott the visit and I was a staunch follower of this command. At school, our English teachers were understandably excited and tried to draw us into their excitement, but we were far too involved in the Resistance Movement and far too angry with the teachers.

While we changed the words of popular songs and wrote, for example, '*When Naicker was in Smuts's land – let my people go. Go down Dadoo, go down to Pharoah's land – let my people go*', our teachers read choice bits from Macaulay's essay, "*. . . as the sting in the bee so is deceit to the Bengali*". We were daggers drawn to the insults. Our teachers, though insensitive to our anger, could not remain blind to our mood which suddenly pierced the classroom air.

The mathematics teacher, Mrs Morel, was known for her close association with AI Kajee, the leader of the conservative Natal Indian Organisation which we thought of as a bunch of sell-outs. Kajee was busy putting up a Taj Mahal canopy at Curries Fountain for an Indian reception for the royal family. In our minds, his hands were dirty. Later there were pictures in the press of him shaking the hands of the King and Queen, his hands gloved in white.

Mrs Morel liked to sit on her desk during class. We considered this uncouth, partly because we didn't like her and were happy to find fault with her. She smoked a great deal and that too we thought coarse. She, for her part, viewed us with cynical superiority. I remember one morning in particular when I felt particularly cowed by her since she was sitting on the desk directly opposite me.

"So you are boycotting the royal visit?" she asked. It came out like a snarl, or that's how I heard it. She was representing the other side, but she was doing so unfairly. She was the teacher. We were only pupils. We were obliged to respect her, lacked the courage to confront her, and worse, we could not clearly articulate why we were boycotting. We hated the British – they had enslaved India, and we saw the white government in South Africa which daily humiliated us, as part of that British system. We knew our feelings but we were unsure of articulating them clearly enough to take care of her cutting remarks. She knew her advantage and she used it mercilessly, every time.

Days later, on one of our family drives into town we saw cheering crowds at an intersection. The royal family was in town and my mothers were keen to see them. Our driver, Khan, slowed the car, and stopped at a convenient point. I experienced the excitement of the oncoming procession. I saw the princesses, Elizabeth and Margaret, delicately coloured and perfectly lovely. I was charged with the excitement of the crowd and my mothers' admiration of the royal family. I had never questioned why they had to be boycotted. I just knew that they had to be. I had my commitment in this respect but it was not strong enough to deter me from looking. I was in fact happy I had seen the princesses who were about my age.

At the end of 1946 I wrote my matric but failed. I was to repeat the matric examination but the principal, Miss Guy, gave me an ultimatum. If I wanted to continue at her school I had to get a written undertaking from my father that I would not involve myself in politics and in particular the Passive Resistance Campaign. My father refused to give such an undertaking and I was proud of him. So I did not return to Girls' High and instead, in 1947 I studied on my own.

My big problem was mathematics, so I dropped mathematics and replaced it with botany. With the help of a family friend who tutored me, I completed a four-year botany syllabus – standards seven to ten in one year. I registered to write two matric exams, the Senior Certificate Exam and the Joint Matriculation Board Exam, as a private candidate in the small coal-mining town of Dundee in the interior of Natal. This time I passed.

I enjoyed my brief stay in Dundee. I stayed at the home of Big Ismail's sister, Buddie. She had a family of seven sons and one daughter, and she was a wonderful manager. At the breakfast table we were each given our allocation – a cup of tea, two slices of bread, a teaspoon of butter and a teaspoon of jam. It was adequate and evenly distributed. I also spent some time at YC Meer's house managed by his mother, Bhabi. Here breakfast was whatever we wanted – there were dozens of eggs, any amount of ghee to fry them in, as much butter and jam, bread and milk. But amid such abundance, one could go hungry because there was no allocation and no even distribution.

During this time I was very friendly with Bibi Mall, née Bismillah. She was from Potchefstroom where her family owned a shop, and she had married our relative and friend Dr Dawood Mall. I often went to their flat in Durban, before heading for the station and our home in Pinetown. Bibi invited me to accompany her to her sister Zuleikha's[29] wedding in Potchefstroom. My mothers were happy for me to go, and put out the money for the airfare. It was my second trip by air, my first being the plane ride in Maharaja Man Mohan Singh's plane when I was eight years old. I flew to Johannesburg with Bibi and her baby Junaid. I enjoyed the wedding and appreciated getting to know something of the Potchefstroom Muslim community.

In Potchefstroom, the entire Gujarati Muslim community, mostly shop keeping Vhoras and Mehmons, were closely knit. Other communities lived outside of these, both socially and spatially, even though this was before the Group Areas Act which would enforce the separation of communities. The Bismillah's customers were mainly Afrikaners. Both Bibi and Zuleikha had worked in the shop before their marriages. Now that Zuleikha was marrying Mohamed Mayet from Durban, the family was about to lose another shop assistant.

III

A HEART AFLAME

A Career and Family of My Own

CHAPTER 10

University Days: 1948–1950

There had been a lot of discussion between my parents and Big Ismail about my post-matric studies. Big Ismail had long chats with my parents about my talents and my career. As the only member of the family who had ever attended university, his advice was valuable. On Big Ismail's advice, my parents decided that I should study social science at the University of the Witwatersrand (Wits University) – the institution that Big Ismail attended.

Big Ismail talked to me about his work and his studies at the University and he fired my imagination with his account of the Young Communist League and a young girl who was at the head of it. She was studying social science, he said, and he advised me to do the same. I realised later that the young girl he eulogised was Ruth First.[30]

I flew to Johannesburg and boarded a bus to the terminal in town where I was met by my father's cousin-in-law, Hawa Bhabi (Mrs GH Meer) and her daughter Afoo, at whose home in Fordsburg I would be staying until more permanent accommodation was arranged.

Big Ismail fetched me from their home and took me to the University where I met Ruth First. She commented on the fact that I had flown from Durban, and appeared impressed by this. She and Ismail exchanged smiles about me, not with me – I was the outsider. Ismail left me with Ruth who helped me with enrolling for a social science degree.

A few days later my parents came to Johannesburg by car to settle my boarding and lodging. Ismail was adamant that I should not stay with Hawa Bhabi. He warned that I would be most unhappy there. Ahmed Limbada[31], a medical student from Dundee, was staying with her and she made him chop wood and do all sorts of chores. Ismail took us to Choti Bhai Bayat's house, where I could share a room with another student. I liked that arrangement, largely I think because Ismail had recommended it.

My parents, however, had financial constraints and so my father arranged for me to stay at Fakir Hassan Mayat's in Doornfontein, instead. Fakir Hassan Mayat had purchased a three-storey house. On the ground floor there was a large kitchen and several reception rooms. On the upper two floors were the bedrooms, each with a washbasin. I was allocated a room on the first floor. Fakir Hassan Mayat's three sons lived on the second floor with their wives and children.

I spent the first half of the year living with the Mayats. When not at university, I spent most of my time in my room. The Mayats, from their perspective, did everything to make me comfortable, but we were on different wavelengths. The problem was old Mrs Mayat. Actually, she was not very old, and she was Fakir Hassan's second wife. She dominated everyone in the house and her domination extended to me.

All the Mayat women were confined to their house. They rarely ventured out of the front door and did not even tarry on the pavement. When they did leave the house, they went straight from the door into their car and to their destination, usually a wedding or funeral. They did not go shopping – this was done by the menfolk. They hardly ever sat together and joked, and they never used the telephone. The telephone was something the men used. The women did not have anyone to phone. They had no friends outside of their home with whom they could gossip. I doubt that such friends would have been tolerated.

The only men the women of the Mayat household knew were their husbands and even with them, they kept their intimacies completely private, within the rooms to which they retired for the night. Occasionally when the old Mrs Mayat was asleep, the daughters-in-law sneaked away with their husbands. The sons and their wives crept out of the house to take a drive and get a treat of ice cream and tiptoed in again, taking the greatest care that the old people did not wake and discover them for then there would be hell to pay.

In stark contrast here was I, a young girl, almost twenty, making my way by myself by train to go to the University where I met lots of strange men of different races. Mrs Mayat and I were just so totally incompatible. I had the impression that Mrs Mayat was incapable of envisaging any relation between the opposite genders except sexually, so she questioned me each month on whether I was menstruating!

These were strange, anxious, exciting days. I had decided to attend university in my ethnic clothes my ijar, kurta and awdnie (trouser, dress and scarf). Ma had spent weeks on the Singer sewing machine on my clothes. I had designed the embroidery on one of my wide-legged trousers, right up to the knee, in a motif I adapted from the mural of Avalon Theatre, the best non-European cinema in Durban. I had never had so many clothes in all my life and I thought myself very smartly dressed.

At Wits that year there were four of us Indian girls from Durban Girls' High: Fatima Mayet (not related to the Mayats I was living with), Dhun Rustomjee, Khatija Shaik and me. We would have remained isolated as an Indian group but for Nana Weinberg, dark-haired, warm and beautiful, who was to become my dearest friend on campus. Nana took us into her circle of friends and ignited a life of fun outside of the lecture theatre. The fun continued off campus into Nana's home. Her parents were holidaying in Europe at the time, and she was in total charge. We felt free to gossip and giggle. We giggled a lot in those days. It was delicious and it bonded us. With her savings from the allowance her parents gave her, Nana bought a painting by Gerard Sekoto. We admired it, largely because she had spent £10 on it.

I was an active fundraiser for the student RAG (Raising and Giving) campaign that year selling £5 raffle tickets for a car. One day I arrived at a shop where the owner seated behind his desk exclaimed in excitement, "Amina's daughter!". It was an old family friend, a Mr Desai, who recognised me and he pleased me by buying several raffle tickets.

My landlord, Old Fakir Hassan Mayat, told me that Big Ismail was going out with the daughter of a very wealthy Jew. He appeared to be approving of the relationship because her father was wealthy. I thought Mr Mayat must surely be mistaken. Big Ismail had mentioned nothing like that to me, nor had I heard it mentioned in the family. It never occurred to me that the old man was referring to Ruth First.

One Sunday, Big Ismail came with Ruth in her small green car to take me out. We picked up Fatima Mayet from her lodgings nearby. Fatima and I sitting in the backseat became aware of flirtations between Ruth and Ismail. We spent a very pleasant and rewarding afternoon at the home of

Hilda and Rusty Bernstein. There was such a free atmosphere. I saw Ismail drinking alcohol. I had never imagined he would do such a thing, but I did not feel I could be judgmental. Fatima and I were offered alcoholic drinks – probably wine – but we declined. Even if Ismail approved, I was not about to start drinking alcohol, for I knew our family's attitude about the matter.

I remember an incident in my first year involving my curfew. There was a classical music performance at the University conducted by the very celebrated Sir Thomas Beecham. A medical student friend and brother of my friend Bibi Mall, Abdul Haque Bismillah, known as Bis, was very excited about the performance and invited me to go with his group. I asked Mrs Mayat's permission and told her my uncle would be there, although this was not true. She was reluctant to grant permission but did not prevent me from going and so I went. Fatima Mayet also joined us.

After the concert, our group visited Edoardo Villa[32], an Italian sculptor who lived in the backroom of a suburban white-owned house. Both Fatima and I knew that it was already late and that we should go home, but we were caught up in the mood of the party. We were ashamed of raising our restrictions and keen to identify completely with the group. We sat on Edoardo's double bed and nibbled at the salami that was passed around on the lid of a tin. It was all very exciting and very delicious and very haram.

When the party ended, Fatima and I were in a quandary. I could not go home so late. I suggested I would stay at my uncle Ismail's flat. Bis flipped.

"You can't do that," he said, "You can't go there!"

"He is my uncle," I argued, "Why can't I go there?"

Bis assured me I would be in greater trouble if I did so. My only alternative was to go with Fatima to her house. We invented a story. We told her landlords, the Dadhabhais, we had been knocking on their door for two hours and they hadn't opened the door. I don't think they believed us but they let it go, and gave me a place to sleep. When I returned to Doornfontein the following day Mrs Mayat said nothing except that my uncle was not really my uncle. He was just called my uncle. That set me thinking. I think she must have decided that day that she would not have me staying with them the next term.

Around this time I joined the Non-European Unity Movement (NEUM)[3]. The NEUM had launched a campaign against the establishment of the Coloured Affairs Department. I was tasked with putting up posters in the Indian area of Fordsburg with fellow student and NEUM member Seymour Papert.[34] I was foolish to take on this challenge. Talk went around that Moosa Meer's daughter was shamelessly fraternising with a white man. My parents waited for me to return home before they questioned me on this.

Big Ismail left for Durban in June 1948. He had graduated with a law degree (LLB), and had started his articles in Johannesburg earlier that year but was now forced to leave because the Government declared him a prohibited person in the Transvaal[35]. He was in fact extradited. He had to leave the flat he stayed in at 13 Kolvad House in Market Street in the centre of Johannesburg which had been a hive of political discussion,[36] his political work with the Transvaal Indian Congress and his close friends and comrades – Anton Lembede, Nelson Mandela, Walter Sisulu, Moses Kotane, Yusuf and Molvi Cachalia, Yusuf Dadoo, Ahmed Kathrada, Bram Fischer, Joe Slovo[37] and many others.

The last time I saw Big Ismail in Johannesburg he was unwell. I think he had telephoned and told me so. So I went to visit him, buying him a present on the way – two little cartoon characters in wood. I enjoyed that visit and for the first time found him attractive. There was something very warm about him. He told me later, maybe a year later, perhaps even after our marriage, that that was the first time he had stopped thinking of me as his niece, that that was in fact when he had fallen in love with me. I had no such reciprocal feelings at the time. He was very much my uncle, my favourite uncle, and ten years older than me.

My friends used to drool over him and he was considered very desirable on campus. Once I had taken my pretty young Chinese friend, Peggy Lee to the Mayat mansion and we sat in the sitting room on the top floor where we found photographs of the eldest Mayat son, Chota Bhai, in athletic poses. I said I thought Chota Bhai very handsome, but Peggy, to my surprise, said, "If you want a handsome man, that's your uncle!" I had said to Ismail, "I don't know what these girls, my friends, were about. They think you very handsome."

In July when we had a break from university studies I went home. I enjoyed my vacation, basking in the warm winter sun and visiting and entertaining my Durban friends. My Durban friends liked coming to Pinetown. They invariably took the train. We walked on our grounds, swung on the monkey ropes across our little stream or waded in the water. Not far from our home, in Marianhill, there was a much larger stream which we bathed in. My mothers were most hospitable. They were interested in my friends, welcomed them, and put out a good lunch or prepared a wonderful picnic hamper which we would take to the stream. Once some of my friends, out on a long walk, broke their journey at our home on an impromptu visit and my mothers put together a lunch that was better than if they had planned it for days.

I had looked forward to seeing my brother Ismail and meeting his wife, Fafa, and their son, Munir, who had returned to South Africa from India while I was still in Johannesburg. Ismail had been studying in India, and during his holidays he went to Surat and there fell in love with our cousin Fafa, Ma's eldest brother's daughter. Ma, Amina Ma and Papa were happy to arrange the marriage, and they sent a trousseau for the bride. I was very excited about having a sister-in-law and my brother Ismail had written glowingly about "your bhabi". I had picked up a lot of romanticism about a bhabi from the Indian films and yearned to meet her. I was excited to see Ismail who had been away from us for twelve years, and to meet their son, Munir, born in India and now just under a year old. I had saved up most of my allowance to buy toys and a baby dinner service for my nephew and dress lengths for Fafa.

When I arrived home, however, I found that the pleasure of having a daughter-in-law had already worn out for my mothers. They allowed me to give only one dress length to Fafa and put away the rest. They felt, I think, that she had taken away their son Ismail – that the son they expected had never returned. Instead it was Fafa's husband who came home after all those years. Ismail and Fafa were very close and they did not want to open that relationship to my mothers.

I too discovered very soon that my brother was not the brother of my letters and my childhood. One day he quite unexpectedly accused me of being jealous of his wife. That put me on my guard. My mothers and I realised that we could not expect a relationship of complete trust between ourselves and Fafa and Ismail. Papa expected Ismail to join him in the press, which he did and drew an allowance, but his needs increased. Fafa did not want to live with my mothers and she and Ismail moved out to a flat in Durban. Papa now had to maintain two households where before he had maintained one.

While I was in Pinetown, the Mayats contacted my father and said it was not convenient for them to have me return to them after the July vacation. My father therefore made arrangements for me to board with another family, the Laher family, in Market Street in the centre of Johannesburg.

Mr Laher went by the nickname Napoleon. Fatima Bai, his wife, was a beautiful young woman. She had two very young children. Napoleon had a wife and children in India as well but he was unable to bring them to South Africa because he was a condonee, that is, an Indian not considered a legal resident in South Africa but whose illegality was condoned. A condoned Indian had to take care not to stray from the law for he could be deported immediately. He also did not have the right to bring his family from India to South Africa.

At the time I went to stay with them, Napoleon was about to leave for India where he would spend six months with his 'Indian' family. I was welcomed to keep Fatima Bai and her infant children company. They lived in a small flat which had only one bedroom. I slept in the sitting room. There was a veranda which overlooked the street. I liked living with Fatima Bai. She was an exceedingly wonderful woman. Over weekends, her brother would take her to spend time with her mother in Krugersdorp. Once or twice I accompanied her, but I had my studies to attend to so I usually stayed at the flat by myself. Fatima Bai trusted me completely – a very different experience from the Mayats.

It was understood that I would stay at Fatima Bai's only up to the end of that year when Mr Laher would return from India. Since accommodation in Johannesburg was such a serious problem, both my parents and I decided that I would not return to Johannesburg the following year. In addition my parents must have thought that things were going much too far and that they had to protect their daughter after all the gossip about me putting up posters in Fordsburg with a man.

I wrote letters to Big Ismail, now back in Durban. In one letter I made a flippant remark about attitudes emerging from purity and impurity of parental heritage and he rebuked me for my remark. I wrote:

> "The place I live in now is much smaller, but the people are much nicer, the women being impure (meaning of mixed race heritage) like myself. They're the best people to get on with because they're never as dogmatic about doubtful things as you people in your purity."

Ismail pointed out that there was no such thing as pure and impure concerning parental heritage, and that no difference had ever been made between me and anyone else in the family or for that matter in the community. I knew he was correct and I was ashamed of myself.

In another letter I made clear that I had reached a crossroad in my academic career. It is clear from this letter that in 1948 I still saw Big Ismail as very much my uncle:

> I am considering going to India due to all the present upheavals about my board and lodge. Papa suggests that I go and complete in India. It means though that I shall miss out on the liberation struggle for three years and I am only now beginning to get involved in it and it is a contribution I want to make. I'm thinking of going to Natal University College, part-time and working at the press in a small way the rest of the time. What do you think of this? I would only need access to the Europeans-only public library in Durban to be able to study well, which perhaps I could do through Mrs Hammond.

Big Ismail had previously been insistent about me enjoying university life fully, but he now supported the proposal that I complete my social science degree as a part-time student at the University of Natal which held special lectures for non-Europeans in the afternoons at Sastri College, since we were not allowed on the main campus.

Big Ismail was by this time settled into his articles with Ashwin Choudree, involved actively in the NIC and occasionally writing for the *Guardian* – a newspaper set up by trade unions and members of the Communist Party in South Africa. Among other things, Big Ismail became involved through his activism with the crisis in Indian education – a crisis created by government's neglect of Indian education and the lack of sufficient schools for the 30 000 Indian children seeking school admission.

I returned home at the end of 1948. That December was full of excitement. My university friend, Nana Weinberg came to visit our home in Pinetown during a holiday in Durban. The only white people we had entertained in our home before this, were the white wife of a friend of my father's, who came to stay with us with her friend. The two white women occupied my mothers' bedroom. When they left, they gave us two monster bottles of eau de cologne as presents, one each for my two mothers. The cologne lived with us, it seemed, for years. Nana was different – she was my friend. While living in a hotel in Durban, Nana spent much of her time with me during that holiday.

My family went out of their way to entertain her. Nana remarked on Fafa's beauty and that surprised me. I had taken her for granted. I enjoyed hosting Nana and introducing her to Indian cuisine. We went to Fatima Mayet's house for dinner on one of those days.

Nana and I "borrowed" my father's car to teach ourselves driving – a dumb thing to do since neither of us could drive. We got the car under false pretences. I asked my father for the loan of the car so that Nana would give me a driving lesson. I omitted to tell him that Nana couldn't drive either. He assumed she could and gave us the keys. The deception was worth the exhilaration that went with it.

We drove out of our poinsettia-lined driveway, up Bamboo Lane to the station and all went well. Then, as we were crossing the railway tracks through the boom gates, we heard a train whistle. Nana, who was at the wheel, panicked and went crashing into the Rahmatullah's wood and iron house. The kitchen shuddered, the crockery fell off the shelves lined with newspaper cut into patterns, and the car came to a standstill. We were badly shaken, Nana more than I because she felt responsible.

The Rahmatullahs came out and instead of being angry, were concerned about us. I took over the driving, putting up a very brave front of being in total control and declining the offered assistance from the family. I reversed with some trouble – to the obvious consternation of the Rahmatullahs – and returned home without further incident.

We couldn't keep the accident secret, so we reported it to my father, except that I said I had been driving. After all, my father had assumed my friend could drive, so how could she have caused the accident, I reasoned.

Nana said nothing. My father comforted us. Nana returned to her hotel that evening, and I to bed, overcome by a delayed trauma brought on by the accident and the fibbing, and ran a temperature.

Nana could not contain her guilt and the next morning she came to see my father and told him that she was responsible for the accident and that she didn't have a driver's licence. My father comforted her and suggested that the family driver, Khan, give both of us driving lessons so that we could obtain our licences. I never got my licence until well after my marriage.

On 13 January 1949, Durban suddenly exploded into violence. Over the next few days, 142 people died and over 1 000 were injured.[38] Both Big Ismail and I, separately and differently, became involved in rescue work. According to one rumour what were called the Durban Riots started when an Indian adult assaulted a Black youth, another version said that the Indian adult had killed the youth.

The NIC office coordinated a plan of action working all through the night and over the following days. Big Ismail organised for the NIC and ANC to jointly patrol central Durban, addressing the gathering crowds together with ANC Natal President AWG Champion through a loudhailer atop a van provided by the Mayor of Durban. The violence spread to the areas around Durban and only subsided when the navy was called in. Over the following days Big Ismail co-ordinated relief work from the NIC offices, with refugees fleeing the violence and living in refugee camps. I became involved with refugees who had fled to Pinetown.

My friend Jessie was also affected. She telephoned one evening in great agitation.

"They are drumming and dancing and they are coming for us. We'll all be dead. Fats help us!"

I told my father and he sent his panel van in which we delivered flowers to the florists and Jessie's family came to stay with us in the main house. We also sheltered other refugees in our home in Pinetown, with its large grounds and group of empty buildings – servant's quarters, a dairy, a double garage and stables. Among those who we sheltered were our driver Khan's distant relatives. The Pinetown Primary School was also converted into a refugee camp.

I became involved in forming a committee to work with the refugees in Pinetown. One of the committee members had a lorry, so we went into town and collected groceries. I went to Ritson Road to make contact with the NIC through Big Ismail who was coordinating the organisation's relief work. Big Ismail was pleased that I was helping out. I had not seen him for a while and he told me that he had missed me. He looked at me, his eyes holding mine in a way that embarrassed me. He then looked away saying nothing more, leaving me with a strange feeling.

That year I had considerable difficulty trying to get the Natal University to recognise all my Wits University courses but eventually this was settled. All my lectures were at Sastri College in Durban, since non-European students were not allowed on the main campus. They were held in the evenings, beginning at three in the afternoon when the lecturers had completed lecturing to the white students on the main campus and ending at nine in the evening.

My mornings were free, and I was keen to fill this time with useful activities so I took on the position of temporary teacher at Pinetown Primary School. I enjoyed teaching very much. I loved the pupils and they loved me back. When my placement ended, two of the boys, young Rawat and young Lockhat, presented me with a huge cake which I very proudly took home.

I travelled to my classes at Sastri College after my teaching duties. On the days that I did not have lectures, I ran a class in adult literacy in our garage. It attracted students from the neighbourhood – male Black house servants. They were keen and tried very hard.

On the days I had lectures I stayed over at Gora Papa's at 62 Ritson Road, not far from Sastri College. Big Ismail was also living there and we saw a great deal of each other during this time. He walked me to my evening classes and he returned to fetch me. I worked at the writing desk in his room while he was away at work or at meetings. In addition to completing his legal articles he was reporting for the *Guardian* and putting in a regular stint at the NIC office.

I was very proud when Big Ismail sent me to conduct interviews for the *Guardian*. I recall in particular interviewing Chief Albert Luthuli from the ANC,[39] and taking him to Crown Studios for a photo-shoot. At this time, the National Party was very busy fuelling animosity between Indians and Blacks, encouraging the rise of the anti-Indian Bantu National Congress, led by SS Bhengu, an inyanga who they cultivated and used to make the most rabid anti-Indian statements. I was instructed to interview the then Natal President of the ANC, AWG Champion, on the matter.

We had our time as students cut out for us at the non-European section of the University of Natal. I had my studies and sufficient extra-mural activities – I was on the Students Representative Council and several other student committees and participated fully in the University's RAG fund-raising activities.

The fundraising efforts of our non-European RAG Committee included a dance, a concert and requests for straight-out donations. We had collected funds equalling those collected by the committee made up of white students on the main campus. The Joint RAG Committee included us non-European students and the European students from Durban and Pietermaritzburg campuses and in 1950 we attended a meeting of the Joint Committee in Pietermaritzburg.

When the meeting adjourned for lunch our host RAG Committee invited the European committee members for lunch. We non-European students looked at each other and watched our white colleagues leave for their lunch. The white students had taken for granted that we knew our place, and that we accepted that we could not be entertained on a white campus beyond the committee room. There was not a hint of embarrassment or shame on their part. The chairman of the non-European RAG Committee, NG Moodley, got us moving. He said we had better take a bus and find an Indian restaurant that would serve us and that is what we did, finding a restaurant some five kilometres away.

When the meeting continued, we concentrated our attention on getting the Joint Committee to accept the principle that, apart from making small allocations, RAG would each year have a focus and make a major allocation to some worthy institution. We accordingly made a substantial allocation that year to the David Landau Community Centre, a centre in the Springfield area of Durban providing support to, among other things, creches, undernourished babies and health programmes.

There were many ways in which non-European students were discriminated against and we organised against the racist practices we encountered at the University. For example, non-European students were not allowed to wear the College blazer, the rationalisation being that the blazer was only worn by those participating in sport. So to qualify for the blazer we first had to qualify for the College sports teams, but we were not interested in sports. We insisted that the blazer belonged to the University and we as students of the University thus had the right to wear the blazer. We insisted that the rules regarding the wearing of the blazer be changed to make it accessible to all students.

We were also not allowed to be members of the National Union of South African Students (NUSAS) in those days. Phillip Tobias,[40] as I recall, was then the president of NUSAS and he held a NUSAS meeting at Sastri College. I made a point of attending the meeting and I challenged him on the exclusion of non-European students from NUSAS. Mabel Palmer, the Fabian socialist who organised the non-European section of the University and was one of our lecturers, had the task of ensuring that the NUSAS meeting remained pure white. She sent her secretary to check whether there were any non-European students present and the secretary, on finding me present, asked me to leave. I refused and criticised NUSAS for its racism.

The University used to have dances but they were petrified that there would be "mixed" dancing between European and non-European students and so the senior marms used to be put on duty to ensure that rule was never infringed. The expedient explanation was that it was in the interest of the non-Europeans that these rules were observed because if the white community heard of mixed dancing on the campus, they would insist on closing down the non-European section of the University.

The Drama Department staged a play by Shakespeare at the main campus and free tickets were offered to the non-European students. However, these were for segregated performances and the non-European Student Representative Council took the decision to refuse the tickets. Mabel Palmer called me in together with a few other students and tried to persuade us to attend the performance. Her final argument was to recite the dictum 'All work and no play made Jack a dull boy'. Our retort was that none of us were 'Jacks'. We were 'Fatimas', 'Vassies' and 'Muthumas'.

That year the officials of the non-European SRC called on the non-European graduates to boycott the graduation ceremony until such time as the University eliminated their practices of racially segregated seating of parents and of presenting graduates by race (rather than in alphabetical order).

The first two names on the statement protesting the segregation were those of fellow student activist Vasi Nair and myself. Mabel Palmer called the two of us into her office. She argued that we had accepted segregated classes, why then did we object to segregation at the graduation ceremony. We told her that we needed the education and it was only available to us through segregated classes. Attending segregated classes was degrading, but we were prepared to concede that degradation out of necessity. However, we could exercise a choice in attending the graduation ceremony or not. Our view was that this liberal white university had every freedom to desegregate its student body.

All in all, that graduation ceremony was farcical as students heeded our boycott graduation call. The non-European students were just not there. As the graduation ceremony began it became clear that this was a "whites only" ceremony. The City Hall was clearly demarcated between non-European and European seating. As always the academic procession was all white. There was an awful emptiness and silence as the names of non-European students were called out.

No other university had pretended to offer post-matric education to non-Europeans. Every other university had obsequiously heralded the apartheid logo of the racist government. In my exhilaration, I felt sorry for the Trojans like Mabel Palmer, Florence McDonald and Elizabeth Sneddon who had set up the classes for non-European students. I wished they were equally victorious with us because in fact they sympathised with us, even though they did not articulate that sympathy.

When the National Party came into power in 1948 it began reorganising the racial map of South Africa with a vengeance that shook us all. Among the most pernicious of its laws was the Group Areas Act which came into operation in 1950. We were all highly disturbed by the clear signs that our lives were going to be shockingly changed by this law.

Black people would be removed to rural areas and allowed into the cities only when required for their labour under a system of strict influx control which exposed them to police harassment and arrest. Indian and Coloured people were threatened with mass removals and expropriations of residential and business premises, as racial ghettos were set aside for them. The Durban municipality seemed most enthusiastic about implementing the Act and developed plans for racial zoning and to remove and restrict Black people to the rural areas bordering Durban.

National Party ministers made it clear that the Act was designed to force Indians out of South Africa. The Natal Indian Congress organised protests and actions against the Group Areas Act, challenging it legally wherever possible and organising mass protest action when legal protest was not possible. I became heavily involved with the campaign, as did Papa, my uncles and Big Ismail. We organised meetings in every Durban suburb, drawing thousands of Indians, all threatened with loss of property and relocation of residential and business premises. The Durban City Council made public its tentative plans for racial zoning and we gathered together to study and interpret these.

While the family remained focused on the problems faced by the community, we were suddenly struck by a far more personal challenge. Papa suffered a heart attack and was admitted to St Aidan's Hospital. It became Fafa Apa (my sister-in-law) and my responsibility to care for him and in particular to provide for his dietary requirements. Papa was pleased with our service in this regard and once remarked with his typical twinkle that Fafa and I were outdoing each other in looking after his comfort.

CHAPTER 11

Falling in Love: 1950–1951

Big Ismail was always in my life. He was there when I became aware of myself as a person and as a woman. I was as aware of him as I was aware of my parents. Ismail was my father's first cousin but considerably younger than my father – so in a way suspended in our kutum between my father's generation and mine, somewhat alone in the constellation of our clan where everyone else was neatly slotted in the age scale.

Ismail was ten years old and living in Waschbank when I was born. He met me before I started walking. For the first 21 years of my life I knew him as one of many uncles and he acted like an elder, teasing me, indulging me and advising me. Our relationship started to change after I spent considerable time with him while I attended university – both in Johannesburg and Durban. In Durban, when I had evening lectures I would stay over at Gora Papa's where Ismail was living. I would work at the desk in his room, we would have discussions, and he would walk me to and from my evening lectures.

I had experienced Ismail's concern for me and I felt I could depend on him. On one occasion, I had been dropped off at Sastri College for an examination which was actually being held at the City Building in Warwick Avenue. I was frantic and did not know how I would reach my examination on time. I did the only thing I could. I took a brisk walk to 62 Ritson Road to plan something from there. To my great surprise, Ismail got totally involved in my predicament. He called a taxi, and in his pyjamas accompanied me to the examination venue.

One of the first purchases I made in Johannesburg, perhaps the only purchase during my year there, was a coat – a fawn coat with deep pockets and a dark-brown peter pan collar. I practically lived in that coat in Johannesburg and I wore it in Durban when I walked to my winter evening lectures, usually with my hands in my pockets. One evening when Ismail was walking me to my lecture, I found his hand in my pocket, holding my hand. He said his hand was cold. I didn't dare put any motive to it. We laughed, but I didn't feel comfortable. It didn't seem quite right, but then I thought I would be narrow-minded if I imputed he was getting fresh. I didn't dare provoke the slightest suspicion that I was misinterpreting an innocent act.

But some three or four evenings later, walking from my lecture his hand in my pocket, we bumped into Bhai Gora Mall, the young son of our former neighbours in Ritson Road. Ismail quickly withdrew his hand. I read consternation and guilt on his face and shock on Bhai Gora's. That left me deeply devastated and I slept badly, wondering at the meaning of that episode and asking myself if I wanted the relationship to move in the direction I now suspected.

My thoughts went round and round that sleepless night. Marriage was something that I contemplated and looked forward to. That was one reason I had not wanted to study medicine. It would take seven years and I could not wait that long before I had a family of my own. I had romantic notions about falling in love but there was no one I wanted to marry.

I had been vaguely attracted to one young man at university but he had shown no interest in me. Two others had shown some interest but did not appeal to me. Three proposals of marriage had come to my parents in the traditional way. They had rejected out of hand a proposal brought on behalf of a family we knew, by our driver, Omar Khan. They had approached me with the other two, and I had rejected both. Then the boy next door had proposed. He was a very eligible suitor, and I liked him very much. He had a fine intellect, but I was disinterested. When he said he wanted to take me in his arms and kiss me, I cringed at the idea.

Ismail, as usual, walked me to my next Thursday evening lecture. During our return walk he drew me to himself and kissed me. He was the first man who had kissed me and I cultivated the idea that he had claimed me and there could not be another man in my life.

A few days later I was working at his writing desk, and needing a ruler, I looked into one of his drawers. I caught sight of an envelope of letters. I read the first lines of one or two and discovered that they were love letters. When Ismail returned that afternoon I confronted him. I told him I didn't understand why he kept those letters if he had finished with those relationships, and if he had not finished with those relationships, why was he beginning one with me.

When I returned from my late afternoon lecture, I found Ismail in the backyard, making a bonfire of the letters. He looked at me with a slight smile on his face expressing unsaid thoughts: *The past is done. I have no baggage. Can we begin now, together*? I was surprised that he had taken my criticisms so seriously.

I think it was after that that I began to be drawn towards Ismail and soon I was in love with him. I had admired him, now I loved him enormously. I always had, the whole family had. After we had developed an understanding that we would marry and live the rest of our lives together, Ismail took me shopping and bought me an engagement ring for a little over £13 from a small jewellery store. He then took me to the beach in Chota Motala's car – a new Baby Austin – and ordered two pink milkshakes. While drinking these, he slipped the ring on my finger. He announced that we were now officially engaged.

When I went home that afternoon and happily showed off my ringed finger and announced that I was engaged, my mothers were horrified. Amina Ma, as could be expected, gave me a sound smack while Ma did not get involved.

I realised that things were serious when my mothers withdrew into Papa's bedroom and there was silence for quite a while and then the telephoning began. There were calls from Pinetown to Ismail's sister Apa Ma in Ritson Road. Angry words were exchanged between my mothers and Apa Ma. How the anger on that level calmed down, I do not know, since I was not party to it. I do not even know whether my father and his brother Gora Papa had any discussion on the matter or whether Ismail was brought to account, but soon thereafter I was informed that there would be a formal engagement.

I got formally engaged on a Sunday in Pinetown. It was a strange engagement, one that included neither Ismail nor me. Nana, my friend, was in Durban when we got engaged. I did not invite her. I explained to her that it was a men's only ceremony and I would not be there.

Fafa Apa arranged sweetmeats on khoonchas – traditional trays– and sent them to Apa Ma, but they sent nothing apart from the ring. The men sat at the table laden with sweetmeats and they sealed the bonding with the traditional Al-Fatiha prayer and the drinking of a syrupy sharbat (sherbet) with cardamoms and almonds.

My mothers were very relaxed after the formal engagement as the custom had now been observed and the groom's party brought into line.

Curiously, although Ismail was getting on in years, his sisters had made no arrangement for him to get married. This must have troubled the cousins and they must have blamed his sisters for their lack of concern, matchmaking being the prime concern of the older women. As Ismail told me later, his sister Ayesha had reported to him a comment made by Ma's sister, Choti Khala Peer, on the day the family came to see me off to my studies in Joburg. On seeing Ismail and me at the station she had commented: "That is a pair crafted in heaven." His sister Ayesha added, "One must take heed of one's elder's advice!" I think that comment set Ismail's mind on me. So Ayesha prepared him for marriage even though his own mind might have been still set on sowing more wild oats.

Our courtship continued under the surveillance of our elders. They had great respect for both Ismail and I, and trusted us not to go beyond the bounds of an unmarried couple. I saw Ismail at 62 Ritson Road. At times we walked to the Botanic Gardens and shared some discreet romantic moments. He came to meet me at Sastri College and on one occasion he took me to the cottage of the caretaker, James, where we had tea and Ismail stole a kiss when he believed the coast was clear, but I doubted it was. I think James knew the purpose of our visit.

On 2 February 1950, Ismail travelled to Cape Town with the NIC to advise a delegation from India who had arrived for talks with the South African government. Ismail and I had been courting for a little under a year, Ismail having declared his love for me around August or September 1949. I now received my first telegram from him from Port Elizabeth, addressed to *Fatima Meer, 68 Bamboo Lane, Pinetown* the message read:

> Arrived safely in Port Elizabeth. Leaving tomorrow for Cape Town. Love Ismail.

That telegram established for me that I had become the most important person in his life.

Once a year, the part-time non-European students at Natal University had a taste of two weeks of "full-time" classes when, during the July vacation, the Black high school pupils of Adams Mission College were on recess. We students looked forward to this opportunity to be together, to attend lectures and hold discussions.

We moved into Adams Mission College on a Sunday. Omar Khan drove me from Pinetown, and Ismail accompanied me. The College was a very frugal campus, fifty or so kilometres off the main road to the south coast through sugar fields, and with the most spartan of living conditions. The dormitories, dining hall, library and church were all scattered on the grounds, with the soccer field as centrepiece.

Some of our lecturers stayed on campus and this gave us greater access to them. We were lectured by Mlahleni Njisane, Professor Vilakazi, Florence McDonald, Mabel Palmer and Elizabeth Sneddon. The library was set up with books from Howard College.

During those July 1950 vacation classes, the campus was seeped in romance – there was our warden, Devi Bughwan, in love with her husband Dennis who ran his family photography business in Durban, the well-known Crown Studios. There was Devi's little sister Prem Singh, brought to help her with her baby son Nalin, falling in love with one of the students, Ben Persad. There were other students in love with each other – Pramda Subran and Jack Ramasar and Muthal Potharaju and Claude Nursoo. There was I, in love with Ismail. We went about our studies and play, floating in a dream world, barely touching the ground of reality.

The Adams Mission post office and the telephone booth became very important to me. But for these, I may not have lasted at Adams. On Monday, Claude Nursoo who was in charge of post brought me a telegram from Ismail. "Did he have to send you a telegram?" he chided. I walked away, seeking some privacy in which to savour my message. I found a quiet place near the sports field and settled down to my post. The telegram read, 'Enjoy yourself and put on weight'. I was very thin and Ismail used to tease me that he couldn't see me at a distance, as I disappeared into nothingness. That message encouraged me to eat a hearty lunch.

Later that same afternoon I received a letter from Ismail. He wrote how much he was missing me already:

> I miss you even when you are in Pinetown, but Adams is even further away. I did not like leaving you yesterday. I wished I were a student so that I could have spent the fortnight with you at Adams. I do find consolation in the fact that once we are married we will be together and then I will cease having the lonely feeling that has overcome me since I left Adams last night. I love you very much. Yours forever, Ismail.

The last lines thrilled me and I repeated the words in my heart. Ismail was giving me attention – more than enough. I was very pleased. I telephoned him on Tuesday morning and told him about an abscess on my toe. He wrote on Tuesday and said he was sorry about my toe and he hoped I had already seen a doctor and was feeling more comfortable. He went on to say:

> I wish people had not hung around the telephone when you phoned me this morning. It was good of you to have done that. I wanted to tell you how much I missed you. I wanted to see you very badly. If you were in Durban today, I would have asked you to visit me this afternoon at Ritson Road. For the time being, I will have to remain satisfied thinking of you and looking at your photographs. I am most anxious to get home for I am expecting a letter from you, or did you say two letters? . . . Don't shout at me for typing this letter. I have mislaid my pen. See you are not the only one who does things like that. The important thing is to tell you that I love you very much. I love you because you are the nicest person I have met in my life or am likely to meet. Do you feel the same about me?

Could I really be the nicest person he had met in his life? That line meant more to me than if he had said I was the most beautiful person. He was writing from the NIC office which was busy assisting dismissed municipal workers who were waiting to be paid relief grants. The Durban municipality had wreaked this revenge on workers who had responded to the call of the Indian and African Congresses to stay away from work in protest against the racist laws passed by the new Nationalist government. The municipality had also focused more on Indian "dissidents" than Black in order to manipulate a racial divide. Ismail wrote that they were trying to get them back their jobs but it was proving difficult. I looked for his declaration of love and it was there.

The day after my phone call, Ismail was disappointed: The postman had not brought him my letter, but my telephone call had compensated. He would go home at lunch time to see if his letter had arrived. He wrote:

> Your telephone calls are having one bad effect on me. I remain in till late waiting for your phone call. There are too many people hanging around here. They suspect I am writing to you. Darling, have I told you that I am very, very much in love with you?

His letters arrived every day those two weeks I was at Adams Mission. He wrote about many things, including the workers who continued to crowd the office:

> I have to end now. Debi has called me three times already. He wants me to go to Clairwood and pay out relief to the workers there. I am very, very much in love with you.

There was another telegram: '*How are classes progressing? Friday seems a long way off. Love Ismail*'.

I had previously had two notes from him, one in English and one in Gujarati, but these were real letters and they revealed another side to him. His letters were so expressive of his emotions.

My letters were longer than his. I thanked him for his telegram and said it had spurred me on to eat more '*so that I put on weight and look nice for you. I miss you all the time so I might as well shut up, than repeat the same fact and become a bore*'. I wrote that I had grown very conceited – thinking that mine was the most wonderful man in the world and that no other man was worth looking at. I quoted Urdu couplets:

> They weighed you against the moon, and the heavier came to earth, the lighter floated to the heavens. Whether you are with me or away from me, you are always with me. Somebody tell me is this what you call love?

I wrote that I wanted to shout to the world that I am in love, in love, in love with Ismail! I told him that my fellow students were complaining that I see only one man and that I am so immersed in him that I do not mix with them. '*Don't ever stop loving me. I don't know what I would do if you did.*' I painted word pictures of our married life.

I also wrote at length about the long conversation I had with Dr Njisane, our sociology lecturer, about political organisations.

> I hold the opinion that we should have social workers as organisers. Njisane says you need noisemakers (politicians), fact finders and social workers.

Ismail replied:

> I am in no mood to discuss the important political questions you have raised. I will do so in a subsequent letter. But I must say we differ little and that is all to the good.

Soon after my return from Adams Mission, Ismail was ready to be admitted as an attorney. Omar Khan drove us – Amina Ma, Ismail and I – to Pietermaritzburg where Ismail was formally admitted. On our return, we detoured to the newly constructed Midmar Dam. It was a beautiful drive and at one point Ismail asked Khan to stop the car and bought me a Zulu beaded love letter from a young vendor on the roadside.

My confidence in Ismail's love for me deepened further when one day he took me shopping in West Street and asked me to choose a piece of jewellery from Payne Brothers department store. He said that the one pound fourteen shillings and six pence was his very first earning as a lawyer and he wanted me to have it in the form of a piece of jewellery that I could always keep. He was entrusting me with his very first earnings and I was deeply touched. I chose an exquisite opal and pearl brooch that cost exactly the same as his salary. I have given the brooch to our daughter Shamim and she will no doubt pass it on to Maia, her daughter, at the right time. Some months later Ismail also bought me a grey corduroy skirt and a red cotton blouse to go with it. I wore that ensemble with great pride and love.

I also learnt during our courtship that Ismail's temper was not to be played with; it was to be feared, and above all, if I were to commit myself to him, I would have to accommodate it. I had suffered good doses of his bad temper before our marriage and knew exactly what I was letting myself into. My mothers saw this and were anxious about it.

On one occasion, I received such a tongue-lashing from Ismail that I said to him I didn't think I could marry him and we should end our relationship. He agreed without any hesitation. All this happened on the phone and I put down the receiver and began weeping. I told Ma that our engagement was off. She admonished me for arranging my marriage myself.

"You go and do this yourself and you see the result? You did not seek our guidance. If it is over now let it be. But don't repeat your mistake. Don't arrange your marriage yourself. We will attend to it."

Ma was still thinking about it and had not yet informed Amina Ma and Papa when Ismail was on the phone again.

"Behn I love you. No matter what you think. If I do not marry you, I'll not marry at all!"

I said I couldn't go on with all this shouting and scolding: "I am not a child. You have to respect me as your equal, not push me around like this!"

I was crying and he was consoling and muttering sweet nothings in my ear and telling me how sorry he was and how it would never happen again. He said he would become the kind of man I wanted him to be.

Ismail and I started to look for somewhere to stay where we could start our life together. Accommodation was very difficult to come by. My friend Bibi Mall told me of some rooms we could rent in Morningside in Durban. She said we had to decide almost immediately since there were others interested. I telephoned Ismail and told him we should go that evening. I told him I would drive down to Ritson Road with my brother Solly and we would pick him up. Ismail did not like being rushed, and he was in a foul mood when we met him. It got worse when we drove to our destination. I cannot recall what he said, but it was enough to freeze me into absolute silence.

After we dropped Ismail off and were on our way to Pinetown, Solly said: "Hell man, I didn't know Ismail could talk like that. This is too much!" I was deeply embarrassed that I should be so assailed in the presence of my younger brother who respected me as his older sister. I said nothing. Of course Ismail made up telephonically and all was well.

There were other hurtful incidents. Ismail came to see me in Pinetown. Soon thereafter, JN Singh, Ismail's friend and fellow NIC activist, turned up with his wife Radhi in their car. They invited us to join them. I did not want to. Ismail and I were spending one of those fairly rare times together and I resented the intrusion, but Ismail went on with JN and Radhi without me. I was terribly hurt and angry. I saw myself as the most important person in Ismail's life. He told me that repeatedly and so when he placed someone ahead of me, I was furious.

When he left with them, I took off his engagement ring, and standing on the veranda of our house, threw it as far as I could into our expansive garden. I never expected to find it and never looked for it. If I didn't have the devotion he promised, his ring was not worth keeping. I have no recollection of Ismail's reaction when I told him about this.

On another occasion, I found it strange that Ismail did not accompany my father and me to the opening of the renovated Gandhi Cottage. Manilal, the second of Gandhi's four sons who had remained in Phoenix and ran his father's paper, the *Indian Opinion*, had renovated and 'improved' on the original wood and iron cottage. He had done me the honour of sending a personal invitation to the opening. I drove with my father to Phoenix and on the way suffered a pang of pain when I saw Ismail riding ahead of us with JN and Radhi. I was confused. We were engaged. Should he have not travelled with me in my father's car? If he loved me as much as he said he did, should he not be spending more time with me, wanting to do so? I kept at my father's side that day at the function.

That was to become the story of my marriage – tempers and tears, deep hurt and deep love. Ismail was a passionate lover almost to the end of his life, but he was also a possessive, domineering husband.

Ismail and I were despairing of finding accommodation where we could start our married life. Khan, our family's driver, came to our rescue. He reported an empty cottage at 1197A Umgeni Road in Durban. We went to see the semi-detached cottage and found that Myna, the sister of my high school friend Minnie Ramawtar, occupied the other half of the attached cottage with her husband Benny Mangal and their children. Ismail and I spoke to Myna. The cottage belonged to her father Ben Ramawtar, who Ismail also knew. She informed her father that we wanted to rent the semi and it was ours at £7 per month.

The home settled, Ismail needed to start practising law. Rowley Arenstein, a lawyer friend, and also a prominent member of the Communist Party and later leader of the Congress of Democrats,[41] had started a legal practice in Verulam, just north of Durban, and needed a professional assistant. Rowley offered Ismail the job and he accepted enthusiastically.

We were now ready for marriage. We set our wedding date for 11 March 1951.

The lead up to our wedding was an exciting but also emotional time for me. On occasion I sat on the settee in our living room sobbing loudly and uncontrollably. My mothers rushed to my side. I did not know the cause of the weeping, but they did. It happened to most brides-to-be they said. Brides were overpowered by their grief at leaving their families. I was parting with my childhood and the security of my parents and the pride with which they had always protected me. "Our Behn," they had claimed, "was beyond any evil or immorality. She was upright and honest." They had veiled me in the image they gave me. I liked myself in that image, I saw myself as that image. That was who I was, as they made me out to be.

Preparations were made for the wedding which was to be held in our garden. Ma was on her Singer sewing machine much of the time preparing my trousseau – dresses, trousers and scarves embroidered in gold and silver threads.

A few days before my wedding, we noticed Papa pacing our veranda, deep in thought. He would cast his eyes across the vast lawns in front of the veranda and from that we discerned that he was contemplating the coming wedding reception. After his surveillance of the lawns, he came into the kitchen where we were busy baking and asked if it would be a good idea if we served sausage rolls at the wedding. We complimented him on his brilliant idea and sausage rolls were included in the menu and the sausages bought from our butcher, Sirkhot.

We baked hundreds of cupcakes for the wedding. I cut off the tops, levelled each cake, spread on butter icing, and placed the cut off tops on each cake, like two wings. Nobody bothered about what the weather might do to our garden party. Ma comfortably said Behn had never licked pots so it would not rain on her wedding day – and it didn't.

The night before the wedding our house was full of relatives and festivities. Instead of the expected traditional bridal khooncha trays of gifts and jewellery, Ismail's sister Ayesha presented me with a single purple orchid with great flourish and a romantic story that they had climbed a mountain facing many dangers and plucked this rare flower for me. But while this presentation and story delighted me, there were the unimpressed Motala cousins who questioned my mother: "What has Ismail given Behn?" Ma intervened quickly, "Money". That ended further questions.

I had trained the children in our family to perform a musical drama based on the coming of Indians to South Africa. I had taken a number of popular Hindi film songs and put relevant words to them. The musical began with a chorus of men '*Durban Chalo, Durban Chalo, nao jahan bahaduri Durban Chalo re . . . Oh you brave ones, let us go to Durban*'. This was followed by the women's chorus grieving at leaving their motherland and kith and kin. The men's chorus then broke in – detailing the wealth to be earned, and the streets paved with gold. The musical was performed the night before the wedding and was a great success.

The morning of the wedding dawned bright and beautiful. Tables and chairs were laid out on the lawns and on the spacious veranda. My mother busily bathed the younger children, readying them for the wedding. An aunt from Pietermaritzburg took over, saying to me in an agitated voice, "It's getting late and nobody is worrying about you". She mixed some turmeric in water and rubbed this on my body to give me my bridal bath. This upset Amina Ma very much. She had wanted to bathe me, and was simply waiting for the right moment which had now been snatched away from her. I, for my part, was pleased that somebody had attended to me.

Our wedding day.
Photo on the left by Eli Weinberg
and photo on the right by
Dennis Govender.

My dressing followed and my friend Minnie Ramawtar took care of my make-up. There was a lot of teasing and laughing when a number of my school friends crowded into my father's bedroom to see me. I had two wedding dresses. I started off the morning with the white dress so laboriously embroidered by my mothers in gold, but the main dress was a pink chiffon, a copy of Elizabeth Taylor's wedding dress.

The 500 guests appeared very happy and related amicably to each other. My father's sausage rolls were greatly appreciated as were the samoosas and cupcakes. My father wanted my wedding reception to be different from the usual, and it was.

Dr Ahmed Limbada, who was a leader of the Non-European Unity Movement (NEUM) which was opposed to the NIC and ANC, somehow became very involved in constructing a stage for me to sit on. So I found myself led up a short flight of stairs onto the stage where I was seated on a chair. Fafa Apa (my brother Ismail's wife) had styled my hair in a veil of flowers – a romali. She had not taken any note of the weight of the crown of flowers though, and I soon found it far too heavy on my head and unbearably painful. Nevertheless, I must have looked quite resplendent sitting high up there, above the well-wishers who came to congratulate me – among them, Mabel Palmer, who commented, "You look like a queen!"

From the stage, I could hear Molvi Bashir perform the nikkah ceremony in the section of our grounds occupied by the male guests. Ismail was admonished for not having put on his fez and then I heard the Molvi address my male witnesses and they reporting that I had consented to the marriage. My witnesses were Ma's brother, Haji Mamoo, Papa's brother, Gora Papa, and their cousin YC. They had asked me the night before whether I assented to the marriage and this was now duly reported as was the custom. Ismail was then asked whether he took me as his wife. I heard his consent.

One is too involved in one's wedding to be able to observe it from the outside, so I can say truthfully that I did not see my wedding. Eli Weinberg[42], a friend and trade union leader, was one of the guests and he captured some splendid photographs of bride and groom. My brother Bhai's friend, Dennis Govender, however, took more interesting photographs. These were of bride and groom and parents.

After the guests left, it was time for the bida – the traditional farewell of the bride. It was a solemn moment. All my siblings assembled to bid me goodbye. There was a lot of crying all around me. I began crying as well. I heard Ma consoling me: "Look there are tears in your father's eyes. I have never ever seen him cry so you don't cry either."

I was then led to the car where Ismail was already seated and Khan drove us to our new home. We arrived at Umgeni Road and Ismail insisted on carrying me over the threshold.

After Khan left, I suddenly realised that my suitcase had left with him. I informed Ismail of this in consternation. It was beginning to rain, but he took a walk to the nearby garage where there was a public telephone, and he telephoned 62 Ritson Road to intercept Khan. Khan returned a while later with my suitcase. Once we had changed into sleeping apparel, our married life, which would last almost half a century, began.

CHAPTER 12

Umgeni Road: 1951–1952

My parents had given us a bedroom suite as was customary for the bride's parents. It was said that when the Prophet's daughter, Bibi Fatima, married his cousin, Hazrath Ali, the Prophet provided her with a bed and some household utensils, hence the custom.

I had admired a bedroom suite in the window of a West Street shop. It was Swedish, crafted in birch, and the legs were slanted. I told my mothers about it, but did not think it was something they could afford. But they said I should find out its cost anyway. My mothers paid for the bedroom suite and, as I recall, £5 or so a month for curtains and the wall-to-wall linoleum floor covering. Our front room had a couch, bought second hand, that opened up and provided storage space. In our kitchen we had four globe chairs painted white, an enamel table and a stove. We put Ismail's writing desk in the smaller room that led off our bedroom.

Our immediate neighbours were Benny and Myna Mangal. We shared a common address – theirs 1197 Umgeni Road, ours 1197A. Myna welcomed us with a dish of freshly cooked herbs picked from the plot of wasteland adjoining her yard. Later the Mangal children, Anil and Pam, came to visit us and they remained constant callers, offering themselves as our children until we had our own some years later when they became their older siblings. The Mangals had a third child, Anushka, after we moved in and she was closer in age to our children. Anil, the oldest, was all too soon conscious of his masculinity or his seniority or both to play with our girls. The girls, however, got on beautifully with each other and formed lifelong friendships – but I am running ahead of things.

I had moved from a large house to a small one. Umgeni Road was quite the smallest house I had lived in, but then there were only the two of us. Through Myna's help, we added a third, Phoowa, who came to help us daily with the housekeeping and cooking. Phoowa was the Mangals' part-time helper. The Mangals called her Phoowa which means paternal aunt, because she was Benny's stepfather's sister. Her name Swaroop was tattooed across her arm at the time of her marriage to reflect her status. Phoowa was in her thirties when she became part of our household. Her husband worked for the municipality and they had three children.

Ismail arranged with Phoowa that she would help with the household chores and cook one curry and a few rotis for our evening meal. Ismail worked out the week's menu and guided Phoowa on how he wanted his curries prepared. Phoowa took over the housecleaning and cooking. This relieved me of household drudgery and created time for my community work.

As Ismail took me in hand on my food foibles, I fitted into his taste. Up to this time I did not eat fish curry. I also did not eat dhall with rice. On the days my mothers cooked dhall and rice, I ate dhall and bread. I would have quite comfortably eaten dhall, rice and fish, but Ma said I didn't and over the years I had obliged accordingly.

Ismail though brushed aside this fussiness: "You will eat dhall and rice, because I eat it and you will eat fish because I like fish." I discovered that I liked the combination of dhall and rice and that I enjoyed fish, much to Ma's surprise. Ismail was very pleased at having reformed me. "'Our Behn does not eat dhall and rice! Our Behn does not eat fish!' What nonsense. I told Behn, in my house you will eat everything, and she does."

He also taught me how to iron his shirts, the collar last, and I had to be very careful not to scorch them.

Each morning Ismail left for the office in Verulam by train. The station was across the road from our house. In the first few days of our marriage I took great pains to make him breakfast, but soon discovered that Ismail did not eat breakfast. He was very fussy about his morning cup of tea and made it himself. The milk had to be a precise temperature and the tea leaves seeped for just the correct length of time. He made the morning cup of tea for himself and me throughout our married life.

I would make him lunch which he took with him to work. My favourite delicacy for him was sardine chutney, accompanied by bread or roti. A few years later when we bought our first car, Ismail began taking lunch for the entire staff. Phoowa would cook a large pot of food, biryani or curry and rice, and he would take this to Verulam.

In the evenings I would await Ismail's return from work, table neatly laid out in the kitchen. He would be very hungry and would want to eat immediately. He would want his food piping hot, and would emerge human after having calmed his hunger.

We would retire on our beds and Ismail would regale me with accounts of the events of his day. He invariably had a new case each day, and he would relate it to me like an exciting – and very often funny – story, making me laugh endlessly. The thought went through my mind that his court stories should be recorded, but I was too timid to think I could do so. So those stories remain unrecorded and have disappeared.

I missed Ismail when he was at work in Verulam during the day or at meetings on the odd evening or over the weekend. There was though significant time to be together and we grew very close and very dependent on each other for our happiness. Some evenings Ismail and I took the tram into town and walked down West Street[43] and then round the City Hall and the gardens adjoining it. At other times we went to the cinema. Our friends were Devi and Dennis Bughwan, JN and Radhi Singh, Debi Singh, Cassim Amra, Hilda and Leo Kuper and Violaine Junod.[44] We exchanged visits and shared common political concerns.

These were our pleasures during the early days of our marriage.

I recall the early days of our marriage, when Ismail, to my great embarrassment, held me at parties and asked his friends: "Isn't she beautiful?" I doubted that this was correct behaviour but did not question it since it came from him and he was perfect. I never thought myself beautiful. When Ismail cupped my face in his hands and looked into my eyes and said "you are so beautiful" I knew I was beautiful in his eyes because he was in love with me.

"How proud I was of you at that party! You looked exceptionally beautiful that evening. I kept telling everyone about that," he remarked once.

We spent many weekends with the family in Pinetown. Sometimes Myna, Benny or Violaine came with us. We always enjoyed our time with the family. Khan would fetch us and then return us to Umgeni Road and then he would retire to his home in Overport.

Visiting my family in Pinetown: Top left, Violaine, me, Ismail, Myna.
My mothers are in the second row from the top. Photo by Dennis Govender.

I spent a lot of time with our neighbour Myna sitting on the steps of one or other of our houses. She was a great one for looking for lice and she would search through my hair and declare it clean. Sometimes we would be joined by Manon who lived two doors away.

I liked my student friends and continued my contact with them, happily entertaining them in our small house. Ismail did not approve of this and he showed his chagrin one late afternoon when he returned from Verulam. Walking up to our house from the station across the road, he espied me in a pair of slacks swinging from the rail that bordered our veranda, tête-à-tête with young Soni. The fact that I was in my gardening slacks aggravated Ismail further. I stopped entertaining my fellow male student friends thereafter.

I had brought my bicycle from Pinetown to give me greater mobility. I thought nothing of cycling to the market. Ismail did not consider this sedate travelling for a married woman and when he saw me cycling one day down Umgeni Road, he forbade me to cycle ever again, and to ensure that I didn't, he returned the bicycle to Pinetown.

Quite early in our marriage Ismail lost confidence in my ability to manage our house or adequately entertain our guests. Added to this was my early disastrous attempt to do our laundry and as a result irreparably damaging his wedding suit. I ought to have sent his suit to the dry cleaners. Instead I washed it by hand and he came home from work to find his much loved suit ruined. He didn't take to my cooking either. He thought that my time would be more profitably spent in community work and academically.

I invited one of the social anthropology professors from the University of Natal to supper one evening but on the actual day forgot that I had. Eileen Krige arrived to find Ismail and me already in bed for the night. Forgetfulness was one of the embarrassing things I repeated in my life, very much to Ismail's embarrassment.

Another of our early, very honoured guests was Mabel Palmer. Both of us admired her greatly, though Ismail even more than I because she had been his teacher. I planned a menu of very traditional dishes, kudie kichrie and karela. We did not usually serve these dishes to visitors and Ismail was dubious about the menu, but had not as yet lost his confidence in me despite the Eileen Krige setback. He let me make the final decision on what to serve, which was a huge mistake.

It was not my menu though that at least initially irritated Dr Palmer. Ismail and Khan had arranged to fetch her but lost their way and eventually turned up at her house an hour or more later than the appointed time. Dr Palmer had given up on being fetched by then.

She had sufficiently regained her humour under Ismail's charm by the time she reached our home and was holding forth on her feminism. "You don't have to train a woman to cook," she said. "If she is educated, she will read up the recipes and turn out a gourmet meal." Ismail joked about it for months after the event. "There was Dr Palmer, hungry and expectant, and Behn placed bitter karela and kudie kichrie before her, both of which are acquired tastes."

Dr Palmer herself didn't say anything but went hungry that evening. She must have also mentally withdrawn her statement about women and recipes.

Soon after our wedding I received an invitation to an afternoon tea from the University Women's Group. I attended enthusiastically but was somewhat confused by the main topic of the afternoon – 'Have you trained your husband yet?' Nobody explained what the training was about, and when I repeated the discussions to Ismail he was highly amused at the idea that husbands needed to be trained, and never stopped repeating this to his friends. He never asked me how I would want him trained.

We settled down to a marriage that was deeply involved with community affairs. Ismail was the more active participant. I went with him to public meetings. Ismail was also fairly heavily occupied with the NIC, attending committee and executive meetings. He was in charge of publicity and after each important meeting, he was at his typewriter typing out the press release and then delivering copies to the newspapers – the white-owned daily newspapers which usually ignored statements and the Indian news-papers, the *Leader*, the *Graphic* and the Communist Party's *Guardian*, which could be counted upon to publish them.

Ismail was very close to Monty Naicker, president of the NIC, and his wife Marie and we often dropped in on them to discuss NIC resolutions and statements. Both Monty and Marie were very hospitable. On many Sundays, as people gathered at the Naicker home after a meeting to assess its impact and make further decisions, Marie would get together a potluck supper. I thought the pot truly lucky for her food was always delicious.

Since my debut at the Red Square some five years before, I was in de-mand as a speaker. Both the Child Welfare Society and the Friends of the Sick Association were forever having annual branch meetings in dozens of centres and always in need of a speaker. I gladly accepted invitations to these meetings and in this way came to understand a great deal more about the community than if I had remained at home cooking and cleaning. Ismail supported my activities in this regard and was even proud of them.

I was very concerned about relations between Blacks and Indians. I had lived through the 1949 riots and I was anxious about building positive relations between the two communities. I was very friendly with Bertha Mkhize, the President of the ANC Women's League in Natal. Together we formed the Durban and District Women's League in 1952 basically an amalgam of the women from the ANC and NIC. I was the secretary, Bertha the president. We decided to work in Cato Manor, where the worst vio-lence had occurred during 1949. Bertha found a church building and we established a pre-school and a milk distribution centre. I set up contact with the bus owners in the area and collected money. We distributed milk each morning. We bused out each morning and spent an hour or so there.

Bertha ran a tailor shop close to the municipal beer hall[45] and the Victoria Street Market in town. I went to see her there quite often and each visit was an adventure. I went through the Cathedral Road entrance, next to the old age home for white men. I always wondered how Durban's European community which lived in exalted isolation from non-Europeans had abandoned their old in the heart of a non-European complex. I passed the many inyangas who traded their muti laid out on the floor of their market stalls, before I came to Bertha's shop window. She sat on a chair beside her Singer sewing machine. I stood at her window in the passage and we discussed our business.

The government threatened to impose passes on Black women[46] and the Durban and District Women's League organised a meeting on this issue at the Bantu Social Centre. The women bristled with anger. They turned on the men from the ANC who were attending the meeting, and accused them of being the cause of the situation in which the women found themselves. "If you had fought the passes the amaboere[47] would not have dared to extend these passes on us. But you accepted the passes and now we'll suffer like you."

Of course the men had never accepted passes. They had even waged passive resistance against them, but the women were in no mood to delve into history. They saw the men carrying passes and now they saw passes coming to them. I realised that the war of the women was just beginning.

I had completed my first degree before my marriage, with majors in sociology and psychology. After our marriage I enrolled for an honours degree in Sociology at the University of Natal. I was one of three students: Two of us Indian and the third white. At the end of the year, both of us Indian students were failed and the white student, who in our view was the least intelligent, was the only one who passed.

Our lecturer was an Afrikaner belonging to the ruling National Party. Both of us Indian students were active in resistance organisations. We knew that our failing had nothing to do with our ability and everything to do with discrimination against us. My academic life seemed doomed as university regulations at the time did not allow one to repeat the honours exam.

Following this unfortunate outcome, Professor Krige in the anthropology department at the University of Natal (of the forgotten dinner appointment) encouraged me to study two years of anthropology with a view to my proceeding to honours in the subject. After I completed a year of anthropology, the possibility of rewriting the sociology honours exam arose as a result of representation made on my behalf by the new head of the department, Leo Kuper. I rewrote the exam and passed with flying colours.

CHAPTER 13

Starting Our Family: 1952–1956

After just over a year of marriage we became anxious about my failure to fall pregnant and decided to seek medical advice. Ismail was the first to be examined. He found the whole affair very embarrassing. He had to run to the gynaecologist's surgery with a handkerchief full of freshly produced sperm. He returned very proud as if that examination had confirmed his manhood. The gynaecologist reported that Ismail had very virile sperm.

My examination followed and it was established that I had a problem. My fallopian tubes were blocked. The doctor injected some gas to free the tubes – a painless and simple procedure. Soon thereafter, in August 1952, I became pregnant with our daughter Shamim. My first three months saw me miserable, nauseated, and salivating profusely. The only way I could control that, short of spitting all the time, was to chew consistently on a carrot.

We chose Mohamed Mayet as our gynaecologist. He had just set up his practice. He was married to my friend Bibi Mall's sister Zuleikha, and I had gone with Bibi to their wedding in Potchefstroom. He proved to be both supportive and full of humour in his attendance upon us.

We made two major purchases while awaiting Shamim's birth – a fridge and a car.

A Frigidaire agent canvassed the sale of the fridge with us. He brought the catalogue and dropped in fairly regularly to see if we were ready to purchase. Ismail was averse to buying anything on hire purchase. He felt he had to pay the entire amount in cash. With Shamim on the way, Ismail decided we couldn't do without a fridge. He had the cash and we bought our first fridge.

While fridges were available during those years not long after the war, cars were not. The only car we could afford was a Volkswagen. It was an unknown car and the family questioned our choice, but we needed it and so we bought the VW, probably the first Indians to do so.

Ismail took a month or so to learn to drive and get his licence. The same driving tutor, Sewpersad, then helped me to get my driving licence. Benny, our neighbour, and Khan my father's driver, drove us until we became licensed drivers.

Ismail reported that the first day he took the car to work and parked it outside his office, his landlady's young daughter came to inspect it and after very careful consideration stepped back and pronounced "flat nose!" Ismail found this very amusing.

We now began getting ready for the baby's arrival. I prepared Shamim's nursery in the space we had used as a study – the little room, leading off our bedroom. I moved Ismail's writing desk into our front room and I painted murals on the walls: An African *Peter Peter Pumpkin Eater* in a field of pumpkins on the large wall, *Little Miss Muffet* and *Mary had a Little Lamb* in the spaces on either side of the window. Ismail was pleased and proud of my handiwork.

I was so delighted when my Uncle Cas (Amina Ma's brother) made a little upholstered chair and dressing table matching mine for Shamim's nursery. To complete the nursery, Bibi Mall loaned me her baby's wicker basket. I covered it with satin and spent days embroidering little roses and edging the scallops with lace. Ismail was as pleased as I was with the nursery. It gave our little house a sense of Shamim's presence before her birth.

I had one or two false labour alarms in the early hours of the morning and Ismail – an over anxious husband – called in Mohamed Mayet who said it was worth the call for the excellent cup of tea Ismail made him.

My labour pains proper started the morning of 11 May 1953. To cope with the pain, I began ironing our laundry. Ismail consulted Mohamed Mayet who advised that I be taken to St Aidan's Hospital where he had booked a private ward. When Ismail returned from his office to see me at the hospital he found me walking the grounds with doctors Goonam and Mayet on either side. They beamed at him and announced "See how good she is and in labour!" This was about 11 am. The baby would not be born for some time. My mothers arrived from Pinetown in the afternoon and took their position in my private ward with Ismail and me. At about 5 pm I was moved into the delivery ward and Shamim was born at seven that evening. I did not experience that greatest of all pain that had been spoken about all around me during pregnancy.

Ismail went to see the *Student Prince* on the night of Shamim's birth. He came to see us after the movie, and regaled me with the whole story. I was too exhausted to enjoy my daughter that night. Amina Ma slept with me in my ward and I awoke in the morning to hear Amina Ma and Uncle Cas talking about the wonders of birth and how a human comes from the body of another human. I found myself absorbed in their conversation.

My mothers took me to Pinetown after my discharge from hospital. That was the tradition and they were certainly not ones to deviate from it. Everyone in Pinetown – my mothers, my father and my brothers and sisters – were very excited about the baby. My mother slept with me in the middle room. Fareeda, my father's cousin's daughter who had come to stay with us when I was in high school, still lived with my parents. Fareeda shared Amina Ma's bed. My mother, holding the baby, said to the infant very lovingly: "This is my baby."

"It is not your baby," retorted Fareeda. "You didn't lay in the hospital to get this baby." We laughed.

The three grandparents would sit on the side veranda, in the warm winter sun with Shamim in her crib. I would join them. I saw their great happiness and felt very proud of my contribution towards it.

Ismail, however, did not appreciate the tradition that his wife and baby should be away from him with his in-laws. He could not protest against it, but he could sabotage it, so I began getting phone calls about Phoowa's incompetence and how I should return. Suddenly I became the indispensable, competent housewife. Things were going from bad to worse, he complained. I resisted him.

Shamim was perpetually at my breast. She cried when taken off. Ismail's sisters, Apa Ma and Choti Khala, came to visit. Shamim cried all the while she was not on the breast and they kept saying "She is hungry, feed her". I wondered how she could be hungry, when she had just come off the breast, and I thought of them as protecting *their* baby and giving me no consideration at all.

Then came yet another call from Ismail and this one I could not ignore. Phoowa had cooked tinned fish with sem, a green bean like vegetable, or papdi as my mothers called it.

"How can you cook tinned fish with sem?" he asked. "How can I eat such food?"

Suddenly he was turning to me as the expert cook. He had propped up my vanity and I caved in and I told my parents I would have to cut short my stay because Ismail was finding it very difficult and insisting I return. My parents would not stand in Ismail's way and I was duly returned to my home.

Shortly after I returned there was a day when Ismail did not return till unusually late from work. Phoowa had left our home as she usually did, at five. My breasts became painfully engorged, my nipples were cracked. I was running a high temperature, my baby was crying, she was hungry. I put her to my breast. Every suckle was an agonising pain. She didn't get enough. She remained hungry. The end of that saga was that I realised I could not breastfeed my baby and she was put on the bottle.

The situation brightened. We loved being parents. Our lives were now focused on Shamim. We lived anew through her, rediscovering our world through her pleasures and her delights. We watched her first steps and hung onto her first words and my parents shared our excitement. Ismail made a song, the one and only in his life, and he sang it to his daughter: "*Oh my mama. Look at the moon. It is round like a balloon.*" The beach and Mitchell Park became Shamim's favourite places. She and I would go to the station in the afternoon to meet Ismail on the days he took the train to work.

My first job, when Shamim was about two months old, was as anthropologist Hilda Kuper's research assistant[48]. This was a half-day job, based at the Institute of Community and Family Health in Newlands. I got lifts to and from work with a colleague Dr Zelda Jacobson. We had a helper who looked after Shamim while I was away, but I was comfortable leaving my baby and going to work only because of the very responsible and motherly Phoowa. Looking back, I am convinced that without Phoowa's support I could never have gone to work, for apart from caring for Shamim, I would have had to cook, do the housework and the laundry.

Shamim never objected, never cried, or expressed any protest, but I saw her tense little face when I left her. Maybe I should have stayed at home and looked after her, but that was when I had this job offer. My great ambition was to do research and here I had a job with a renowned anthropologist who was doing research among Indians.

I enjoyed the job immensely. I walked about Newlands, dropping in on families and taking particular note of all ritual celebrations. I got invited to celebrations and observed them. I enjoyed myself tremendously and made many friends. The community was largely Hindustani, so I was picking up a lot of information about Hindustani traditions.

The Newlands of the early 1950s I roamed in was a huge tract of land owned jointly by the Paruk and Lockhat families. They donated a big portion to found the FOSA (Friends of the Sick Association) TB Settlement which included a hospital and accommodation for patients. The rest was leased to private extended families – parents, sons, daughters-in-law and grandchildren all living under one roof – at nominal rates of £10 per annum. These families built their houses in wood and iron and grew vegetables.

It was the age of the mother-in-law and mothers-in-law ruled with an iron hand, some silently, others lugubriously, their voice and words constantly raging throughout their homes. They were also gatekeepers of their homes and families and to enter these I had to go through them – so my friends were the mothers-in-law.

The food served to me was delicious. The most delicious fried sardines I have ever eaten were cooked for me by a Newlands mother-in-law. I still remember also the wonderful curried dishes served at a daughter-in-law's chhati ceremony welcoming a newborn baby.

Births may have occurred frequently in a family, but they were always treated with respect and ritual. For six days mother and baby remained isolated from the family on a strict diet that built her body and encouraged the milk flow. On the sixth day, they rejoined the family and the baby became part of it. The mother was then reintroduced to her usual diet and six curries were placed before her. The whole family joined in the chhati feast and so did I.

Then there were the bride-fetching parties during which young people from the groom's side and the bride's side engaged in a mock battle trying to rub powder and turmeric onto each other. This demonstrated the delicate and vulnerable nature of the bride and groom's newfound relationship.

One Sunday I returned in a very agitated state. I had attended a South Indian Kali Puja ceremony, dedicated to the goddess Kali, where the head of a goat had been slashed off and the key worshipper, a woman, had taken its head and drunk the blood streaming from it. Ismail wondered whether I should continue my fieldwork if it upset me so much. I, of course, went on because of the pleasure it gave me.

I probably earned £20 a month or so, and I was very happy for the entire amount to be put into Ismail's account. We saw ourselves as earning everything together. We never had a sense of mine and yours. I recall just before our marriage Ismail had an antenuptial contract drawn up to give me independence. It had upset me greatly when he had brought it for me to sign. I had reacted to it as a document of separation when we were about to come together. He had taken the document away and we never discussed it again.

Around this time my parents decided to leave our Pinetown home. Two factors led to their giving up our Pinetown home – the looming attack on our right to continue to live in Pinetown given the passing of the Group Areas Act and my mothers' loneliness. All the children had completed primary school and were enrolled at high schools in Durban. They left home in the morning with Papa and returned only in the evenings.

Papa sold the Pinetown property for less than its value and the family returned to 84 Ritson Road. Papa extended the house to double its size with three additional bedrooms and a new bathroom and toilet. His mode of extension was by trial and error. I would arrive one day to see a wall and the next day, the wall would be down. It was eventually a comfortable, large house. The house now teemed with people and burst at the seams when the entire clan, about forty of us, gathered for supper on Sundays.

Apart from my research and enjoying Shamim, I was also very involved in attending and organising political meetings. The threat of the Group Areas Act united Indians in a continuation of the sort of unity that the Passive Resistance Campaign had engendered. I recall a mass meeting at Curries Fountain Sports Ground. The sports ground was filled with people.

We addressed them from the stadium – Monty Naicker (prominent activist and NIC president), Alan Paton (author and founder of the Liberal Party) and I. There were probably other speakers, but these are the ones I recall.

I was in a bus a few days later and I heard two women passengers discuss the meeting. The one referred to the woman speaker: "She spoke! She said things that shook everyone." The reference was to myself and I felt proud.

We held many meetings at which both Ismail and I were speakers, alongside Monty Naicker and at times alongside Yusuf Dadoo. I became a new recruit for the attention of the South Africa Police Force's Special Branch which focused on attacking and undermining any anti-apartheid work.

I continued my work with Hilda Kuper, filling in dozens of the reporter's notebooks with my observations. Then suddenly about a year into a job I was enjoying very much, I received a letter of dismissal from the government department responsible for the research. No reasons were given and Hilda was as shocked as I. Her reports had always commended my work highly. The reasons for the dismissal became all too clear as my notice month came to an end.

It was 11 November 1954 and I was two months pregnant with my second baby, just overcoming my nausea. I was in the bathroom, washing my hair when Phoowa called out, "Behn, there are some white men. They want to see you".

"Let them sit in the sitting room," I told her, "I'll come just now."

I wrapped my hair in a towel, wound it round my head like a turban, and entered our sitting room. The men announced themselves as members of the Special Branch – the section of the police dealing with political dissent – and served a document on me.

"It is a banning order," they said.

I was flabbergasted and flattered. I was being served with a banning order! I was growing in prestige. I was being noticed. I couldn't wait to inform Ismail and as soon as we had shut the door on the police, I phoned him and told him the exciting news. He received it with a mixture of misgiving and surprise and immediately phoned Monty Naicker. Monty, thinking he'd play a joke on me, phoned me and said in a voice disguised as an Afrikaner:

"This is Captain van Niekerk speaking. Have my men served you?"

Then this voice changed to his own. "Sorry Fatima. They have come for me as well. I'll phone you later."

As a result of my repeated appearances at mass political meetings, I had become a prime suspect in the eyes of the Special Branch, and I was honoured with my first banning order ahead of Dr Naicker himself. I became quite a celebrity and had a special photograph taken which appeared on the front page of the *Leader*.

A day after I received my banning order, Ismail was banned. Both our banning orders were for two years and prohibited us from attending political, social or family gatherings and from publishing. Despite being barred from meetings, we continued to make our contributions as best we could during this period.

By the end of 1954 a very large number of leaders of the Natal and Transvaal Indian Congresses and the African National Congress (ANC) were banned under the Suppression of Communism Act countrywide. In the first week of 1955, a five year long banning order was served on my father's brother, Gora Papa (AI Meer). He had been Joint Secretary of the Natal Indian Congress between 1945 and 1947 and of the South African Indian Congress (an umbrella of the NIC and TIC) in 1948 and 1949. He had served a term of imprisonment during the 1946 Passive Resistance Campaign, and had represented us at the United Nations in 1947.

The bannings were intended to sabotage the political summit, The Congress of the People, which was to be held in Kliptown in Johannesburg in June 1955. However, despite the state's actions the Congress of the People took place as planned. One of the main objectives of the summit was to develop and adopt a manifesto – the Freedom Charter – for the ANC. Even though many responsible for drafting the charter were not able to attend the summit, it was adopted and endorsed.

Ismail was one of those who could not attend as he was banned. Technically I was too, but even without the banning I would not have attended – I was heavily pregnant and just three days after the Congress of the People I gave birth to our second child, Shehnaz.

Shehnaz was born on the 28 June 1955, two years after Shamim. Ismail and I decided I would have our second baby at home. We discussed the matter with our doctor, Dr Davidson, who agreed to deliver her at home. We arranged with the Salvation Army's Mother's Hospital to provide the home nursing. The arrangements turned out to be perfect and I had my best confinement.

Amina Ma was my constant support. She was with me on the morning when my labour pains started. Ismail fetched the nurse from the Mother's Hospital, very pretty and young. I liked her. Dr Davidson came at about 11 am and decided there was time for him to attend to another patient, but Shehnaz was in a hurry and probably shared my partiality to the pretty nurse. Within minutes of Dr Davidson's departure, she was ready to be born. It was the easiest birth I had. Dr Davidson came in time to deliver the afterbirth. He was very pleased with the young nurse's delivery of Shehnaz.

Amina Ma was very happy with her second grandchild. She declared her perfectly beautiful, breaking her rule not to praise children as it spoilt them. She probably realised that Shehnaz was too young to realise the praise and would not be spoilt. Ismail was informed and he rushed from the office to his next new daughter. We had no concept of the first baby resenting the second baby and did not take any steps to brace Shamim against that, nor did she need any. She too had no such concept of the first child/second child syndrome. As far as I recall she had no trouble relating to Shehnaz. She took to her new sister in the stride she was expected to, with no psychological hang-ups.

Naming a new baby was a big performance in our kutum. Everyone participated. A list was drawn up and names considered for their sound and meaning. My generation were named after the prophets or their family members. For example, I was named after the Prophet's daughter. My brothers, Ismail, Sulaiman, Ahmed and Mahomed were all named after prophets. My younger brothers, Siddiek and Farouk, were named after the companions of the Prophet.

The trend had changed when we were having our children – the fashion was for Persian names. My father chose Shamim's name and both the sound and the meaning 'fragrant breeze', had the approval of everybody except

With Ismail at Charles Johnson Memorial Hospital in Nqutu, 1971.
Photo by Dorothy McLean.

Being interviewed in the 1970s.

On publishing Portrait of Indian South Africans *in 1969.*

Addressing a protest meeting in the 1970s.

*Photographed in the 1970s in front of a wall mural
I painted in our home.*

In my study at Swarthmore College, 1984.

Above: With Dr Goonam at Curries Fountain, Durban 1970s.

Top: With Coretta Scott King in Durban.

Above: Receiving an Honorary Doctorate from
Swarthmore College, USA in 1984.

Opposite: Cover of the Harper & Row edition of Higher Than Hope
published in 1990.

HIGHER THAN HOPE

FATIMA MEER

"THERE WAS NO BETTER PERSON
TO WRITE SUCH A NARRATIVE
THAN FATIMA MEER."
—WINNIE MANDELA

The Authorized Biography
of Nelson Mandela

Portrait taken in the 1980s.

With Archbishop Denis Hurley.

Above: With Rashid in his London flat in February 1990.

Opposite: Nelson Mandela visiting our home after his release from prison.

Above: With Nelson Mandela when he visited us after Rashid's death.

Opposite top: With Ahmed Kathrada.

Opposite bottom: With Sonia Gandhi on the launch of my book
The South African Gandhi *in 1995.*

Photo by Gisèle Wulfsohn.

our close friend and Shamim's Godmother, Violaine who didn't like the crowding together of so many m's in Shamim Meer. As if passive resistance was to continue endlessly, she said she would have difficulty standing before the magistrate and saying "my name is Shamim Meer".

Naming Shehnaz was not so easy. We wanted to name her Yasmin. We liked the sound and we were happy with the meaning – the jasmine flower. But my father liked Shehnaz which he translated to mean 'the chief of our pride' – naaz-pride, sheh-chief. We ended up giving her both names, but my father won – we called her Shehnaz.

It was during the anti-pass struggle in January 1956, with Shehnaz only around six months old, that I fell pregnant again. My friend and colleague, Dr Zelda Jacobson, offered to give me an abortion, but such thoughts never entered my mind and I told her that was quite unnecessary.

I don't recall Ismail's reaction to our third pregnancy. We could not say it was unexpected because we were not practising any birth control. I think Ismail took the pregnancy in his stride.

I coped far better with my third pregnancy. I discovered at one point that I had a depression in my tummy and went to see Dr Davidson about it. His first impression was that I was having twins, but there was no such luck. He confirmed that it was a breach baby and he could not turn it.

Rashid was born at St Aidan's hospital on 2 September 1956, a beautiful big baby, but neither his size nor that he came legs first caused me any problems. Everyone in the family was pleased that we now had a boy. I recall a member from the community, Mrs Jalbhai, pushing her head through my ward door when Shamim was born. "What did you get?" she inquired. I told her a girl. "You must first give birth to a babaw," she said, "then the bhabies can follow" – as if the process was in my hands. I had thought her quaint because we were so pleased with our daughter.

We named our son Rashid because we liked the sound of the name.

The only time in my life I suffered from asthma was during the time I was pregnant with Rashid. Rashid was asthmatic in his early childhood.

We were now a compact little family living in a compact little house at 1197A Umgeni Road. Ismail and I occupied the only bedroom and the children slept with us on the twin beds most of the time – though there was a cot in the small annex to our bedroom and when asleep, we would at times move one of them into it.

During my research in Newlands I had met the Maharaj Family, whose daughters Laila and Sharda were to take care of Shehnaz and Rashid respectively. When I first met the family, the parents and eight children lived in one small room. They had applied for a house in Springfield but were patiently waiting to be allocated one by the municipality. I discussed their plight with my boss, Hilda Kuper, and through her influence we managed to get the Maharaj family moved into one of the four-roomed houses in Springfield. This made a dramatic difference to their life and they never ceased to thank me for this.

When Shehnaz was born, I needed help with her. So the eldest Maharaj daughter Laila came to help me. Laila was a very pretty buxom young lady. She fitted in beautifully with our small family. She brought in her younger sister Sharda, a very pretty slim girl, to help look after Rashid when he was born. Sharda lived and slept in the sitting room.

Phoowa came each day to cook and clean the house. She often brought her baby, Pingla, with her. The baby lay quietly, undemanding, on the bed.

With our family expanding, we needed more space and we decided to look into buying or building a home. Land was hard to come by in those days, as the Group Areas Act restricted us to our racial zone, creating scarcity and inflated prices.

We found land in Burnwood Road in Sydenham north of Durban almost purely by accident in 1956. We had gone to see a house in Kennedy Road on the opposite hill and the estate agent, seeing that Ismail was quite unhappy with that house, pointed to plots of land opposite. We examined the land. There were two plots adjacent to each other along a corrugated dirt road, Burnwood Road. There was neither electricity nor sewerage available. Nonetheless, Devi and Dennis Bughwan, who were also looking for land at that time to build their home, decided to purchase the land with us. We planned to build our houses next to each other. The plots were offered at £800 each.

Alan Lipman, an architect and member of the Communist Party and the Congress of Democrats, had drawn the building plans for the Bruntons Arcade in West Street, the first shopping complex in the city. I visited his office. He was most receptive, and showed me his working drawings. I suggested to Ismail that we engage him as our architect.

Ismail fell in enthusiastically with my suggestion. Alan, after all, was a comrade and it was good to pass business on to him rather than looking for an unknown commercial architect. We then started discussing the kind of house we wanted, showing Alan pictures of a few we liked. His response was, "That's easy! I'll do it far better than that!"

However, Alan found that the property was not big enough for two houses and advised that one of us should take over the two plots and build one house on it. The Bughwans very magnanimously handed over their plot to us.

Alan's first proposal was for a single-storey, ground level house. We did not like this and he drew up a second plan: A two-storey house, with an entertainment area on the ground floor, bedrooms on the first floor and a sunken study. He talked about "burrowing into your den and working there". Adjacent to the study was the garage. We approved of this plan, although Ismail's friend, the Verulam Town Clerk, warned against the flight of stairs and old age. Nonetheless, we went ahead since it was attractive and very different from the existing conventional houses in the area.

The land and the plan now in place, we needed money to build the house. Alan did the first sketch plans and we put this to tender. This proved too costly and we eventually decided, on the advice of Gopal Hurbans, a businessman and NIC activist, that we would save tremendously if we became owner-builders. Hurbans offered to get us building material at a reduced rate. He also introduced us to a suitable builder, Jivan, who we gave the contract to.

Our next hurdle was finding the capital. The building societies and banks in those days did not give housing loans to non-whites. Leo and Hilda Kuper came to our rescue. They had shares in a prominent building society and they managed to solicit a loan for us and stood guarantor for the loan.

CHAPTER 14

Treason Trial: 1956 – 1958

The end of 1956 brought an unexpected turn in our lives. In early December Ismail had his appendix removed at St Aidan's Hospital. He had returned early from work one afternoon complaining of stomach ache. He was lying down when Dr Davidson came to see one of the children, probably Rashid, who was not yet three months old.

"Why are you in bed?" he asked Ismail.

"I have a pain in my stomach."

"Let me see," Dr Davidson said and within minutes had located the site of the pain. "It can only be one thing," he said, "your appendix."

The operation was arranged. My cousin Unus and I were with Ismail at St Aidan's when they took him to the theatre. He was already groggy but calling for me. I was conscious of Unus's presence, but I kissed Ismail as he wanted me to and he was returned an hour or so later.

Ismail's operation occurred in the midst of our preparation to stage a massive Women's League anti-pass march on the central administration offices in Pietermaritzburg. We had already held a mass meeting in the city – the capital of the Natal province – a week or two previously, and I had attended it, driving up with Violaine. As League Secretary, I had done a great deal of the organisation. I was now torn between Ismail's need for me and my responsibility to the march. Ismail would never forgive me if I left him and went on the march, so I stayed with him in the hospital.

The march resulted in high drama when they arrested all the women, over 6 000, and then, not having sufficient prison accommodation, held an emergency court outside the court building in lights beamed by cars. I was proud that I had a hand in planning it, but disappointed that I was not part of the protest.

After Ismail's discharge from hospital, we went to 84 Ritson Road, our plan being to stay with my family for the period of Ismail's recuperation.

Within days the house was invaded by police and Ismail was charged with treason alongside 155 others. On the morning of the arrests on 5 December 1956, I grabbed my chance and dashed to the Umgeni Road house to clear and secure as many of our papers as possible from the police. I was certain that after arresting Ismail, they would raid the house. I felt a sense of victory as I moved whatever I could into the house of our immediate neighbours, the Mangals.

Back at Ritson Rd, Ismail's legal partner and fellow political activist, Rowley Arenstein, together with our doctor, Dr Davidson, arrived. Dr Davidson was adamant that Ismail was in no condition to be moved, and the police had no option but to comply. This gave us some time together and more importantly gave Ismail the necessary time to recuperate before embarking on a train journey under police custody and being exposed to prison conditions. The police arranged a constant vigil outside our bedroom door.

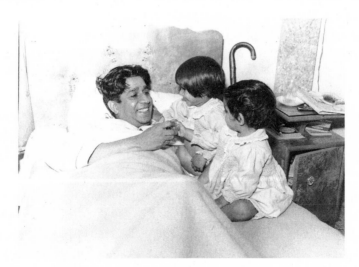

Ismail with Shamim and Shehnaz in 1956. Ismail was recuperating from an appendix operation under police guard as a treason trialist.

Once Ismail was strong enough, he left 84 Ritson Road amidst much drama – family, friends and neighbours gathering to bid him goodbye. The police kept their travel plans secret from us, so we did not know that he was leaving by train, though the NIC got wind of this and organised welcome receptions at the stations where the train stopped.

Ismail's arrest for high treason in December 1956 forced our separation – he in Johannesburg standing trial and I, at home in Umgeni Road. We had no idea how long the trial would continue, nor what would be the outcome.

The preparatory examination to test if the state had sufficient evidence began at the Drill Hall in Johannesburg on 19 December 1956. A few days later on the 23 December the trialists were released on bail. Ismail went to live with close friends and fellow activists Goolam and Amina Pahad while he attended the preparatory examination daily. He visited us in Durban on average once a fortnight, spending weekends with us.

As it happened, this was to be our lives for the next twelve months, with Ismail returning to resume his normal life with us in January 1958 when the charges against him were dropped. He was one of the more fortunate ones. Charges against 92 of the original 156 trialists were only dropped three years later in 1961, after great cost to the state, our organisations and the trialists' personal lives.

The Treason Trial[49] took its toll on us. Ours was a very small family, with deep emotional bonds and we relied on these for our day-to-day well-being and sense of security. The Treason Trial threatened all of this. For Ismail, there was the trauma of being wrenched away from his newly found family in which he was finding so much happiness. For the rest of us, it was a period during which we learnt how very much we depended on and loved each other.

That period of our lives is well recorded in the letters that survive. Ismail and I wrote to each other at least once a day and sometimes twice. We had been married just over five years and the letters depict the very strong bonds we had developed and that we were more in love than ever before. They also reveal that our married life was not without its stresses and strains but that we recognised these and committed ourselves to overcoming them.

My life, at age 28 was suddenly full of newfound responsibilities which included caring for the children, running the home, looking after Ismail's office (or at least keeping an eye on it), working out ways to curb household expense, looking for some employment and over and above this, supervising the building of our new home.

I had the support of my family – my mothers, my sisters and the cousins who lived with them. Leila and Sharda Maharaj looked after the children and Phoowa kept the house and cooked. Our cousin, Minnie, came to live with us. She was a student at ML Sultan Technical College and she helped with the children on evenings and over weekends.

I was determined that Ismail should return to an office that was intact and running. I went to Verulam as often as I could. We had to convince potential clients that even in his absence we could give them the service they required by engaging other lawyers. We had very good support from a number of eminent lawyers and advocates, two of whom, Hassan Mall and John Didcot, went on to become judges. I relied on Ismail's staff, Cassim Amra, Aubrey Naraidoo, Puran Maharaj and Mr Sithole, who were all committed to him.

Building our house in Burnwood Road was an adventure in itself. In Ismail's absence, I took charge of the building process – finding, signing up and overseeing the subcontractors. We were very excited during the building process. On the weekends Ismail was in Durban, we inspected our house-in-the-making. We climbed up the stairs to the upper floor and looked out all around us. The children were particularly excited and we had to watch them closely to avert any accidents.

All members of our family were also invited to some of these inspections and we even took our close friend, communist party and anti-apartheid activist Yusuf Dadoo to see it. He liked the location of the home and admired the view from the top floor. Ismail was happy with the progress.

The trial pushed me into looking at our financial position and taking some responsibility for it – something I had up to now ignored, leaving everything to Ismail. I tried to work out some measures of economy in our domestic expenditure. On 25 March 1957 I wrote to Ismail and made several suggestions. Our household expenditure was about £40 a month, including running our car. I calculated that if we moved in with my parents, we could save £18 a month on rent, electricity, home help and telephone. Our rent was £7, electricity £2, housekeeper £6, and telephone £3. The other proposal was to keep the house and still move in with my parents. Then we would save £11 a month. Our highest expenditure was food at £20 a month. I thought of selling our car. Secondhand Volkswagens were advertised in the showrooms at £400-£450. The first garage I went to offered me £200! I felt insulted.

My father asked whether I was managing and if I needed help. His own resources were dwindling but his offer was genuine. We had not though reached the bottom of the barrel, so I thanked him and said we were fine.

I began to make plans on how I could contribute economically to ensure that we would not end up in a situation where I would become dependent on the International Defence and Aid Fund (IDAF) – a fund set up by Canon L John Collins of St Paul's Cathedral in 1956 to work towards a peaceful solution to the problem of apartheid through raising and distributing funding to victims of apartheid laws.

Work was difficult to find. I heard that there was a vacancy at a madressa. I applied for a post but was turned down. Maybe they thought I was not Muslim enough, or not sufficiently versed in Urdu and Arabic. The salary was a pittance, as were the salaries of all madressa teachers, but I was rejected for even that job.

Leo Kuper came to my rescue, offering me a job at the University. Leo had previously encouraged me to rewrite my honours examination and to enrol for my master's degree. The Kupers, Leo and Hilda, had joined the University in the sociology and anthropology departments respectively. They identified wholly with anti-apartheid politics and Leo's study of the Defiance Campaign was published in 1957 and subsequently banned.[50]

Leo was a liberal and non-racist in the true sense of the word and unlike other academics, he did not stop at talking. He was not prepared to pamper the European patrons of the university. Leo was trying to deracialise his department. He appointed a black academic, Mlacheni Njisane to teach sociology at the medical school and took on a number of senior black students to conduct tutorials. Now that we faced real financial problems, he took me on as a tutor and promoted me to the position of temporary junior lecturer, thereby launching my career in sociology. I enjoyed tutoring and lecturing, but perhaps more important at the time was the fact that I earned some money.

There were hiccups, but I handled them as gracefully as I could, playing down the belligerence and challenging the liberal conscience of the white university establishment. This was particularly my tactic in dealing with Leo Kuper's replacement, Hansie Pollack, after he left for California. Hansie had been most helpful to me when I was an undergraduate and I had looked forward to working with her when the Kupers emigrated. Apart from knowing her as a teacher, we met socially at the Kupers, and later, we were also regulars at Hansie's parties.

When Hansie succeeded Leo, she had to handle the *problem* I created as a black member of her staff in a white university. The first year she cut my salary, already quite humble at twenty pounds a month. I protested and told her I'd work for nothing, but it would be against both her grain and mine to be party to what was clearly an instance of racial discrimination. My salary was reinstituted.

Hansie was also the supervisor of my master's thesis, and that too was a bad experience. She blocked me from submitting the thesis, I suspected, because the senior lecturer in the department only had an honours degree at the time. I was however, allowed to submit the thesis the following year when the senior lecturer was awarded a doctorate. She concurred with the external examiner and I was awarded my master's degree with distinction. But with all that, she remained a friend, loyal and concerned.

The trial sorted out our true friends from those who were simply fairweather friends. My most constant friends during the Treason Trial were the Kupers and Violaine Junod. In addition Margo and Martin Russell and Nana Weinberg were people from whom we drew strength and support. Alan Paton also emerged as a good friend in those days.

The letters exchanged between Ismail and me, those that survive, chronicle something of our thoughts and our relationship. They also chronicle our anxieties, responsibilities, and the love and the pleasure we derived from our children. Most of all, the letters emphasise our love for each other which had grown over the years, and our frustrations with each other's shortcomings. When I look back on our letters, I am moved by our strong identification with each other, and how we mirrored each other in idealistic terms.

Our regular letters to each other reflect a very unhappy Ismail. Throughout his absences from home during the Treason Trial, Ismail was homesick. He suffered bouts of depression. His letters were full of his loneliness and his yearning to be with the children and me. In his letters he declared his great need for me, his inability to live without me, his dependence upon me. My letters during 1957 express my deep concern about Ismail's loneliness and his physical health. They also express my own loneliness. I found my life quite empty because of Ismail's absence. I depended on him for my self-confidence and well-being.

What we probably wouldn't have talked about, we wrote copiously in our daily letters. On 11 March 1957, we celebrated our sixth wedding anniversary. I wrote to Ismail on 9 March. We both acknowledged that the intervening six years had brought us closer to each other, but in my letter to him I also included what I did not like about him, carefully following with what I did like about him. I wrote that he more often than not exasperated me with his temper changes. He could be as loving as anyone could wish in one moment and then be painfully horrible. I pointed this out in the hope that he would change, but that was a hopeless hope. Ismail remained Ismail and if I wanted him, I had to accept him as he was.

On the weekends he visited us in Durban, Ismail would come home happy, but in a short while his mind would travel to his worries and his anxieties and the little things that he found out of order. Our short times together would be marred by these fault findings. He would realise the time he had wasted in this manner, and on his return to Johannesburg he would beg forgiveness. But come the next visit and it would be the same. Ismail wanted me to be like him – disciplined, tidy and orderly. As much as I loved him, I did not want to become like him. I was I, the woman he had married.

And yet we loved each other passionately. I longed for a love that was free of all hurts. He took our relationship as it was for granted. He took me into his arms and reassured me when I was reduced to tears, but went right ahead and treated me as he had before I had dissolved into tears.

While I recognised the problems in our relationship and wanted to discuss them in the desperate hope that we could solve them and be the happy couple we could be, there was no question of us not loving each other. I believed in Ismail, I loved him as much as I admired him. I saw him in heroic proportions. Our letters were full of darlings and sweethearts and of missing each other. Ismail denied we had any problems, he

Me on my own and me with Shamim, Shehnaz and Rashid – photographs
sent to Ismail during the Treason Trial in 1957. Photos by Ranjith Kally.

ignored them. He would be very contrite and very apologetic when I
pointed out specific instances of hurtful behaviour. He promised it would
not happen again but it almost always did.

The letters also created an opportunity to chronicle the growth of our children – Shamim four years old, Shehnaz two and Rashid one-year-old – since
I felt it my responsibility to keep Ismail in touch with their development.
      In one letter I wrote:

> At the Blue Lagoon, Shehnaz saw the moon and met the moon and dis-
> covered the moon for the first time. She stood, the little figure, excited
> with the new felt joy, flinging her arms and jumping as she pointed at the
> magnificence of the moon nestling in the bay that was the sky encircled
> by a coast lightly flecked with clouds. She shouted 'moon moon' and then
> somebody gave her the idea that Papa was in the moon and she could say
> hello to him and so the little one stamped her feet with increasing excite-
> ment and shouted 'Papa Papa'.

In another letter I wrote:

> 12:15 am- the night is quiet, the house is still and your children deep in
> sleep, and Rashid. He lies next to me. His bottle propped on a pillow, his
> mouth suckling away at the teat, a more wonderful baby is yet to be born.

He is so contented and so happy, his chubby strength so charming, his inviting smile appealing, like his father's.

Yet another letter I shared with Ismail on my return home from visiting him in Johannesburg:

I returned on 8 May 1957 with Mr and Mrs Bana. I travelled with them in their car from Johannesburg. Mrs Bana and I sat at the back, Mr Bana sat in front with his driver. If they had not been as nice a couple as they were, I would have known only impatience to be with my three children. Mr and Mrs Bana passed their middle years and were like two friends, there was such understanding between them and such enjoyment of each other's company. Mrs Bana came well packed with food. We stopped at Standerton at a garage for petrol, tea and buns which Mrs Bana topped up with chevda and chops. We stopped an hour in Newcastle and reached Mooi River for lunch, fried chicken from Mrs Bana's basket and coffee from a garage and we were on our way headed for Durban. The driver was good, the car performed beautifully, and it was wonderful flying down down down from the Transvaal Plateau to green wooded coast and our glorious Natal. I have never entered this province with such expectation and happiness as I did on that afternoon and when Maritzburg came it was like entering the gateway of heaven.

An hour more and we were cruising down Botanic Gardens Road and turning from Mansfield into Ritson Road, and then the house 84! Mr Bana and his driver helped me with my baggage. I was met by Minnie at the door, and then I saw Rashid, mouth open, looking at me, looking and looking without quite understanding. Then he knew and his face broadened with a smile and his hands stretched out and dived into me. Oh what joy, mother and son at our reunion.

A little face with an incredible smile looked up at me. It belonged to a tiny figure in a checked skirt and a little check bolero. 'Mama you're not looking at me'. I was, I was, with Rashid in my arms, I bent down and kissed my Shamim and holding her hand and holding Rashid, I went to the backyard, a sweet face with melancholy eyes, lit up and smiled and after that Ismail, it was pandemonium. I did not know who I was carrying, or who I was kissing and which considerate member of the family, removing which baby from my arms to give another a turn. Shamim,

Shehnaz and Rashid, all of them wanted to be in my arms at once. The doll distracted Shamim briefly but not Shehnaz. She let the doll drop and stretched her arms, and insistently demanded, 'cally me, cally me'. Oh the joy of it, this wonderful welcome, they had missed me as much as I missed them. They would not let me out of sight and insisted in being with me in the bathroom while I bathed. Shamim quietly said to me, 'You know mummy, I was thinking what you were wearing – a dress or a sari. You wear a sari sometimes don't you mummy?' Shamim informs me you are coming for her birthday!

Today my arms are sore from the excitement of carrying the children. And now my love I don't know whether I am happiest with you or with the children? It is so confusing yesterday in the car I knew what I wanted most of all in the world. But now that wish being fulfilled, my heart again yearns for you. We are happiest when we are all together.

A little more patience, my heart was sure, and we would be in Durban. As the car sped so my heart soared. I had forgotten what Shamim looked like, I didn't know how fat Rashid was. The thought that I would have all three children in my arms made me deliriously happy.

In May 1957 our house seemed to be wrapped in colds. All three children were ill with colds and coughs and no matter how much cough mixture I thrust down their throats, the colds never left them. It was a difficult period for me, I had to bundle the children very warmly and take them to my mothers where I left them while I went off to attend to my tutorials and lectures. Leo was most sympathetic of my problems and Hilda urged him further so that his sympathy compounded.

I wrote to Ismail:

Shamim has made a beautiful bed on the floor at the foot of my bed with the help of Sharda. Shehnaz who has been folding and refolding a comic, now wants to sleep with Shamim. Shamim doesn't want her and there are arguments. Shehnaz returns to my bed. Shamim asks her for a pillow ever so sweetly that she obliges. Shehnaz says 'cheep Tamien', Shamim says 'come my baba' – so the two settle down. But Shehnaz wants the bed. So she is back with me and Shamim's bed has to be made all over again. Shamim says she didn't want Shehnaz because she wanted her doll to sleep with her.

Almost as suddenly as the Treason Trial had turned our lives upside down, we were released from it. The trial had invaded our lives for over a year, now it was over. Ismail returned to us to resume his normal life in January 1958. He was one of the 65 trialists against whom the charges were withdrawn at the end of the preparatory examination. Though happy in ourselves, both of us regretted that others close to us and equally innocent or guilty were still trapped in the trial and there was no indication when their torture would end.

CHAPTER 15

Burnwood Road: 1958 – 1969

S oon after Ismail's return in January 1958 after all charges against him were dropped, we moved into our newly built home in Burnwood Road, bringing our old furniture from Umgeni Road. I very much wanted us to buy a lounge suite but Ismail said we couldn't afford it. We had two deep chairs which our cousin YC Meer had given us as a wedding present. We put these in our new lounge and for a settee we used a divan which we had now dressed up anew. For the girls' room I bought some pink linen curtains, printed with Degas' Ballerinas. We bought a bed for ourselves and our old bedroom suite was put in the girls' room.

Though Ismail had helped me on his visits to Durban during the Treason Trial with managing the building, it was left mainly to me to develop some kind of garden on this barren plot. I planted lawn, trees and shrubbery wherever I could.

Me with Shamim, Rashid and Shehnaz outside our new home.

We found that since our house was high up on a hill, it was very windy and the first time we experienced the ferocious wind, it ripped off the asphalt tiles from the roof and dumped them in the valley below. There was a solitary thorn tree on the land and that too was ripped from its roots and flung to some faraway place. Ismail consulted a gardener from Mitchell Park about this wind problem and the gardener advised that we plant *Eugenia Jambolana* trees. We planted these along with two fistula trees towards the end of our back garden.

I continued lecturing at Natal University, to both European and non-European students. By now the government had changed its attitude to advanced education for non-Europeans and as per the University Extension Bill opened separate ethnic universities for non-Europeans. Natal University became a "whites only" campus and could not enrol Non-Europeans. The non-Europeans already enrolled could continue but any further enrolment of non-European students was prohibited. The current non-European students were part-time students, receiving their lectures in the City Building near the market.

Phoowa continued to take care of the cooking and running of our home in Burnwood Road. She lived close by and we spent practically every Diwali with her family at their home.

Phoowa suffered from backache and because Rashid was a breach baby, she believed he could cure her back or give relief to it by walking on it. And so she would lie stretched on the floor on her tummy and invite Rashid to walk up and down her back. He did this fairly regularly until he was eight or nine years old.

In March 1960 Ismail was again detained. His detention followed the wild shooting by the police into the crowd gathered in peaceful protest against passes in Sharpeville in the then Transvaal, killing 69 people. The government attempted to nip in the bud what it saw as a revolution in the making by declaring a state of emergency and by banning the African National Congress and Pan African Congress. The police went about picking up people willy-nilly throughout the country and dumping them into prison.

It was just before dawn when the police charged up our garden path, anxious not to lose their quarry. We were startled out of sleep. Ismail was taken to the Durban Central Prison.

Rowley Arenstein made an urgent application for the release of the Durban detainees on the grounds that their detention was illegal, since the police had acted before the law permitting the detention had been gazetted. The application was successful and the detainees were to be released, but we knew that the police would soon return with the necessary orders to re-arrest them.

I waited for Ismail outside the prison and as soon as he emerged we rushed to the car. Ismail's plan was to take advantage of the release to make the necessary arrangements for his office, and then hand himself over to the police the next day. This meant we would have to leave the prison gates without delay.

I was, however, distracted on seeing Bertha Mkhize, who had also been detained, coming out of the women's section. I impulsively ran to hug her, while Ismail called after me not to delay as the police would be upon us. Even as he called, the police pounced on Bertha and marched her back to prison. I ran to the car where Ismail had already started the engine and we sped off, escaping the police. We spent the night at my brother Ismail's house in Reservoir Hills, while Amina Ma looked after our children at Burnwood Road.

During their second dawn raid on Burnwood Road the following day, the police found Ismail missing. They vented their anger on Amina Ma, and she was petrified and still shaking when she reported the ordeal to us.

Looking back, I realise how callously I had treated Amina Ma, dismissing her fears as petty and expecting her to put a brave face on it all. She had no business to be afraid. After all it was I who was suffering, she was merely supporting. It was her duty to look after her grandchildren. I literally dumped the children – Rashid, three years old, Shehnaz four and Shamim six – on Amina Ma throughout that detention, while I ran around organising the detainees' support services. I explained nothing to her. My husband was in prison, my first duty was to him and my mother's duty was to support me in every way. I was attending to a crisis which would pass, but my mother, I believed illogically, would be there for me forever. Now that she is gone and can never be accessed, I am overcome with unbearable remorse.

Ismail's detention, this time round, was different from the Treason Trial. Whereas he was out on bail during the Treason Trial, he was now solidly imprisoned. The detention came as a shock and the worst aspect was that we did not know how long it would continue. As it was, they were detained for three months.

Ismail was imprisoned at the Durban Central Prison. I was allowed three visits a week and I took every one of these, as eagerly waiting at my end as he was at the other. The prospect of the first visit so excited me, that I did not sleep the whole night before, and as visiting time drew near, I was the first wife outside the prison gate, a whole hour before it opened for visitors. Five of us took our visit together in one room and so ten of us shouted at each other simultaneously across the two grilles that separated us. I wondered how the warder sitting in the alley between the grilles could monitor our conversations when we ourselves found such difficulty in understanding each other. Ismail looked well, and I was happy to see that he was his usual self, grumbling about the blanket and the pillow. If he hadn't grumbled, I would have worried.

The next day when I returned home, I found a letter awaiting me and I became childishly happy. I wrote to Ismail that it was the best letter I had ever received from him. We had reached a situation where we expected so little, that we became jubilantly happy when the little came.

We, the wives of those detained, decided we would keep a 24-hour vigil outside the prison to monitor any moving of the detainees. The prison guards and chief warder watched our vigil threateningly. We stared back at them even more threateningly. The chief warder was the last to avert his eyes, turning away his face, tinged with fear. We continued our vigil.

Come Saturday, three days after the original detentions, we arranged a prayer meeting on a vacant plot opposite the prison. This holding of prayer meetings opposite the prison continued for a few weeks. We then met to organise a march to the mayor's office. We were determined that our suffering would not be forgotten. The march would be a strategy to keep the public mind focused on it.

However, at the meeting to plan the march, Zulie Christopher, the wife of detainee Enver Hassim, rejected the march. They were both members of the Non-European Unity Movement (NEUM) which was very critical of the Congress movement. They criticised our mass action as exploitation of the masses. They insisted that the people had to be educated before they could be involved in a revolution. The revolution seemed to be some far off goal, as distant as heaven itself, and the educational process was an end in itself. Zulie supported her rejection of the march with some Trotsky-ite theory beyond the reckoning of most of the wives.

The march by contrast appeared simple and straightforward, and the women supported it. The wives of the Congress of Democrats detainees joined us and we planned to march with our children.

I phoned my mothers and asked them to bring my children to the corner of Grey and West Streets. We began our march from the ANC office in Saville Street, a short distance away from the mayor's office. Some mothers wheeled their babies in prams. Others carried their babies on their backs. Those with older children held them by their hands. To evade the law on illegal processions, we kept our distances walking in rows of ten. The media was there, and as we began our march we had already achieved a part of our purpose – keeping the detentions in the public eye.

I saw my mothers at the corner of Grey and West Streets smiling at me nervously, but my children were not there. Deeply disappointed, I continued on the march.

We had just turned into West Street when the police came up:

"This is an illegal procession. You are under arrest."

We retorted: "This group is on its own. We are not connected with the group behind us."

The police insisted: "Just come along with me, I am arresting all of you."

We were herded into the vans. I saw dismay on my mothers' faces. Amina Ma had stepped close to me. I whispered to her, "Move back. They'll arrest you too." She was flustered.

"Why didn't you bring the children?" I asked.

"To be arrested?" she responded.

She stepped back, realising that she now had to look after the children and guard against being mixed up with the procession.

We were taken to the police station at the corner of Smith Street[51], a very plain old colonial residence. About 200 of us were herded into the back veranda and called into the office one by one to have our particulars recorded and our finger prints taken. One woman was pregnant and needed a toilet urgently. Either the police station did not have a toilet for black women or they did not respond on time. Seeing the woman's distress, we formed a cordon around her and told her to relieve herself right there, which she did, leaving a puddle for the police to mop up.

We were eventually all discharged with instructions to appear in court the next day. The African National Congress and Natal Indian Congress got busy with our defence. Rowley Arenstein engaged advocate Douglas Shearer who gave his services pro deo. We met in the Natal Indian Congress office in Lakhani Chambers to work out our strategy.

I felt very strongly that if we were given the choice of a fine or imprisonment, we should choose imprisonment. There was heated debate on this. Margaret Hathorn, a member of the Congress of Democrats adamantly opposed this, her argument being that our husbands were already in prison and if we now volunteered to be imprisoned we would lose all community support. "That may be the attitude of the white public", I countered. "It wouldn't be the attitude of the non-white community."

Black women were being picked up all the time and hurled into prison for passes. As for Indian women, they had been brought up in the tradition of seeking imprisonment through passive resistance. The non-European community would applaud us. Margaret did not change her position. Vera Ponnen was in conflict. As a fellow member of COD she should stand with Margaret, but she knew that I was correct. Eventually it was decided that the matter should be put to vote and the majority position would be binding on all. My position received majority support. It was decided that we would not pay the fine, and Margaret left the meeting. Vera Ponnen remained with us.

The following morning we arrived at court – the first floor of a commercial building, the original courthouse having outgrown its space. The entrance to the courtroom was through a long passage. All of us women, Indian and Black lined the two walls of the passage, waiting to be called in by our counsel. Margaret walked past us into the courtroom where she told counsel that we would pay the fine whatever the amount. I was flabbergasted, shocked and enraged. There were some 200 non-European women. We had had a full discussion on that matter the day before. Margaret herself had undertaken to stand by the majority decision and then flouted it. Now she went further and instructed counsel to follow her decision. I intercepted and told Advocate Shearer that we women would go to prison but not pay any fine. I could not but see Margaret's behaviour in race-class terms. Had she discussed this with the COD or was she simply imposing her own personal will ignoring everyone?

As it transpired, Advocate Shearer argued our case with such skill and humanism that the magistrate discharged us, imposing neither a fine nor a prison sentence.

When we were arrested, my immediate concern was Ismail – that he would be very upset. He had written to me:

> If anything should happen to you, it would break me. I am somewhat adjusted – perhaps only superficially – to the present situation but that adjustment has been possible only because I have the fullest confidence in you to look after our home and children and the office. Without you present, my heart would be sore and life would become completely unbearable. It would break me. I am so thankful to you that you have managed so well. You are now doing both your work and mine. I know how hard it is for you.

We, the women, had taken the only honourable decision, but this would mean that I would not be able to do the things Ismail was relying upon me to do and of which he was so proud. Ismail would certainly not *break* as he professed, but suffering was hard on him though he bore it with dignity and I admired and loved him for that.

I wrote to Ismail about the march and our arrest. I was sure Ismail would agree with my reasoning. I was proven right when at my first visit after the arrest I was met by a beaming Ismail. "We are all proud of you," he told me, despite the presence of the warder. He went on to praise my spirit and the spirit of my sisters. Ismail may have had anxieties if I had been imprisoned, but I believe I would still have had his support.

We wrote to each other often over this time. After a visit from the children Ismail wrote:

> It was indeed a pleasure to see you all. I only hope the children were not too disturbed. Shehnaz seemed quite shocked, while Rashid appeared

to be the least disturbed. And my grown daughter Shamim looked all understanding.

The weekly visit is something to live for and look forward to. Did the children go to Ahmed's wedding? How is the new bride? Convey my heartiest congratulations to the couple. Tell me all about our garden in detail. Have the cassias blossomed forth?

My sweetheart, I love you so deeply. I wish this long separation will soon end. I miss you so terribly and look forward to seeing you – I hope the business meeting will come off tomorrow. Shehnaz appeared to be a bit shy with Amina Ma carrying her. Tell her she is a beautiful girl and I was pleased to hear from her that she received a nice Easter egg.

Tell Shamim that she looked very charming when she came to see me. Is she working hard for her half-yearly exam? You must do your best to help her. And now that talkative Rashid – I am sure he must have thought that I had sweets in my little tin. He must look after the family while I am away from home.

Darling please look after yourself and the family well. I love you all so very much and I want to feel assured that everything is alright at home. Yours forever

Ismail

In a letter dated the 27-05-1960 Ismail wrote:

What a lovely letter you sent me. I was deeply moved and felt that you were so close to me. I don't think that we have been so close to each other as we are now, nor has our love been so deep as it is now. My darling I wish I had the capacity to tell you how deeply I feel for you. Every moment of my existence I long for you and how proud I am of my wife, my beautiful wife.

I gave Ismail news about home, about the children, about our dog Rishi, and the garden:

The Cannas have flowered vigorously again and it would do your heart good to see the cassias in bloom. There are empty beds below our living room under and in front but I hope to have these replanted for your return.

I wrote to him about my brother Ahmed who had just got married in the Transvaal and had returned home to a family welcome.

> You were sorely missed by all. The new couple looks very happy. The family seems proud and satisfied, especially at 84.

Shamim sufficiently educated, gave her own news of the photos taken with the bridal couple:

> Shehnaz and I had on our off shoulder dresses yesterday and took photos with the bride and Rashid wore his long trousers and a white shirt. And in one photo I was giving the bride the bouquet. On Saturday we all went to Brighton Beach. There was a pool and no waves in it. Even Shehnaz was bathing in it. From your daughter, Shamim.

Ismail, along with the other detainees, was released after three months.

In July 1962 Ismail was listed as a communist in the government gazette. He was one of 102 persons whose freedom to participate in political activity the government sought to curtail through the listing. But the name and address that appeared in the gazette was not his. He was listed as Meer, Ismail Chota, alias Meer, Ismail Cassim. He was Meer, Ismail Chota and not alias Meer, Ismail Cassim. The address given – 15 Market Building, Etna Lane – had never been his residence. Ismail objected to the listing on grounds that the name listed was not his, but he never heard from the Department of Justice in response to his objection.

Persons listed as communists were prohibited from taking part in political activities and from publishing anything. Thankfully the clause of the law striking listed lawyers off the attorney's roll was held in abeyance and Ismail and others were able to continue to practice, although with some level of insecurity as they did not know when they might be struck off, and be thus left without their livelihoods. The listing changed his life. He was cut off from practically all his former activities and forced to resign from the organisations in which he was active, including the NIC.

Later that year we organised the marriage of Sharda Maharaj who had been with us at Umgeni Road taking care of Rashid since his birth. A young man, Teddy Goordeen, who lived on a road joining Umgeni Road, had courted Sharda during those years. He was the nephew of Ashwin Choudree, a prominent lawyer and a leader of the Natal Indian Congress but he was of a lower caste than Sharda's family. Sharda's father, who was a Maharaj of the highest caste, objected to the relationship because of Teddy's low caste status, and when the young couple wanted to marry, he adamantly refused to have any part in it. So Ismail and I acted as her parents in arranging the marriage and Rashid performed the ritual in the Hindu marriage ceremony as younger brother.

Then, in April 1963, Ismail was banned for five years. His movement was now also restricted and he could not leave the magisterial district of Durban unless to travel to Verulam to his practice. Faced with restrictions of movement and activity, Ismail turned to gardening.

It was around this time that Zwelinye was brought to us by his father Chief Goba to work as our gardener. The three men – Chief Goba, Zwelinye and Ismail sat on the back terrace and the father gave his teenage son firm advice. He then left his son in our care. Zwelinye was industrious and dependable and he hugely respected Ismail. Ismail was keen on gardening and spent a lot of time with Zwelinye who learnt to be a good gardener from him. Ismail acquired a taste for growing roses. He put in a bed of roses bordering our front path. His roses flourished. Pruning was a very busy time for him, and the only time I received roses which I arranged in several vases. Ismail's beautiful rose garden was his pride and joy.

Since Ismail's roses dominated the front garden I focused my gardening aspirations on the back garden. I had planted the front lawn when the house was still under construction. I now also planted the back lawn.

We had just the one car at that time, the Volkswagen, and each morning Ismail dropped me off at the University and then dropped the children off at their school. He proceeded thereafter to his practice in Verulam. At times, when I kept the car, I would pick up the children after school and take them to the beach for a picnic lunch before returning home.

During school holidays when Ismail left for Verulam in his Volkswagen, we, the women and children of the house, had to stand in a line at the entrance and on some mornings before leaving, he would present each of us with a wild rose from the rose bush that grew near his more cultivated roses.

I arranged for the children to have swimming lessons at the Asherville pool, the only pool available to Indians in Durban. I never learnt to swim but went into the pool with them in a yellow and white swimming costume that I acquired for that purpose.

During this time, I was for the first time allocated my own office in the Sociology Department at the University. My children painted me curtains with colourful Egyptian motifs and my office was the prettiest in that corridor. I was very proud of it and took my mother, Amina Ma to see it. I wanted to share with her my newly achieved status, observable now in its own space.

Phoowa left us when she became arthritic and couldn't make the walk from her home to ours. Irene Ngcobo came looking for work and contacted our neighbour Kay Ramjathan, who knew we needed a housekeeper and sent her to us. So Irene started working for us. She learned to cook our Indian cuisine, phoning to confirm the recipes with my mother, cousins and aunts. She made beautiful rotis every day. She made samoosas and during Ramadan made all the necessary delicacies with which we opened our fast and she made the best biryani in the family.

My parent's home at Ritson Road continued to be a focal point for all of us, where the extended Meer family came together at Eid celebrations and weekend lunches, but there were now also signs of my parents failing health. We worried about Papa when he suffered a heart attack. He told me then that he was very worried about Amina Ma's high blood pressure and we should take account of that. "She is inclined to be careless about her health," he said.

Amina Ma learnt to drive the car and for a while after Papa's heart attack, took over collecting the subscriptions for his newspaper. Her brother, Uncle Cas accompanied her on these trips. Amina Ma was happy then, happy for the opportunity to travel and help with the business, happy for the time spent with her brother. On one journey travelling through the Karoo, they espied three tortoises moving slowly across the road in the way of tortoises. They brought them home for the children.

Papa died in 1964, and two years later, in 1966, Amina Ma died. We all went through a very traumatic period. I was no longer a child, but a young mother myself. After Papa's death I grew kinder towards Amina

Ma, but not kind enough, and when she died, for the first time I felt a certain resentment towards Ma and Papa. Amina Ma had never been allowed to lead her own life. I bore my own burden of guilt on this.

When Amina Ma died, Ma looked at me helplessly and said, "Now I am all alone." It was both a statement and question: Am I expected to live alone? The life she had founded with Papa and Amina Ma had ended.

In 1966 I started working on my book *Portrait of Indian South Africans.* I wrote about Indian South Africans in the hope that they would reach out and make contact with other South Africans, in the hope that South Africans would recognise themselves in the lives of their fellows. I felt that there was a need for those who shared the country to know each other.

As segregation had crystallised into apartheid, barriers between communities had grown wider. Opportunities for interpersonal contact were less than in earlier times, as each community was residentially barricaded into its own little homeland or group area. The written word seemed to me important as a channel of meaningful contact.

The book written, I struggled to get a publisher. But this was only one among several sagas that frustrated my attempts to publish the book. Hansie Pollack, head of department at the University of Natal was disparaging about the book. She said the book would reflect poorly on my academic status. Ellen Hellmann, head of the Institute of Race Relations, rejected publication of the book on grounds that my Indian characters spoke bad English!

Hilda Kuper on the other hand, considered the manuscript so good that she canvassed the head of department to award me a doctorate for it. Professor John Blacking, head of the Anthropology Department at Wits University at the time, was also complimentary and urged me to publish.

Struik, a publisher specialising in Africana, accepted the manuscript, and I spent all of 1967 working with Struik and a photographer. But when I fell out with the photographer over credits, Struik withdrew. I then went to another publisher – Balkema – who was excited by the script and photographs. Another year went by, planning and adding new material. Then Balkema dropped the bombshell that the book was politically risky and his printers would not handle it. He was dropping it. I then decided to publish the book myself. A group of young friends gave me enthusiastic support – Saths Cooper, Subash Maharaj, Strini Moodley, Zubie Seedat. They helped with proof reading and layout, and the book was out in 1969. It was well received by critics and the community. We sold thousands of copies.

In 1969 I started work on a book on the life of Mahatma Gandhi who I had long admired. In this book, *Apprenticeship for a Mahatma,* I traced Gandhi's life from birth up to his departure from South Africa. It was published in 1970 by the Phoenix Settlement Trust which I had worked with closely, and on whose board I served. Proceeds from these two books went towards the building of the Gandhi Museum and Clinic.

Many years later I worked on a screenplay based on my book on Gandhi for the movie *The Making of the Mahatma* directed by well known movie director Shyam Benegal from India, and released in 1996.

IV

GLIMPSES:
1970 to 2004[1]

---

1   This last section is different from the previous ones. While the earlier sections of this book were written before her stroke, my mother only started working on this section in 2006 after having a stroke. Much of it was therefore dictated rather than written by her. It does not include a detailed account of her life after 1970 but rather deals with individual meaningful moments, events and people in her life. Her memories captured here are enhanced where relevant by extracts from her book *Prison Diary One Hundred and Thirteen Days 1976* (Kwela, 2001).

CHAPTER 16

A Trip to India – 1970[52]

After years of repeatedly having applications for travel documents refused by the apartheid government, I at last obtained a passport in 1970. Our principal at the University of Natal, Professor Owen Horwood, who later became a Minister in the National Party Cabinet,[53] had persuaded the authorities to issue me with a passport to take up an invitation as a visiting professor in the department of sociology at the Delhi School of Economics.

Towards the end of my stay I was joined by my children – my daughters Shamim and Shehnaz, seventeen years and fifteen years respectively, and my son Rashid who was fourteen – and my sister Ayesha, whom we called Gorie. The children and Gorie joined me in Hyderabad in December of that year where I had attended the All-India Sociological Conference, and we took a train from there to Madras. We had our own coupé, separated from the other compartments, with its own toilet and washbasin. The only door in the coupé opened out onto the station platform.

We stopped at the Warangal station and the vendors came shouting 'garum samoosa, garum samoosa' (hot samoosas), and 'garum chai' (hot tea). We made our purchases. The train took off and we were soon trundling away. We were very relaxed. The sun was setting and night was approaching. We changed into our sleeping attire. I turned into my pink pyjamas with matching cotton gown. I was stretched out on the seat, talking to Shehnaz. Rashid was sitting in the open doorway, his legs dangling out, happily listening to his transistor radio. He seemed so happy. I didn't want to interfere with his happiness.

My back was turned to Rashid – Shehnaz was facing me and bringing me up to date on the news at home. Suddenly she screamed; Rashid had fallen off the train and the train was steaming away. I flung myself across the open door and reached out to the window in the next compartment shouting, "Mera baccha! Mera Baccha! Train se gir gaya. . ." (My child! My child! He's fallen off the train).

"Pull the chain! Pull the chain!" someone yelled. In my half demented state I went and pulled the lavatory chain, but my sister Gorie had the presence of mind to pull the right chain. The thought flashed through my mind; this country of 400 million, what would they care for one life? But the train stopped. A senior official was on the spot. We explained our tragedy. He said the train would wait; I should go look for my son and he sent an attendant with me with a hurricane lamp.

We began walking on the railway tracks. Shehnaz came after me, needing to be with me. I scolded her and sent her back. She left me crying. The attendant and I walked in the black night, on the tracks, and the thought that rang through my mind was that I couldn't leave India without my son. If anything happened to him, I could not return to South Africa. I could not face Ismail without Rashid. We walked some distance with no sign of Rashid. As we neared the Warangal station, my eyes fell on the criss-crossing steel tracks and my heart sank as I thought of the fate of someone falling on that. A chill ran down my spine. I froze in my tracks unable to breathe.

Then I heard a distant voice calling, "Are you looking for the boy who fell off the train?" There was a sudden gushing of blood in my head and my breath returned in short gasps. The voice came from the signal box. "They found the boy and took him to the clinic. Come up and you can telephone the clinic." I felt hope limping back. I climbed up to the signal box, the attendant with the hurricane lamp following me. Wonder of wonders, the man in the signal box put me through to the doctor at the clinic. "Your son is well," he told me, "and he is asking for you." Hope now came bouncing back and I was relieved, though still tense.

The signalman, who introduced himself as Vaithalingam, made arrangements for me to go to the clinic. I asked the attendant to go back to the train and return with my handbag. I would need money. He returned quite soon without my handbag, saying the other passengers had remonstrated with my sister for trusting him with my bag. I was exasperated. He said the train was leaving now and my family would alight at the next station in Kazipet, and I could meet them in the waiting room. He had been instructed to accompany me to the clinic.

We walked together, crossing the railway tracks, the hurricane lamp casting its long light ahead of us. We passed through a village with its night sounds of gossiping women, quarrelling men and crying children, and reached the clinic. I found Rashid lying on a bench, shivering. The doctor told me he had given him emergency aid. He needed to be taken to the hospital. He had called the ambulance, but he didn't know how long it would take. Perhaps I would like to take a rickshaw. He was just about to arrange for one when the ambulance arrived.

As providence would have it, the ambulance service was called *My lady of Fatima* and I was being taken to Mahatma Gandhi hospital in Kazipet. Both names had meaning for me and I felt comforted. We got into the ambulance. Rashid was very cold; I asked if we could keep the blanket. They said they couldn't spare it – it was the only one they had. So I lay over Rashid to keep him warm. The hospital was twenty miles away. I shuddered to think of that journey by rickshaw and gave up a prayer of thanks.

The service was efficient. Rashid's lip was cut. They stitched it. They said he was concussed, but they could not ascertain what internal injuries he might have suffered. He would have to be hospitalised and they would observe him. They put him to bed in the general ward and once he appeared comfortable and asleep, I hired a bicycle rickshaw – there was no other mode of transport available in Kazipet – and went off to the station.

My daughters and my sister ran towards me, tense with anxiety. I told them that Rashid appeared to be safe. We piled our luggage and ourselves into five rickshaws and went looking for a hotel. The two better ones were full. We found a room in Gopi Lodge, a third rate and rundown affair. The room opened out into a sort of lobby with a service counter. There were a number of men hanging around and this made us nervous. I told my sister to lock the door, pile the suitcases against it and get what sleep she and the girls could. Then I returned to the hospital to be with Rashid.

The hospital allowed relatives and some made their beds on the floor. I asked the nurse on duty if I could have a chair. She gave me a surly look and said nothing. Meekly, I took my position next to Rashid's bed and remained standing for an hour or so. Then the nurse took pity on me and brought me a chair. Rashid slept fairly peacefully.

In the early hours of the morning, I returned to the lodge and after a wash and breakfast of sorts, we all rickshawed back to the hospital. Rashid was awake and greeted us as cheerfully as he could, with his mouth all stitched up. The hospital turned out to be a teaching hospital. Mid-morning the professor came around with his students on their rounds. They were quite clearly intrigued by us. The students returned later and offered to assist us. Their advice was that we should take the evening train to Madras and have Rashid seen to by India's renowned neuro-surgeon, Professor Ramamurthi, who also attended to the President of India.

In the meanwhile, they said they would take us to see the splendid ruins of a castle dating back to the fifteenth century. One of the students volunteered to remain with Rashid. By now the signalman, Mr Vaithalingam, had joined us and he produced a car. The ruins, dating back to the Vijayanagar period, were as splendid as promised. We had a hurried lunch at a restaurant and then, emboldened by our newfound friends, we returned to the hospital to discharge Rashid. The hospital discharged him very reluctantly and at our peril.

We knew the train was full; the stationmaster had told us that it was not only full, but overfull. However, on the strength of the students and Mr Vaithalingam, we set off for the station, determined to board. The train would only halt for a few minutes, they warned, and we would have to be quick if we were to get on. We looked at each other in despair, but Mr Vaithalingam's instruction was to get on, regardless, and let the officials deal with the problem we would create.

As the train came to a stop, our helpers loaded our bags in the passage and we all got on, they and us. The conductor came striding towards us and told us to get off at once. Now the haggling started. The conductor insisted there was no way we could remain on the train. Mr Vaithalingam and the students were equally insistent that there was no way we could be left stranded in Kazipet. We had a seriously ill patient and he had to be taken to Madras to see Professor Ramamurthi. We had an appointment to keep. We couldn't miss it. It was a matter of life and death.

Their pressure and Professor Ramamurthi's name won the night. Gorie, Shehnaz and Rashid found berths in the ladies' compartment. The ladies complained about the intruding male (Rashid), but I reassured them he was only a child and a very ill one at that. Shamim and I were left standing in the passage, which we considered a small price to pay for being on the train at all.

We did not have time to thank Mr Vaithalingam and the students and we never saw them again. They were there to do a good deed and their satisfaction lay in having done it.

Shamim and I did not stand in the passage too long. The conductor gave us his bunk at the end of the coach where it coupled with next coach. We curled up together and dozed off intermittently rocked by pushing and pulling of coaches.

Once in Madras we found a good hotel on the marina. The doctor came to see Rashid and made a grand entrance with his portly gait and an entourage of bearers who impressively carried his instruments as if bearing royal gifts. He examined Rashid, dressed his cut, arranged x-rays and said there was nothing for me to worry about. It took a few days, but Rashid recovered and began to enjoy the trip.

Surat

My first visit to Surat, the place of origin of us South African Meers, was during this visit to India. We visited the town in December 1970. We had travelled from Delhi by train, reaching Surat early in the morning. I was very excited. I was setting foot in the city of my forebears for the first time.

The porters came charging into our compartment and before we could hire any, several had hired themselves and were racing off with our baggage atop their heads, under their arms and in their hands. We followed them up the stairs, onto the street, and into several bicycle rickshaws. I paid the porters tenfold more than they expected, and seeing their pleasure, I told them: "We are celebrating. We have arrived at the place of our Baap Dada – our fathers and grandfathers."

We gave the rickshaw wallahs our address and they cycled through narrow streets, passed a gully where a bevy of decorated ladies stood expectantly on their verandas, and deposited us outside a house, which stood out distinctly in size, style and beauty from all the others on the street. It was not the ancestral home I had seen in Ma's photographs. It was, as we learnt soon enough from the very warm welcome we got from its occupants, my father's cousins, the Variawa's, *Kimberley House,* built circa 1911.

We said we were looking for our grandfather's house.

"But this is also your grandfather's house," they said, "your paternal grandfather's. He and your paternal grandmother lived here. We are your father's first cousins. You will be more comfortable with us."

I accepted their hospitality somewhat reluctantly, somewhat ungraciously, for we were anxious to see *Raja Wadi*, which had taken on fairytale proportions in my mind. I insisted we wanted to go *to Raja Wadi*, the Meer ancestral home.

"Leave your baggage here," they said. "The Meer home is just behind ours, you can walk to it, and we will arrange for your baggage to be brought to you."

We approached *Raja Wadi* now, 55 years after Ma had left it, not from the splendid front entrance she had described, but from a shoddy back entrance, up a rickety flight of stairs. There was no indication of that palatial haveli my mother had talked of. Our cousin Kader, the only Meer who had remained in India, bearded and in kurta, in his forties, met us.

Kader, his wife and young children occupied two rooms, both furnished with beds. My mother had talked of her four-poster bed in carved mahogany and her wardrobe. I asked after the bed and he said, "You are sitting on it. We cut off the legs for the convenience of the children." Her wardrobe was in the next room. I found it dilapidated and dusty. In my mind's eye I tried to fill her shelves with her beautiful karchop, gold embroidered suits that she had described. It was difficult. My imagination gave up.

The room was large, there were ornamental niches on the walls, a patterned pressed ceiling, and arched windows with shutters that opened onto a veranda. The balustrade was old and weather worn, but along the ridges, flowers of stucco pushed through their heads and kept faith with Ma. I saw the filigree she had described. Ma's haveli came to life as I filled in the colours.

My cousin Kader was saying: "This room opened out into two other adjoining rooms in our Grandfather's time so that it made up a hall. The floor was carpeted, bolsters lined the walls and our elders sat here against them with their friends and passed the hookah and held mushairas – the poets gathering to read their poetry."

I recalled my cousin Salehjee Motala's description of the hall: "Moham-

med Meer's dream house was completed during my stay in Surat. We all
gasped in wonder at the splendid edifice, with its ornamentation picked
out in gold glistening in the sun. There were many rooms within, and
the main hall had a glittering chandelier and was carpeted in deep pile.
Silk covered bolsters lined the wall. The room also had a large ornamental swing."

I recalled how Ma had described *Raja Wadi* and the joys of her childhood
to me. "The bungalow is large, double storey, with porticoes embellished
with flowers and leaves etched in gold. There are palm trees and fruit
trees . . ."

The bleating of a goat dragged me back from the past into the present.
I stuck my head onto the balcony and saw the goat among its droppings
and its fodder. Kader explained it was his son's pet.

"We have partitioned the hall and rented out the rooms to diamond
polishers. They occupy the whole of this floor, barring the two rooms we
occupy. We need the rent to pay the rates and taxes. The ground floor is
rented out to the post office and the surrounding land is used as a piggery."

I stood on the balcony and searched for signs of the garden my mother
had spoken of, there was only dirt and dung and pigs sluggishly going
about their foraging.

"How big is the land?" I asked.

"About ten acres," he said. "Very valuable but run over with shacks, and
there is nothing we can do about them. They do not pay rent and we can't
evict them. The law is in their favour."

He then told us that since there were no womenfolk in the house, we
would be more comfortable staying at *Kimberley House.* So my dream of
spending a few nights on my mother's bed, in my mother's house, was
shattered.

We returned to *Kimberley House* somewhat crestfallen. Our father's cousins Gorie Apa, Bibi Ma, Raboo and Moosie Bhai were overjoyed and over-
loving. *Kimberley House* was beautiful and the woodwork exquisitely carved,
the floors tiled in intricate mosaic patterns, the furniture heavy Victorian,
the food as tasteful as we had known at home. The house was also flanked
by family history; Halloo Meer's house stood on the one side, on the other
was a vacant strip of land on which had probably stood the first Meer

house in Surat, built by our great grandfather Ahmed Meer and his brother Ahmedjee Meer. The Meer brothers who had migrated to South Africa had been born and raised in that house.

And now, a hundred or more years later after the demise of the founding fathers of the Meer clan, I stood on the narrow strip where it had begun. Where the two brothers, Ahmed and Ahmedjee had plied their trade and raised their families. I tried to put together the house and the people who had lived in it.

The house, I was told, was a double storey, bamboo and daub dwelling under a tiled roof. The ground floor housed the oil press, a cow-cum-donkey shed, a washroom and kitchen; the top floor, the family living rooms. It was both house and workplace, and the work involved grinding nuts, mostly monkey nuts, between two large round stones driven by a donkey, to extract the oil. One imagines the early Meer patriarchs to be long bearded and stern tempered in long kurtas, wielding great authority.

CHAPTER 17

1976[54]

In early 1976, Ma's health failed, and she was moved to hospital. I kept her company there at night, sleeping in her ward. When she improved, I took her with me to Cape Town to settle Shehnaz and Shamim in their lodgings. They had enrolled at the University of Cape Town – Shehnaz to study law and Shamim sociology. Shamim had married Bobby Marie the year before, and he planned to join her in Cape Town later that year.

Ma was by now living with my brother Ahmed. By 1970, the Group Areas Act had taken its toll and forced Ma out of her Ritson Road home. Our second family home had fallen victim to the white nationalist government's racism and greed as it brutally enforced its separate development policies reserving prime land for whites only. The government gave Ma a pittance in compensation for expropriating her home. She could not buy even a plot of land in an Indian area with it.

The four of us – Ma, Shehnaz, Shamim and I – flew together to Cape Town. Ma was very happy on the trip. She recalled her childhood – about her Mother and Fatima Chachie and the swings they would tie on Eid days and the neera they would drink and the cream they would eat "so thick you could pick it up in layers". And she laughed as she recollected this.

Ma and I stayed with Uncle Cas, Amina Ma's brother who now lived in Cape Town with his family. The night of our arrival Ma took ill and I called Ayesha Arnold, the friend who Shamim was lodging with who was a doctor. Ayesha examined Ma, gave her some medication, and advised her to rest. Cas was showing a film in the back room and later that night somebody knocked on the door and Ma got up to open it. I scolded Ma because she was supposed to rest.

The next day Ayesha took us on a drive around the peninsula. I was possessed by some strange mood and I kept aloof from both Ma and Ayesha. We stopped at the Rhodes Memorial. I climbed up the steps and left them at the bottom. Ayesha had brought along some snacks, and when we stopped at Chapman's Peak, the baboons invaded our car and helped themselves to our snacks while we were looking around. Ma got agitated, fearing that they would attack us as well. I calmed her down and we returned to the car.

Uncle Cas bought us snoek (fish) to take home. Ma wanted to know the cost of the fish. I was short with her. "Why do you want to worry over the price?" But I knew full well that she was simply interested.

When we reached Durban, Ismail was at the airport to meet us. He remarked that "Budie" as he called Ma, did not look well. I did not pay him much attention. The next day I resolved to take Ma and Choti Khala (Ismail's sister Ayesha) for drives as often as I could. I was never able to fulfil that. Ma died at Ahmed's house in Reservoir Hills the next day.

Ma's passing saw the end of our parents – only memories remained, of the caring and nurturing, of the days in Grey Street, Wentworth, Convent Lane, Ritson Road and Pinetown. There was no one to look up to. We became our own keepers. We now had the responsibility of cherishing the traditions and values of our parents, keeping them alive and passing them on to our children. We did not succeed in the latter, for we were not good keepers of our parent's lives. We were too full of arrogance of our own.

Bannings and Arrests

In 1976 Rashid was a student at the University of Durban-Westville (UDW) when the Soweto pupils revolted. UDW had been established in 1972 for Indian students. Students at the university, Rashid among them, protested against the police shooting of the children in Soweto on 16 June 1976[55]. Rashid was one of three UDW students singled out by the police for detention.

We had wanted Rashid to have the best education and in the early 1970s had tried to enroll him at the Waterford Kamhlaba private school in Swaziland. We had heard very good reports about the school and so we applied and he was called up for an interview. After a great deal of negotiating with the officials at the Department of Indian Affairs, and anxiously holding our breath, they gave him a passport just for Swaziland, and just for a month, warning that they would review the position if he was admitted. We took our chances.

Rashid was accepted by the school, but the government refused to renew his passport and so he was unable to attend. We kept applying unsuccessfully for a passport for him until for some reason in 1972 the government gave him one to travel to the UK for a year. He was enrolled at King Alfred School in London where he was a day scholar while living with my brother Bhai and sister-in-law Zubie at their home in London.

Rashid with Shehnaz (behind him), Ismail and Shamim before leaving for London in 1972.

Rashid returned home in 1973 for a holiday, just before his passport expired. The government refused to renew his passport despite all our efforts so he did not return to school in London. He enrolled at Sastri College and went on to study Fine Arts at UDW.

When the incessant, impatient predawn knocking on the door jerked us out of our sleep that morning in August 1976, we knew it was the police. We had become familiar with it from the many nocturnal raids since Ismail's arrest in 1956 when they hauled him away for treason. We assumed that this time round they had come for me, since I had been organising protest meetings. We were shocked when they asked for Rashid.

They warned us not to use the telephone. Then they followed us into Rashid's bedroom, close on our heels, nervous lest we forewarn him or tamper with some vital evidence. Rashid did not appear surprised. He was calmly co-operative as they went through his books and papers and looked under his bed and in his cupboard. One of them kept watch over him, another over us, and the others searched the rest of the house. They found nothing incriminating, and we were about to sigh in relief when the chief among them turned to Rashid and said: "Pack some clothes. We are taking you in." We were shaken. Rashid was tense, and I grew tense with him; I could feel his nervousness. I helped him put a few things together. It can only be for a few days, I kept telling myself.

As Rashid came down the stairs with the police following, he stopped momentarily before reaching the landing and asked his father for a ciga-rette. We had no knowledge that he smoked, and even if we had, he would not have done so in our presence. But this was not the time for niceties. Ismail lit the cigarette and then as the police led Rashid out towards their car, called after him: "I am proud of you boy".

Rashid told us later that remark had earned him additional cuffs and jabs during his interrogation, "Proud of you, eh? Proud of your terrorism!"

"When can we see him?" was my sole concern. "Can we bring him some breakfast in the morning?"

As irrelevant as that sounds, it gave me a contact line, even though it was an imaginary one. As the day set in, we realised the meaning of incom-municado detention. Knowing that your teenage son was in detention and entirely at the mercy of the police was bad enough, but not knowing where he was being detained and having no means of contacting him was unbearable.

That night as we lay in bed Ismail said: "Had you not been banned they would have detained you too." I understood what he was saying. I had been banned a few weeks earlier for five years, and he'd rather have me banned than detained, for then he would have me with him.[56]

The next day they detained our son-in-law Bobby Marie, our daughter Shamim's husband. He worked with me at the Institute for Black Research (IBR)[57]. We had just completed production of a journal we were estab-lishing, *Africa Survey*[58], and Bobby had taken it to the printers. He had done a lot of the research and writing for the publication. He was secre-tary of the IBR at the time and ran our office at the Ecumenical Centre. He was also involved in community projects, had started a community newspaper *Challenge*, and was one of the four students expelled from the University of Durban Westville during the student unrest in 1972. All of this had provoked the ire of the Special Branch of the police.

For nine agonising days we had no idea where Rashid or Bobby were or what was happening to them. Then the police told us that we could see them before they were to be removed to Benoni in the Transvaal. This alarmed us, as it meant they would not be released after the mandatory fourteen days, but would be detained indefinitely. We arrived at the Wentworth police station at 2 pm as arranged, laden with eight parcels of prepacked food for Rashid, Bobby and the other detainees. We filed down the stairs together with the other anxious relatives, excited to see our loved ones. Our hour with Rashid flew by without our having said all we had set out to say. Ismail and I drove home from the police station then Ismail left for his office in Verulam.

Later that afternoon the police arrived. I saw them from our bedroom window and was half way down the stairs when they rang the doorbell. The largest of the eight stood in the doorway, darkening it even further in the falling light. He introduced himself as Captain Du Toit. I moved away from the doorway and they moved in and filled the room.

Du Toit informed me that he was arresting me under Section 10 of the General Laws Amendment Act and that a notice would be served on me within seven days. I told him I had to inform my husband. He allowed me to phone Ismail, but stopped me abruptly when I began speaking in Gujarati.

"Speak English or Afrikaans," he ordered.

Ismail arranged to meet me at the police headquarters in Fisher Street. He knew they would take me there first. Meantime he would ask other family members to go to the house immediately. The police ordered me to hang up and to pack a bag. I asked Irene to help me. The policewoman followed us into the bedroom. She advised me to take my coat. Baby, my youngest sister and the last of my parent's nine children, was the first of the family to arrive. She helped with my packing of clothes and the scriptures I could lay my hands on – the Quran, the Ramayana, and the Bible.

Once packed and ready to move, I told the captain I needed to inform my daughters who both were studying in Cape Town of my arrest. He hesitated at first and then relented. I spoke to Shamim. She took the news calmly and said I should hold on while she got someone to call Shehnaz. I continued talking, but Du Toit had by now reached the end of his tether. Technically I was his prisoner and he felt he was conceding too much. I was forced to put the receiver down so I didn't speak to Shehnaz. Later

I learnt that this had devastated her and that she had sobbed uncontrollably.

As we moved towards the car, Ismail's brother AC arrived with his son Salim and his granddaughter, little Shehnaz. I was not allowed to speak to them so we smiled at each other and bade each other Khuda Hafez (in God's care).

I was conducted to the rear seat of the car where I was flanked by the policewoman and the only Indian in the contingent, Nayager. Du Toit sat in the front. Nayager asked me if I was involved with *Challenge,* the newspaper started by Bobby's group. I reminded him I was already banned when the first issue of *Challenge* was published. "But initially?" he asked.

"Yes initially I was, I attended the first meeting of *Challenge.*"

We reached the police headquarters in Fisher Street and I was taken to the top floor. Ismail was already there with his friend, fellow lawyer and activist George Sewpersadh. Ismail said he knew I would be brave. I told him I had taken some of his handkerchiefs and socks. "Well I'll be with you then," he said.

The policewoman surprised us: "He'll be at your feet", she quipped.

Ismail clasped his hands together and bowing before me, said "I am always at your feet". Pressing his forehead against mine he added he would miss me. Captain Du Toit informed us that Ismail and Sewpersadh had to leave, our visit was over. Ismail held me close and kissed me. We said our goodbyes.

I was escorted to the police car. This time I sat alone in the back. The policewoman sat in front with the driver who was also a member of the Special Branch. He became quite chatty. I realised he was keeping logs on us. He said Rashid had told him he had two sisters. He wanted to know what Shamim was doing in Cape Town while Bobby was in Durban. My first reaction was to tell him to mind his business. On second thoughts I felt perhaps he should know, so I told him she was studying.

We were heading for Wentworth police cells. A policeman opened the gate and I heard the clanging of heavy keys, a sound that would keep me company in the days to follow. I was conducted to my new lodgings, the policewoman carrying my coat and bag.

We left the next morning at the crack of dawn for Johannesburg. We reached the Women's Gaol at the Fort Prison complex in Hillbrow at 11 am. My cell was small but clean. There was drinking water in a round large stainless steel receptacle and a small pail served as the toilet. There were two sleeping mats on the floor. It was mid-winter and very cold. The cell felt even colder. I was exhausted and had developed a splitting headache. I lay down on the mats and covered myself with my coat. The cold from the floor penetrated through the mats and felt as if it was biting into my very bones.

Yet again the jangling of keys, my cell door opens and the matron is back. She stands in the doorway. What now, I think. I can't bear any more instruction, so I pre-empt her with a complaint: "I am cold and have a bad headache".

She instructs the warder to bring me more blankets and leaves, bolting the door behind her.

I wonder what exactly it was that lead to this arrest and made mental notes of my public activities in the past months. The Institute for Black Research was of course ongoing. The Tin Town Relief Committee which I headed following the flooding of the shack settlement on the banks of the Umgeni River was a passing responsibility shared with the City Council. I had also worked on the 'Save our Homes Campaign' in the Coloured community of Sparks Estate, where homes were under threat of expropriation. Perhaps the state felt most threatened by our Union of Resident's Associations (URA) which brought together Black, Indian, and Coloured residents and had the potential of developing into a multiracial regional body? All of us who were working together in the URA – George Sithole, David Gasa, Jeannie Noel[59] and I – were in detention.

After I had returned from a visit to the USA where I had met with black women I had initiated house meetings to assess the position of black women's organisations in Natal. In 1973 we had set up the Black Women's Federation (BWF) in Natal and in 1975 we had made contact with Transvaal women and held a meeting at the home of Sally Motlana in Soweto. We resolved to reach out to women in other parts of the country. The inaugural conference of the national BWF was held in December 1975 including some 200 delegates from across the country. The Special Branch had come snooping but we went ahead and elected the first officials. I was

elected president, Virginia Gcabashe secretary, Jeannie Noel assistant secretary, and Vuyi Moloto treasurer. Winnie Mandela was also elected to the
national leadership. A political women's organisation had been formed
under the noses of the police!

It was probably the Black Women's Federation more than any other
single factor that resulted in my detention, I thought. Three of the key
organisers of the inaugural conference – Jeannie Noel, Winnie Mandela
and I – were in prison.

But then, three members of the Institute for Black Research (IBR) –
Bobby Marie, Govan Reddy, and I – were also in prison. The Special Branch
had not interfered with the IBR; no raids, no interrogations. The IBR was
aimed at teaching black people to research and write. None of its publi-
cations to date – *Women Without Men* (a report on rural Black women),
a survey on the Soweto uprisings, or the first issue of *Quarterly Comment* –
had aroused police attention.

*Virginia Gcabashe and Ellen Khuzwayo carry me on being elected
President of Black Women's Federation. Sharing the joyful moment are
Theresa Hendrickse, Zubie Seedat and Sally Motlana.*

I realised that we who had been detained are terribly interconnected, our
organisations and memberships are interlocked.

As president of the Black Women's Federation I had worked closely with

South African Student Organisation (SASO) president Diliza Mji who was also detained. In June of that year (1976) I had had an urgent call from Winnie Mandela:

"Soweto is burning; they are killing the children!"

The next day the news was all over the world. We had called an emergency protest meeting in the church hall in Beatrice Street in Durban but postponed it after Diliza came to see me and suggested we hold it jointly with SASO. I agreed, but said that with much more time on our hands, we had to do better than a few hundred people in a church hall. We should organise a mass rally at Curries Fountain football grounds. He agreed, we printed 100 000 leaflets overnight.

I ended up paying for the leaflets but the rally never took place. The next day the Medical School students distributed the leaflets. We were at the IBR office in St Andrews Street planning the rally when we received a telephone call informing us that sixty medical students had been arrested. Close on the heels came another call from the Special Branch. I was told in a sinister tone that an urgent proclamation had been passed banning all open-air meetings and accordingly our planned rally was illegal.

We took a quick decision to shift the meeting to an enclosed venue. Archbishop Denis Hurley made the Cathedral available, but now Diliza objected to Hurley being a speaker. I challenged Diliza to give me a reason, apart from his colour, for the Archbishop's exclusion from the platform. Diliza did not have another reason. Govan Reddy said we were being unreasonable to impose a white speaker on SASO. I said we were not imposing anything on SASO. SASO was telling us who we could and could not invite to address our meeting.

We could have saved our breath. The police settled the matter even as we argued. There was another call from them. They warned that if they found people in groups of three or more walking to the meeting they would arrest them for forming illegal gatherings!

The violence in Soweto was unprecedented. Durban had to express its outrage, but at what cost? It was already evening and the meeting was the next morning. We had no way of controlling the way people walked to the meeting, but we could not be responsible for mass arrests. We already had sixty students in prison and we were organising food and legal defence for them.

We did not have the organisation to cope with more so we decided to call off the rally and asked permission to use a loudhailer outside Curries Fountain to announce the cancellation. The police were hesitant at first. Then they agreed, but stipulated that we submit the wording of our announcement and warned us not to deviate from it.

That Sunday, hundreds of police and as many police dogs, cordoned off access to Curries Fountain. It was grimly intimidating and enough to put people off. We didn't have to use the loudhailer. People got the message and departed.

Some weeks after this I was banned. My banning orders allowed me to continue teaching, probably because they reasoned that as an Indian I could exert little influence on white students. In contrast Dr Rick Turner[60], a veritable guru on campus, who had enormous impact on the students, was not allowed to continue teaching when he was banned. Clearly the state could not take the chance of Rick's continued contact with the students. The staff association had succeeded in prevailing on the university to keep him on full pay.

A few weeks before my arrest I had met Diliza when he and Abdul Haq Randeree of the NIC had come home to see me, to discuss the formation of a political front. Five of us sat together in our study, constituting a gathering. My presence was illegal as I was banned. This had not bothered us, but then we did not know that Diliza and Randeree had been followed by the Special Branch who were observing us. However, they did not raid us. They thought something more sinister was afoot and were waiting to be led to it. They followed Diliza and Randeree and when their car stopped to let passengers alight, they pounced on them and took them in for questioning, but finding no reason to detain them, they released them later.

Excerpt: Prison Diary 3 October 1976

It must be after 6 pm and it is raining cats and dogs. I find myself missing Ismail more than usual in this rain and thunder. I am assailed by a sense of danger and insecurity and a need to be safe with him. Our meetings are so fleeting. They seem quite unreal. But I couldn't do without them; they are my lifeline. I am very grateful for them, for the regulation that allows them, for Ismail and the girls who travel such distances to be with me. Ismail seems as if he could not do enough. I get the impression he needs these visits as much as I do. They keep us connected, they reassure us of our love, even though their duration is short and their circumstances constrained – with no privacy at all, with every word overheard by others, especially the intruding warder. What we cannot say in words, we say with our eyes. And Ismail's eyes are full of passion, at times embarrassingly so.

Excerpt: Prison Diary 27 October 1976

I write to Ismail: "I loved you so much today, but I was so afraid. Wasn't it terrible, you and I, husband and wife, lovers, and we couldn't make love. You pushed the door a little and there was that slip of a girl restraining you. For me, the touches, even as fleeting as they were, were wonderful. We have been parted for 73 days and have 60 more to go.

How beautiful it was, you and I, sitting there, even though not quite alone, and you saying, "Where are we and what is this?" It was as if we were young again, in the first flush of our discovery of each other. In the common room at Sastri College, in the Botanic Gardens and at the stream in Pinetown with Najma the cow bellowing in the distance and my mother coming down in agitation. She had every reason to fear as we knew.

My yard depends on Durban food. We miss beans and roti and aloo gos (mutton and potato curry). Bring us roast lamb, the way we do it. Sally Motlana, Vesta Smith and Joyce Seroke also receive resplendent meals from home and we all share.

I was released from prison on 10 December 1976.

What did it all mean – the five months in prison and its rules, the police and their authority, the Minister and his power, the wardresses regimented by race and status, the prisoners, awaiting trial and convicted, and the detainees?

We were all women, but so classified and separated that we could not be women together. We were divided by the impregnable barriers of law and custom in addition to race. We were under a common roof, enclosed by common walls, subjected to common rules, but were different. There were awaiting trial prisoners in their own clothes, many imprisoned with their children; there were the convicted prisoners whose children were not allowed to visit them. And they were so divided between black and white, so discreetly, that the one knew nothing of the other.

The black convicts in uniform blue overalls and red socks, no bras, no panties, some in shoes, others barefoot – accepted their imprisonment. The whites appeared defiant and let down by apartheid. We, the political detainees were different. We were proud of our detention. It was the seal of our service to our people, our resistance to injustice and inequality and our commitment to a non-racial democracy. We were there in pursuit of a moral and just cause.

We had our bad days and we missed our families and our lives outside. We were frustrated and irritated with each other and the wardresses. We had misunderstandings and differences of opinion, but we were sustained by our solidarity and our sense of mission. We glowed in the attention we received from friends, followers and families. While the period in solitary confinement was trying, and the uncertainty of not knowing the length of our detention foreboding, we knew it was transitional.

When we were released we made no attempt to get together to revitalise the Black Women's Federation. Too many of us were banned and unable to work openly in the political context. Our detentions had an intimidating effect on many of our members. Then in October 1977 the government banned the organisation together with seventeen others and confiscated its assets.

On our release both my son-in-law Bobby and my son Rashid were also banned, which meant that we now had three members of the family banned. The government gave us permission to communicate with each other – because in terms of banning orders, banned persons were not allowed to.

For Rashid, the banning was particularly pernicious. It amounted to a house arrest because we were confined to our handkerchief-sized group area of Sydenham. Rashid was precluded from joining any university or any institution of learning. The prospect of spending the next five years without any education appeared far too grim for him, and he escaped and went into exile.

Andrew Verster who had been Rashid's art lecturer at UDW became a great help to Rashid when he was imprisoned. After his release Rashid worked with Andrew in his studio. Andrew helped Rashid escape from South Africa by forging a passport for him. He considered this his best piece of graphic work! Andrew was brave and outspoken and that lost him his job at UDW.

Rashid left to go into exile in 1977 aged 21. He remained in exile in London for fifteen years, and during that time we had very little physical contact with him, because Ismail and I had great problems getting passports. Rashid, of course, could never return to his country until the apartheid government had ceased to exist.

CHAPTER 18

Fragments from a Violent Struggle[61]

Arson, attacks and assassinations

In December 1977 an assassination attempt was made on me. We were at home, Ismail and I, telling stories to my young nieces who were staying with us at the time when my daughter Shehnaz sounded the alarm that our garage was on fire. This immediately got me rushing to the door. Fortunately for me, Zwelinye Goba, our former gardener, was staying with us at the time and he preceded me by seconds or minutes to the door. He is a tall man, I am a short woman, and he was shot twice in the shoulder. When I got to the door, Zwelinye was already lying there bleeding and he said to me, "Please go away, they are calling your name, and they are swearing at you".

Had I been the first to open the door, I would have been shot in the head, most likely fatally. Zwelinye was rushed to hospital where he made a good recovery.

About three weeks later, my friend and colleague, Dr Rick Turner, who was also banned at the time, was shot dead in his home. From the description of the car that had left our house and one that an observer had seen at Rick's, it appeared to have been the same car.

Before this assassination attempt, there had been one arson attack on our home in 1972. Years later, in 1985 there was another one. The 1972 attack was purported to be by a member of the Black Consciousness Movement, believed to have become an agent of the state. The 1985 one we assumed to be part of a more general assault by the then government on resistance to its barbaric laws.

In 1985 the Nationalist Government began its death dance. In despair it tried to do whatever it could to change the situation in its favour. That year an intelligence source was reported by the *Sunday Times* of 14 July to have said: "There is a revolutionary assault going on in the country and that government has no instant counter-revolutionary force."

Within days of this statement, the first stone was cast by the government to cause ripples in a situation which up to then was fairly calm. That was the shooting on 1 August 1985 of Victoria Mxenge – an attorney in Durban who defended many anti-apartheid activists and was active in many democratic organisations including the Natal Organisation of Women (NOW) and the United Democratic Front (UDF). Victoria's assassination took place two weeks after she had spoken at the funeral of four Eastern Cape activists (Matthew Goniwe, Fort Calata, Sparrow Mkonto and Sicelo Mhlauli). They became known after their deaths by assassination as the Cradock Four.

Victoria's husband, Griffiths Mxenge, a lawyer, anti-apartheid activist and Robben Island detainee, had been assassinated a few years before in November 1981.

The assassination of Victoria Mxenge understandably provoked a response on the part of students and pupils. There were demonstrations. There was some stone-throwing. There was damage to one or two houses, but generally speaking these actions were low-key. On 8 August 1985 we held a meeting at Umlazi to protest Victoria's assassination and it was at that meeting that the very first mobilised attack by the government, using black people against each other, occurred.

I drove into the township just before 6 pm, and despite newspaper headlines of the day reporting violence raging in the area, found it quite calm. The vast cinema hall where the meeting was scheduled was still filling up. The assembled crowd danced and sang in the way people usually do at meetings to break the monotony of waiting. Every now and again a small contingent of mourners walked up and down the hall bearing a banner which read 'Don't Shoot, We're Not Fighting'.

Speakers took their positions on the platform around 7 pm. Florence Mkhize, a founding leader of the UDF and Natal Organisation of Women, leaned over to tell me that outside the police were like an army, but that they were keeping their distance. She said Inkatha[62] was also there.

By the time the meeting started there was a rumbustious audience of about 5 000 people, some standing outside unable to get in. The meeting was on the verge of ending when attention was diverted by a fearful commotion outside. Like wildfire the message spread through the hall that Inkatha was on the attack and the orderly meeting disintegrated into a swirling frantic mass. People began jumping down from the gallery and clamouring to reach exits. I managed to get out of the hall with the help of one of the UDF members, Chris Hlongwane. We clambered through a barbed-wire fence and scaled up a steep sandbank on to flat land from the top of which we could see the cinema submerged in the smoke of teargas, intermittently lit up by flares flung into the sky.

After a while we ventured to my car which I had parked in front of the cinema. My car was safe although scores of others had been badly damaged. A man lay on the curb bleeding profusely. We got him into my car with the help of Zo Mbele, a UDF member from Lamontville, who volunteered to drive with me to the hospital. We proceeded only a few yards when we were stopped by a blockade of burning tyres and suffocating teargas. Overcome by choking and streaming eyes, I handed over the driving to Zo.

By now the calm road of just a few hours ago had transformed into a battlefield of people confronting each other with whatever weapons they could muster.

We reversed the car into a dirt lane and crossed over onto the main road but were stopped again by groups of people flanking the road on both sides. The passenger door was yanked open and it seemed we were about to be stopped or attacked. However, someone recognised us and called out "comrade" and the call was taken up by others along the road and we were allowed safe passage. It occurred to me that the Inkatha attacks had provoked an instant response and that these were UDF supporters.

The man we tried to save was declared dead on arrival at the hospital, and we were directed to take him to the mortuary. We were required, according to regulations, to witness the officials collect all personal effects from the body. The deceased was without any possession or documentation.

I would learn later that fifteen UDF supporters were killed by Inkatha that night.

As violence escalated all around Durban in the following months of 1985 I became involved in trying to assist people who were under threat. I would go to the police for help, and they would point-blank say to me that the people who claimed they were going to be attacked deserved the attacks that were being made on them. My experience was that the police literally withdrew. My interpretation of this period is that those people who actually attacked and did the killing were instigated, orchestrated by the pernicious system of apartheid to do so. Inkatha, provoked by the disruptions in schools and by pupil mobilisation, provided that counter revolutionary force the state sought.

Refugees were living at the Gandhi settlement in Phoenix, the result of rising racial tensions between Indian and Black communities living in the Inanda area. On arriving at the settlement early one morning, I found looters and arsonists on the premises and I immediately called the police. The police seemed uninterested and so I called the *Daily News* to get them to alert the police. Two Casspirs came soon thereafter and parked in the grounds. The police remained in the Casspirs and the looters disappeared on seeing the vehicles. After five minutes the Casspirs left and it was business as usual for the looters.

I saw the main house on the Gandhi Settlement being set on fire. I phoned the fire brigade for assistance and I was told that they had specific instructions not to go out there and help in any way.

A police statement at the time stated that the police had instructions to keep a low profile to avoid accusations of instigation. Instigation was so real, and they were so conscious of the fact that they had deliberately provoked this whole situation, that they now actually said they wouldn't go there in order not to be accused of instigation.

In that fraught environment, our house was attacked in what was to be our third petrol bomb attack. I was once again a target. I was seen as being a little bit too active in trying to assist, or overcome the machinations of the police and the military, of the system which always remains faceless, nameless. A petrol bomb thrown through our lounge window caused considerable damage to the lounge area. That was the last of the attacks that we ourselves suffered during those times.

A diabolical system

Both racism and tribalism were used to divide people and neighbours from each other. If we do not understand the full scope of the perniciousness, the sort of diabolic planning that went into the massacres that continued in the Natal region from 1985 onwards, we will never really see the full scope and the full cruelty of the system of apartheid.

The national state tried to destroy its opposition and the inevitable revolution in many ways. Perhaps the least innocuous was the banning order whereby a person was isolated from society, in thought and his or her very person. You were banned from all gatherings and banned specifically from some key institutions – educational and labour.

My banning orders meant that I could not attend weddings, funerals and parties and certainly not attend meetings. We had many weddings – my brothers', sisters' and cousins'. It was a family tradition to set up planning committees and I attended these, though strictly speaking I could not do so without breaching the law, but in fact it was left to the banned person to interpret his or her limitations. My self-allocated task would be to decorate the stage and I always carried out my function in this regard, with great pleasure but I did not attend the weddings to see the full effect of my work. I carried that out before the weddings, helped by some younger members of the family who enjoyed the work as much as I did.

In Burnwood Road there was a rise at the end of the road opposite our home and we would often notice an idling member of the Special Branch positioned there wasting his time spying on us. We also knew that our phone was tapped. All they were able to come up with from their spying efforts was allegations of ban-breaking.

I was arrested twice for breaking my banning order. The first time was for attending a dinner party at our friend Andrew Verster's home during Christmas 1977. Bobby Marie, our son-in-law, who was also banned and attending the dinner party, was arrested with me. The second time I was arrested for being outside the geographic area my banning confined me to – I had gone to the craft centre I had set up at the Phoenix Settlement.

On both these occasions I was defended by Ismail Mahomed. I first met Ismail some years before in Johannesburg, when we shared a platform on the subject of Mahatma Gandhi. He took the trouble of finding out where

I was living in Johannesburg, phoned me and invited me to tea in his chambers. He was a Senior Counsel at the time.

Ismail defended me and Bobby brilliantly. He was assisted by his brilliant young apprentice Clifford Mailer, a nephew of the author Norman Mailer.

Arriving to stand trial for breaking our ban:
Our lawyers Ismail Mahomed and Clifford Mailer together with me and our son-in-law Bobby Marie.

During the trial Ismail knew that the main witness for the State, an Indian detective, did not understand Afrikaans. So he began his cross examination of Mr Moodley in Afrikaans and then ridiculed him for being in government service and not understanding the government's language. He tore into the detective and exposed that his understanding of what constituted a social gathering was quite absurd. This gave Ismail the basis of his defence – that the definition of social gathering in the law was void for vagueness since the police and the prosecution itself did not understand it. The case was dismissed on that ground alone.

The state though took the matter on appeal to the Pietermaritzburg high court. During a break in the proceedings, we sat on the lawn of the court and a friend of Shehnaz, Brahmi Padayachee, brought us a most delicious lunch. We clearly constituted a gathering in the eyes of the law but, I think, the government had given up on prosecuting us and no action was taken.

Writing

McGraw-Hill accepted a revised second edition of my book *Portrait of Indian South Africans* for publication. The plates were about to be made in 1976 when I was banned. McGraw-Hill immediately broke their contract to publish on grounds that I was banned. I challenged this stating that they were an international company and I was not banned internationally, only in South Africa. They were in effect collaborating with the government and banning me themselves. The local directors were Afrikaners. There was obvious collusion between the Americans and South Africans.

The good news was that my book *Race and Suicide* was published by Routledge & Kegan Paul in 1976, with copies arriving while I was in prison.

Although not allowed to publish while banned. I self-published two books in the name Y.S. Meer –*Documents of Indentured Labour* and *Apartheid Our Picture*. When my banning came to an end I was able to publish in my own name and in the mid-1980s we at the IBR published a number of books on the political situation in the country and on the lives of working women. I also published two books with Skotaville Publishers – one on Andrew Zondo (*The Trial of Andrew Zondo* published in 1987) and one on Nelson Mandela (*Higher Than Hope* published in 1988).

Andrew Zondo was a nineteen-year-old soldier in the ANC's liberation army, Umkhonto weSizwe, arrested for planting a limpet mine that had killed five people at a shopping centre in Amanzimtoti, south of Durban. I met him in prison at Westville and was very impressed with the young man. I visited his parents and was absolutely outraged when the judge pronounced the death sentence in 1986. Deeply anguished I went home that day and wrote the biography of Andrew Zondo, which was published in 1987.

Nelson and Winnie

My husband Ismail and I had a long and very close relationship with Nelson and his wife Winnie. I first met Mandela when he came with Ismail and Dr Diliza Mji (senior, father of Diliza Mji the SASO President) to my parents' home in Pinetown in 1952. Mandela was at the time a leader of the ANC Youth League and had come to Durban to campaign for a national day of strike, the Gandhian hartal, against the government. Ismail and I had just discovered our love for each other and Ismail had brought his friends to show me off and all three of them teased me.

I got to know Nelson better when he visited our home in Umgeni Road after our marriage. His then wife Evelyn was studying midwifery at King Edward Hospital. We would take Nelson there to collect Evelyn and we would give them our bedroom. Nelson always stayed with us when he came to Durban, which was often since the ANC was becoming very active at the time. Fellow ANC Youth leaders, Oliver Tambo and Walter Sisulu, also stayed with us from time to time as did the then ANC President General, Chief Albert Luthuli, when he was in Durban and it was too late for him to travel to his home in Groutville, north of Durban.

One day, while we were living at Umgeni Road, Nelson phoned and asked Ismail to fetch a Miss Winnie Madikizela from the station. She was arriving by train from Johannesburg to Durban, he explained, and would spend a few days with us. Ismail and I went to receive Miss Madikizela at the appointed time and she emerged from one of the compartments, radiant and beautiful.

She slept with my cousin Minnie in the front room and I left her to spend most of her time with Minnie because they were the same age, I was much older. I discovered that Miss Madikizela carried a batch of photographs of Nelson in her handbag and then surmised that there was a growing relationship between the two. I recall that Winnie had a sister, a nurse, working at the FOSA TB Settlement in Durban. Her sister had come to see her. I do not have any other recollections of Winnie during that visit except that I was struck by her beauty and noted that she was an avid reader. Years later, when we were in prison together, I asked Winnie why she had visited us at that time and she disclosed that Nelson was thinking of marrying her and sent her to us to assess her suitability as his wife.

On my trips to Johannesburg during the Treason Trial in 1957, I saw quite a lot of Nelson, and one evening he invited us for dinner at his home in Orlando, now part of Soweto. His mother was our hostess. I remember her as a very gracious woman who served us our dinner, but did not join us. After dinner we sat in a part of the room which was fitted out as a conversation corner. It was dominated by a large print of Lenin addressing a workers meeting. We retired to this part of the room and chatted away.

Ismail and I were also present at the much-talked-about party at photojournalist GR Naidoo's house in Asherville the night before Nelson's arrest outside Howick. Nelson cut a large military figure in khaki, his laugh booming the familiar welcome as he embraced each friend. We drank and ate and discussed politics. We laughed a lot, excited by the intrigue. The police were looking for Nelson and here we were partying with him, virtually under their noses.

Nelson, after his conviction and imprisonment in 1962 for conspiracy to overthrow the government, had asked us to look after Winnie. I took this as a personal charge and the first time I went to Johannesburg after Nelson's imprisonment, I went to meet Winnie. I saw that she was living in poverty and I promised that I would send her something. I was, at the time, earning £30 a month as a temporary lecturer, and I sent her half of that for a substantial period. Her daughters, Zeni and Zindzi were studying at school in Swaziland at the time, but they spent part of their holidays with us in Durban.

Over the years Winnie and I grew very close. In May 1977 Winnie was banished to Brandfort. During her banishment she had an arrangement to be at the telephone booth for an hour or so at eleven in the morning. Ismail phoned her during this hour daily. I kept close contact with her and visited her in Brandfort during her banishment.

Visiting Winnie Mandela in Brandfort. Photo by Steven Linde.

Winnie once sent friends to me from the Transkei and they told me of something political that she wanted done and they were in Durban to do. I said to them, "One Mandela is enough in prison. We don't want another in there". A few days later I was picked up by the Special Branch, taken to their office and threatened by them. Subsequently they arrived at my house and demanded: "What did you mean by that statement – 'One Mandela is enough in prison we don't want another in there'?" Naturally, I refused to tell them anything, but I gathered from this that these 'friends' of Winnie were indeed spies.

Ismail and I communicated with Nelson over the years through many letters. While in prison, Nelson was very concerned about the education of his children. His son Makgatho's wife was enrolled at Ohlange Institute in Inanda north of Durban. Her fees needed to be paid. Nelson discussed

With Winnie Mandela at her daily telephone hour. Photo by Steven Linde.

the matter with Ismail and he in turn discussed it with Alan Paton and
Peter Brown and the three of them arranged to pay her fees.

Later Nelson needed help for Makgatho to study law. So we got him
enrolled in the law school at Natal University. I had purchased a property
in Umbilo at the time for the IBR office. I renovated and extended the
outhouse and Makgatho was accommodated there.

Higher Than Hope

In the early 1970s I was at a mass meeting in Durban convened by the
Black Consciousness Movement. I recall Steve Biko was on the platform
when a message was whispered to me by a newly released political prisoner. "From Nelson Mandela," I was told. Nelson would like me to write
his biography. The prospect overawed me, although Nelson's confidence
was flattering.

A few months later I made my one and only visit to Robben Island.
Winnie had arranged for me to take up one of her visits to Nelson. She
met me in Cape Town and took me to the docks from where I travelled
by ferry to Robben Island. We spoke about my working on his biography
and Nelson said I should go to the Transkei to speak to Chief Sabata's
mother who was a mother to him.

Then in 1976 I was banned and soon after detained at the Fort in

Johannesburg with Winnie and other women political detainees. Towards the end of our detention Winnie got permission to see me in my cell on the grounds that she needed to consult me on a sociology essay she had to submit as a correspondent student. We spent this time working on Winnie's autobiography. Following our release, we went to our different cities, and the conditions of our banning orders made it impossible to continue working with Winnie on her book.

In the 1980s Nelson requested that we help his eldest daughter Makaziwe continue her studies. So Maki, as she was called, came to live with us in 1983 and enrolled for an honours degree in sociology. This was a time when all our children had left home and Ismail and I were on our own at Burnwood Road, but for our grandchildren Zen and Maia who would spend their days with us while their parents were at work.

Maki was a very pleasant and attractive young lady. She spent her weekends with her sister-in-law who had been married to Nelson's eldest son Thembi who had died in a motor accident. Maki was very good company and both Ismail and I were happy to have her and most happy to help Nelson. Maki passed her course comfortably. I then encouraged her to apply for a full scholarship to the United States to continue her studies. She did so and succeeded, gaining a doctorate from the University of Massachusetts.

In 1984 while Maki was still living with us I arranged with her to go to the Transkei. Maki took me to the persons Nelson had advised I should meet to gather information for the book. Most of my material for *Higher Than Hope*, however, came from Winnie, from our conversations when we were in prison together in 1976, and from my visits to her in Brandfort. Winnie agreed that I should use her interviews for the biography on Nelson. She also gave me letters from Nelson and they proved most useful. I also got letters Nelson had written to his daughters and all this added richly to my biography of Mandela.

Higher Than Hope was published in 1988 both in South Africa and in Britain and sold well. When the South African edition was published Nelson, still in imprisonment, was ill in hospital. In September 1988 I left a copy of the book for him at the Tygerberg Clinic where he was recuperating. I also left one at Polsmoor Prison where he had been moved from

Robben Island. Nelson did not see the book, however, until December. He wrote to my husband Ismail on 10 January 1989:

> Writing a biography without access to the subject of study can be a very difficult matter. There are chapters in *Higher Than Hope* which clearly reflect this absence of contact. But I think that you have done a marvellous job for which the family will remain very grateful.

In May 1989, at Nelson's request, Ismail and I were granted a visit to Victor Verster Prison – the prison he had been moved to from Pollsmoor. We spent a pleasant day together and arranged that I would return in a fortnight to discuss corrections and additions to the second edition of *Higher Than Hope*.

When we next met, Nelson presented me with a neat 39-page folio of amendments and additions typed by the prison department. We decided I would attend to these at home and that we would spend the day on other aspects of his life. We worked continuously except for a lunch break. Two more visits followed so that in all I interviewed him for around eighteen hours. We worked on the dining room table and when the weather allowed on the veranda. On the third visit I was told by the prison authorities that I would have to finish work that day as no further visits would be allowed.

Nelson was frank and open, his memory remarkable. I came closer to him during those three days than I had at any other time during my association with him. The second edition, while benefitting from this contact and being approved by him, was nonetheless still based on restricted contact with him. It was published in South Africa in 1989 and in the UK and USA in 1990. The book has done well and has been translated from English into thirteen languages in Europe, Asia and Africa.

On his release from prison in 1990, Nelson honoured us by coming to stay with us. On his first travels abroad after his release from prison he asked Ismail to accompany him as part of his delegation. The first trip was from 4 June to 6 July 1990, the second from 13 October to mid-November. They visited European capitals, USA, Asia and Australia.

Winnie asked me to advise her when she was appointed Deputy Minister of Arts, Culture, Science and Technology and I accompanied her in this capacity on her visit to China and on one visit to the USA in 1995.

We remain very close. She always stays with me when she comes to Durban and we keep in close touch by telephone.

Post 1994: The struggle continues

After the second democratic election in 1999 I was very concerned that many Indians were not voting for the ANC and so I formed the Concerned Citizens Group (CCG) to try to persuade Indians to vote for the ANC at the next election. We held several meetings in Chatsworth where the largest Indian public was concentrated.

At one such meeting I asked the audience: "Why do you want to vote for your former white oppressors?"

A woman, Orlean Naidoo, spoke out: "We are not concerned about our former oppressors. We are concerned about our present oppressors."

I was shocked by this response, and began to engage with community members to learn more about their living conditions and struggles – working closely with Orlean. I found appalling poverty and learnt that the poorest community members occupying the sub-economic flats in the Bangladesh and Bayview areas of Chatsworth constantly had to deal with evictions and disconnection of their water supplies by the ANC-led local government. I attempted to make representations to the Council but found it difficult to get through to officials.

We conducted a survey so as to confront officials with evidence of the appalling poverty in these two areas. The survey of 504 families in the Westcliff and Bayview areas of Chatsworth revealed that 75 per cent of them lived below the poverty line, 58 per cent were unemployed and 42 per cent dependent on welfare grants. My greatest difficulty though was trying to get our report to the municipal government. The secretary at the time was a young woman who had worked diligently with the community during the apartheid years. Now in her role in the post-apartheid local government, she blocked the report from reaching the relevant elected officials on the local Council.

A few months later in 2000, I had a second heart attack and surgery, and a few weeks after my discharge from hospital I had an urgent call from Orlean asking me to come as there was a crisis. Ismail was most protective of me after my heart attacks and I knew that he would be terribly agitated if I went to Chatsworth so soon after an operation, but since he was at his office in Verulam, I took the opportunity of going to Chatsworth with Ramesh Harcharan, the deputy director of the IBR, and community activist Ashwin Desai who was working with us in the area.

The sight that met us was horrific. The City Council–appointed security men were trying to force the residents out of their homes, using guard dogs, tear gas and the threat of rubber bullets to aid their efforts. We decided to bring an urgent interdict against the Council to stay the evictions. I pleaded with the head of security to call off the attacks by dogs and teargas, while we applied for an interdict. He refused, stating that he had orders from the Council to get the tenants out. I asked him to put me through to the authority at the Council and I spoke to the person in charge but to no avail.

Meanwhile, there was absolute pandemonium in the poorest part of Bayview known as Bangladesh. The security company attempted to evict a tenant in the area but when they got to the home women neighbours surrounded the house and successfully prevented the eviction of the Black tenant who was away at work.

Over the following months community members were empowered to fight their own battles, with the Concerned Citizens Group (CCG) playing a supportive role. Residents of Bangladesh and Bayview formed residents committees to lead their struggles against the local government. They held mass meetings, marches and they negotiated with Council. I felt highly gratified at the people's recognition of their own power, and at seeing Satyagraha or peaceful protest at work spontaneously.

Government for its part would not admit the poverty-stricken nature of the townships it administers and did not come up with sufficient subsidies. Housing remained in a deplorable condition and services in the townships equally deplorable if not unavailable.

The CCG became well known as a group that could be depended on for help. The Isipingo community (also in the Durban area) approached us to help them. We were also approached by community members from Mpumalanga, a rural township outside Hammarsdale in KwaZulu Natal, where, like in my old days in the Natal Indian Congress, I climbed onto a lorry to address the crowd.

We decided that there were so many townships with common problems that we should have one large body. The different communities –
Indian, Black and Coloured were working together. They looked at each
other and said 'well we are all poor together that's what we have together –
our poverty; our race makes no difference'.

Cry the beloved country

Many things have improved since 1994. For one thing racial laws have
disappeared. However, the aspirations of the Freedom Charter – the only
historic document that we have registering people's voices and dreams – have
not been realised. By the year 2000 we do not have a leadership committed
to fighting poverty – we have a corrupt leadership. That is our tragedy.

If resources are reserved for only the wealthy, if government shows a
commitment only to the middle class then all I can say is 'cry the beloved
country, and cry and cry and cry'! And those of us who can shout no matter how many years we have lived on this earth, we must get up and shout.

I have always stood for the poor and the rights of the poor and though I
and all my friends have been in the ANC for over 60 years, if I have to
stand against the organisation to address the needs of the vast majority
of South African citizens then I will unhappily do so. We have to be in
the process of perpetual revolution to progress and guarantee the rights
of people.

There can be no peacetime so long as there is poverty and hunger and
so long as basic human rights are trodden. The cause of rampant crime
in our country is inequality. We are the second most unequal country in
world. More than half the population lives in poverty. Can we call this
living in peace? The definition of peace is equity, harmony, not starvation.

Alternative futures

I also became involved in a range of international initiatives to address
inequality in society. I was invited in 1999 to serve as patron of the Jubilee
2000 movement. This was an international coalition calling for third world
debt to be cancelled by the year 2000. I agreed enthusiastically to work
on publicising the plight of third world countries unable to alleviate their
poverty as a result of their debt to first world countries and the World
Bank. South Africa was among the indebted countries, but our govern-

ment opposed our efforts in alleviating the debt burden of the third world. Nonetheless we struggled on.

I was also a keen supporter of the World Social Forum which brings together grassroots and civil society voices from across the world to discuss alternative futures. I believe we need to strengthen the numerous community based organisations in our country and increase the voices of civil society and was therefore part of setting up the Durban Social Forum in 2001 and attended the World Social Forum in Mumbai in 2004.

The Durban Social Forum organised a series of engagements during the World Conference Against Racism held in Durban in 2001. Around 20 000 of us marched against the anti-poor policies of the ANC during this conference under the banner of the Durban Social Forum.

I have also been privileged to be invited to get actively involved in women's tribunals around the world. In this I have worked with Corinne Kumar, from the Tunis-based human rights advocacy group, El Taller International. I have served as a juror on the World Court of Women Against War, for Peace in Khayelitsha, Cape Town in 2001 and the World Court of Women on US War Crimes in Mumbai, India, in 2004. In addition, I was a juror at the International Tribunal of Cuban Women Against the Blockade in Havana, Cuba in 2002. These courts and tribunals are unofficial, symbolic forums to engage through public hearings with those who are traditionally excluded from formal political and legal proceedings and a way of bringing attention of governments to their concerns.

CHAPTER 19

The Joy of Grandchildren

A new generation of Meers entered my life with the birth of Shamim and Bobby's son Zen on 26 February 1980 at 11.30 am. He was born at McCord Hospital in Durban, a beautiful baby boy. Shamim became a mother effortlessly and both Ismail and I were very excited with our first grandchild. Maia, Shamim's daughter followed a year and bit after Zen. She was born on 23 October 1981 at St Aidan's Hospital where Shamim had also been born.

Shamim and Bobby were living in a flat in Sparks Road not far from our house in Burnwood Road, and since they both worked, they would leave the children with us each morning. It was a great joy to have them! Sometimes, when they were little, I would take both Zen and Maia to my office at the University, and Maia would crawl around in her baby grow suit, looking much like Popeye's baby Sweet Pea.

They spent their early years playing with our neighbours' children in the back garden. Zen, at five, and I built a fowl run in our back garden with the help of Zwelinye. We went to Pinetown and bought a whole lot of day-old chicks which we thought we could grow into chickens. Zen used to feed them responsibly each day, but unfortunately the Silvahns (predators of chickens) came and made a meal of them before they could show any growth. Ismail, the great pacifist, brought Zen a toy gun and they would drive about in our beetle and, cowboy-like, shoot the imaginary Silvahns from the car window. I think grandfather enjoyed the game more than grandson.

Papa, as Zen and Maia called their grandfather, bought Maia an embroidered crepe de Chine dress, which her mother didn't particularly care for but Maia, I think, loved. It made her so dressy.

Zen became addicted to Indian movies, particularly to those featuring Amitabh Bhachan. Ismail would bring these movies home quite regularly. Maia joined in the viewing, but had none of Zen's addiction. He would want particular scenes, usually very macho sequences of Bachan beating somebody up, or crashing a car, to be replayed dozens of times.

Shehnaz married Joel Krige in 1981. Her marriage created some problems because of the Immorality Act which defined inter-race marriages as immoral and therefore, illegal. The event drew the attention of the media, and the editor of the *Sunday Tribune* was insistent on making a story out of it. I was equally insistent that the marriage should be kept out of the public arena and in particular not draw the attention of the Nationalist Government, whose police may decide to take some action or other. I spoke to the editor of the newspaper and expressed my concerns and his remark was that "When the grandson of General Smuts marries your daughter, it is news".

I told him: "There is no news for you. My future son-in-law is not the grandson of General Smuts. He is the grand-nephew of Uys Krige, whose relative had married Smuts."

The editor then agreed to ignore the event, saying "Well in that case, it is not of public interest".

Shehnaz and Joel had a nikkah (marriage) ceremony in our study, following which they went to Lesotho where friends of ours had arranged for their marriage to be registered. They began their life together in Cape Town where Shehnaz practiced law with the Legal Resources Centre, while Joel established his practice as an advocate.

Shehnaz had her first baby, Nadia, on 5 July 1985. I travelled to Cape Town to be with Shehnaz over this wonderful event. Joel's mother, the adept Mei (fondly referred to by the granddaughters as Granny Mei), had expertly lined and draped a crib for Nadia. It was though large and the little baby felt cold and lonely in it after her nine months in her mother's womb. She cried and would not fall asleep. I brought the baby and laid her beside me under my warm duvet. She promptly stopped crying and was soon sound asleep.

When she grew into a toddler my greatest pleasure, when I visited Cape Town, was to wheel Nadia in her pram and take her to the Company Gardens, where she loved feeding the squirrels, holding out peanuts in her little palms. I used to tell Nadia stories. We would sit in the back garden in the sun and I would tell her stories and play a game that I remembered from my childhood: Akka Bakka.

When Nadia was two years old, Khiyara made her appearance and four years later Ayesha arrived. Shehnaz visited us in Durban with her daughters, and Zen and Maia, considerably older, would come to play with them.

The best time I had with Shehnaz's three girls was when their parents went on a visit to India and the girls stayed with us. Nadia, Khiyara, Ayesha and I struck beautiful bonds during that period. I had to sleep in between four-year-old Khiyara and six-year-old Nadia, placing little Ayesha, around six months old, in the wooden crib which I had bought initially for Zen but which had been used successively for the other four grandchildren as well. In the middle of the night Ayesha would get lonely and would insist on sleeping with us, and we somehow made room for her as well.

My grandchildren with me: Zen, Ayesha (on my lap), Maia, Nadia and Khiyara sitting in front.

Both Ismail and I were very fond of our grandchildren. We would take them often to the beach to play in the sand and to Mitchell Park to see the animals and enjoy rides on the swings. We had started life afresh with our three children and now we were enjoying a third lease on life with our grandchildren. That was perhaps the best part of my life. They gave me immeasurable love and as much pleasure and happiness.

Shamim and her family moved to Johannesburg in 1987 and whenever I visited their home, she and Bobby vacated their bedroom and their double bed so I could sleep with Zen and Maia. This was something my grandchildren insisted upon. I would have to sleep in the middle of the two.

When the grandchildren visited us in Burnwood Road, all five insisted on sharing our bed. Ismail found this very uncomfortable and I ended up buying a second double bed and putting it in our second bedroom where I would sleep with all the grandchildren.

I was fortunate enough to make trips with my grandchildren to Disney World in 1990 and India in 1994 and 1996. Ayesha was not yet born when we made the trip to Disney World. Khiyara was in a pram and Zen loved to push the pram. When Khiyara found that he and not I was pushing her, she would object. At one point I found myself with Nadia on my back and Khiyara in my arms in Disney World.

I was lecturing at the University of Oregan in the USA at the time and the children travelled to meet me in the USA with Granny Mei, Shehnaz's mother-in-law. On their way to Disney World they stopped in London and Rashid met Shehnaz's daughters for the first time, and was enchanted with them. He had met Zen and Maia some years before when Shamim had taken them to London and was as taken with them.

CHAPTER 20

Our Son Rashid

In 1995 I suffered a heart attack. I collapsed while at home with Irene, and was removed to the St Augustine's hospital. Ismail was alerted and he came to see me, and both Shamim and Shehnaz arrived that evening from their respective homes in Johannesburg and Cape Town.

Shehnaz tried to keep my mind away from my physical condition by engaging me in a long story about some incident with her friends, but I could not concentrate and I collapsed into a state of semi consciousness. My belief is that I died then. The nurses confirmed this when I came to and I found a doctor pumping my heart.

The next morning Rashid arrived from Johannesburg. He was in the process of relocating to Johannesburg after returning the year before from London where he had been in exile since 1977. I saw Rashid standing at the door of my ward. I signalled for him to come in and he did. He stood next to me and cried. I asked him why he was crying and he said he didn't like to see me like that.

With Rashid in London
(Feb. 1990).

Rashid came to say goodbye to me the following day as he had to return to Johannesburg to work as he had a contract with the public broadcaster, the South African Broadcasting Corporation. He held me in his arms before he left. And that was the last time I saw my son Rashid.

Some days after I was discharged from hospital, Rashid

phoned me at home early one morning and Mrs Singh, who had come to help with my care, answered the call.

"Who is Mrs. Singh?" Rashid asked

"She is here to help me."

"Why should Mrs. Singh help you? We should be there to help you . . . I am coming home to help you."

That was the last time I heard him. Rashid never came.

I was at home painting, waiting for Rashid, when my brother Farouk came. He held me very close, not saying a word. He cried as he held me, as though his heart would break. I thought something had happened to his children. Then he told me that Rashid had been killed in an accident while driving to Durban.

That evening Ismail returned home from Ulundi – he was a member of the provincial legislature which then sat at Ulundi and he had left on hearing news of Rashid's accident. The sitting room was full of people. I was in bed waiting for Ismail. My sister Baby was with me. I heard Ismail's car and got up. Baby tried to restrain me but I would not be restrained. I met Ismail at the door and asked him how we were going to live without Rashid. Ismail took me to our room and comforted me. Here we were parents and we had lost our youngest child. It was a terrible fate.

Shamim had the task of attending to Rashid. She got in touch with the local Muslim society and their hearse brought Rashid to us in the early morning, with Shamim, Bobby and their children following in their car. We prepared the sitting room to receive Rashid. Many friends and relatives had collected. My son's dead body was brought to lie on the floor in front of me. A little later Winnie Mandela arrived and she sat with me the entire day and was a great comfort.

Rashid was buried that evening. Ismail gave me details of how the burial went. It is not customary for Muslim women to go to a burial, so Ismail explained how our grandson Zen and Ismail's nephew, Salim, had gone down into the grave to receive Rashid's body and that they had laid the body to rest. Zen had said that when he and Rashid had attended the burial of my brother Solly, some months before, Rashid had said he would want Zen to go into the grave to receive his (Rashid's) body and Zen had done just that.

We comforted ourselves that night because there was nothing else we could do but it was very hard for both of us to adjust ourselves to our loss.

Every Sunday we went to Rashid's grave and placed flowers there. We had a tombstone made for Rashid and I placed two black urns on either side of the tombstone. Ismail recited the fateha, a prayer, filled the urns with water, and I put flowers in the urns.

CHAPTER 21

Thoughts of Ismail: 11 March 2002

The most important relationship in my life was and is with Ismail.

It is today, 11 March 2002, our 51st wedding anniversary. If there is no thought after death, then his marriage with me ended with his death and he lived with me for 49 years, but my marriage with him continues. It is not of the day itself I think, but of the love that that day brought into my life for all of the years I lived with Ismail. I thank him for those years.

Today when I recall my relationship with Ismail, it is the loving that dominates. I think of all the loving and the companionship, of his great patience with me, and his tolerance of my faults, which are many. We had a remarkably happy marriage.

When the Molvi Saheb intoned that we had taken each other as husband and wife, two very different personalities were committed to live together for the rest of our lives. Separation was a strange word that never entered our consciousness.

I remember clearly the beginning of Ismail's inability to use his left leg. We were driving to the airport early in 1999 some months after his 80th

Ismail and I in our garden at Burnwood Road, 1991.
Photo by George Hallett.

birthday, and at the robot that preceded the turning into the airport the car suddenly stopped and Ismail was not able to use his leg. We consulted many doctors over the following year and he was subjected to many tests. Eventually Ismail was advised to take a brain scan. He resisted, saying to me that the problem is in my leg and they want to examine my head, what foolishness.

One night around March 2000 Ismail got out of bed to get something out of the cupboard. He had become unsteady on his feet, had held on to a weak doorknob unable to support his weight and fell.

In the morning I called my brother Farouk to come and examine him. That morning I was due to leave for Johannesburg to visit our close friend Ismail Mahomed who was terminally ill with pancreatic cancer. We did not feel that I should cancel that visit. On my return from Johannesburg I rushed to the hospital where Farouk had arranged for Ismail to be X-rayed. I found Ismail anxious to get home. The ambulance took a little while to come but we eventually reached home.

The X-rays showed a number of fractures, but the orthopod's instructions were that Ismail should lie flat on the bed for three weeks and then he would consider the next step. After the three weeks the orthopod decided to operate. We moved into St Aidan's, the hospital where the orthopod practiced, and I made a sort of bed for myself on the floor against the wall in Ismail's private ward. We were then moved into a double ward with two beds and I had a bed opposite Ismail. Family members brought supper, but Ismail did not eat.

Ismail had the operation early in the morning while I waited anxiously outside the theatre. Afterwards, our doctor was anxious about bedsores and insisted that Ismail had to be turned hourly. Ismail grumbled about this.

Ismail never really recovered from that fall and he died on the 1 May 2000. I don't know to this day why he had not called to me for help rather than get up himself that evening. I was only a few yards away, but I expect he did not want to trouble me.

He was buried in the same grave as Rashid. I added his name so now both Ismail and Rashid's names are on the tombstone. I go as often as I can and I read the fateha for both of them – the two most important men in my life, my husband and my son. I hope to be buried in the same grave.

Glossary

Achkan	Long coat
Afrikaner	A person who speaks Afrikaans
Allah Pak	God
Amaboere	Slang term for the government and/or the police; literally means 'the farmers'
Apa	Big sister
Awdnie	Scarf
Badla	Gold thread
Babaw	Baby boy
Bhabies	Baby girls
Bhabi	Sister-in-law
Bida	Traditional farewell for a bride
Casspir	An armoured truck used in South Africa by the army and police
Chevda	A snack of cereal, nuts and legumes
Dai ma	Traditional midwife
Eid	Muslim festival of breaking the fast
Ghazal	A poem (generally a love poem) with a recurring rhyme and a limited number of stanzas
Gor paprie	A fudge-like sweet
Hadis	The words, actions, or habits of the Prophet Muhammad
Haram	Forbidden
Hartal	Strike action
Hoors or Houris	Female companions for faithful Muslims in paradise
Ijar	Trousers
Inyanga	Traditional healer
Jhorie	A hammock-like baby's cradle

Kalimah	Significant parts of religious belief
Karchop	Intricate embroidery
Karela	Bitter gourd, a vegetable
Kathi mithie	Sweet and sour
Khoonchas	Wedding trays and gifts
Khuda Hafez	In God's care
Kokam	Dried fruit
Kudie kichrie	A rice and yoghurt dish
Kunwar	Prince
Kunwarani	Princess
Kurta	A long loose garment (like a shirt) worn in India
Kutum	Clan
Madressa	School for study of Islam
Marms	as in 'school marms', indicating a strict disciplinarian woman teacher
Mithai	Sweetmeats
Molvi Sahab	Muslim religious scholar
Moulood	Observance of the birthday of the Prophet Muhammad
Muti	African traditional medicinal herbs
Namaaz	The ritual prayers prescribed by Islam to be observed five times a day. Also called salaah.
Namazi	One who prays five times a day
Napak	Impure
Natak	Dramatic performance
Neera	Nectar of palm extracted before sunrise
Navjot	Ceremony to intitiate a Zoroastrian child into his or her religion of birth
Nikkah	Signing of marriage contract
Nimbar	The platform at the mosque from which the Molvi speaks
Padkos	Food for the road or journey
Purdah	Seclusion

Puruna bangla	Old house
Qawali	Form of devotional music
Raas Lila	Story of Krishna from Hindu scriptures
Ramadan	The Muslim month of fasting
Scotch cart	A two-wheel cart
Sehri	Pre-dawn meal before a day-long fast
Shariah	The body of Islamic law
Sirdar	Supervisor of labour on a sugar estate
Soomyathie	Abiding evil
Telis	Oil pressers
Vadamrie	Gift
Wuzoo	Ritual performed in preparation for prayer

My Family

The Meer Ancestors

Cassim Meer	The earliest known Meer ancestor
Ahmed Meer	Cassim's son
Asmaljee Meer	Ahmed's son
Ahmedjee Meer	My great grand uncle (Asmaljee's son)
Ahmed Meer	My great grandfather (Asmaljee's son)
Sarah Amin	My great grandmother

My Parents

Moosa Meer	My father (Papa – also known as M I Meer)
Rachael Farrel / Amina Meer	My mother (Amina Ma)
Khatija Meer	My mother (Ma)

My Siblings

Ismail

Solly

Ahmed

Mahomed (Bhai)

Ayesha (Gorie)

Siddiek

Farouk

Razia (Baby)

The first Meers to arrive in South Africa

Mohamed Meer	My grandfather (Ma's father)
Fatima Amin	My grandmother (Ma's mother)

Ismail Meer	My grandfather (Papa's father)
Khatija Variawa	My grandmother (Papa's mother)
Chota Meer	My granduncle and also my father-in-law
Rasool Naroth	My grandaunt and also my mother-in-law

Amina Ma's Family

Charlie Farrel	My great grandfather
Amelia Van Vollenhoven	My great grandmother
Hannah Farrel	My grandmother
Koplan	My grandfather
Wally Bailey	My step grandfather
Cassim/ Lionel Farrel	My maternal uncle

Meer Family

Ahmed Mohamed Variawa	My father's maternal uncle
Ahmed Meer/ Gora Papa	My paternal uncle (also known as A I Meer)
Apa Ma	Wife of Ahmed Meer and also Chota Meer's daughter
Unus	My cousin (their son)
Abassi	My cousin (their son)
Ahmed Meer / Uncle AC	My brother-in-law and also Chota Meer's son
Ismail Meer/ Big Ismail	My husband and also Chota Meer's son (also known as I C Meer)
Hoosen Meer/ Gora Mamoo	My brother-in-law and also Chota Meer's son
Gorie Apa	Wife of Hoosen Meer
Zohra	My cousin (their daughter)
Ayesha/ Choti Khala	My sister-in- law and also Chota Meer's daughter
Essop/ Chota Mamoo	My uncle (Ma's brother)

Cassim Meer	My father's cousin (son of Suleiman/Haloo Meer)
Y C Meer	Son of my father's cousin Cassim Meer
M C Meer	Son of my father's cousin Cassim Meer
Chota Motala	Son of Cassim Meer's sister Fatima

Chronology

Fatima Meer contributed to the struggle against racial rule and apartheid as a public speaker, campaigner, political and community activist and as a public intellectual. She lectured in sociology at the University of Natal from 1956 to 1988.

1928   Fatima Meer is born in Grey Street, Durban South Africa

1932   Starts madressa

1937   Starts school

1942   Attends Durban Indian Girls' High School

1944   Fundraises for the Bengal Famine

1946   Becomes involved in the Passive Resistance Campaign led by the Natal and Transvaal Indian Congresses;

Is one of the founding members of the Students Passive Resistance Committee set up by high school students;

Makes her first speech at a political rally and leads a march alongside leaders of the Campaign

1947   Rejects pressure from her school to stop her political activism and is therefore not allowed to return to school. Writes and passes matric as a private candidate

1948   Enrols for a Bachelor of Social Science at the University of Witwatersrand;

Joins the Non-European Unity Movement (NEUM);

Is involved in fundraising for the student Raising and Giving (RAG) Society

1949   Continues her degree at the non-European section of the University of Natal;

Member of the Student Representative Council and the non-European RAG Committee;

Supports refugees affected by the Durban "Riots";

Starts an adult literacy class for male domestic workers;

Interviews Chief Albert Luthuli for the Guardian newspaper;

Becomes engaged to Ismail Meer

1950   Graduates with a Bachelor of Arts in sociology and psychology

1951   Marries Ismail Meer;

Enrols for honours degree in sociology at the Univeristy of Natal

1952   Co-founds and is secretary of Durban and Districts Women's League with Bertha Mkhize as President

1953   Birth of first child, Shamim;

Starts working as research assistant for Hilda Kuper at the Institute for Community and Family Health

1954   Banned for two years in November 1954 together with husband Ismail and many leaders of the ANC, NIC, TIC and SACP as government attempts to sabotage the Congress of the People planned for June 1955

1955   Birth of second child, Shehnaz

1956   Birth of third child, Rashid;

Husband Ismail is arrested on 5 December with 155 others and stands trial in Johannesburg in the Treason Trial

1958   Husband, Ismail, is released, charges against him are dropped;

The family move to their new home in Burnwood Road, designed by friend and architect Alan Lipman

1960   Husband, Ismail, along with other activists across the country is detained without trial following the Sharpeville Massacre and the declaration of a state of emergency;

Meer helps organise weekly vigils outside the Durban prison, a march of wives and children of the detainees, and a week-long vigil and fast at the Gandhi Settlement in Phoenix, led by Sushila Gandhi

1962   Ismail is listed as a communist along with 101 others cutting him off from political activities and forcing him to resign from all political organisations

1963   Ismail is banned for five years

1969   Fatima publishes her first book, *Portrait of Indian South Africans,* and gives the proceeds from sales towards the building of the Gandhi Museum and Clinic at Phoenix Settlement where she is a member of the board

1970   Travels to India on invitation as visiting lecturer to universities there;

Publishes *Apprenticeship of a Mahatma* on Gandhi's year in South Africa.

1972   Founds the Institute for Black Research (IBR) based at the University of Natal

1973   Visits Mandela in prison;

Founds the Black Women's Federation in Natal

1975   Organises inaugural conference of the Black Women's Federation of South Africa and is the first president;

Founds and heads the Natal Education Trust which raises funds to build schools for Black children;

Presents a scathing attack of the apartheid government at a conference of
the Black Studies Programme.

1976   Is involved in rescue operations for flood victims of Tin Town – a shack
settlement on the banks of Umgeni River and heads the Relief Committee;

Organises a rally with Steve Biko's South Africa Student's Organisation after
the Soweto student uprising in June but outdoor gatherings are banned
and rally does not take place;

Banned for five years in August but allowed to continue teaching;

Detained for close to four months soon after her banning;

Son Rashid and son-in-law Bobby Marie are also detained;

Her book *Race and Suicide* is published

1977   Black Women's Federation together with seventeen other black consciousness organisations is banned;

Son Rashid goes into exile in London;

Charged by state for breaking her banning order;

Assassination attempt in November – her house is petrol bombed and a
family friend shot in the shoulder

1978   Friend and colleague Rick Turner is assassinated at his home in January

1979   Establishes Tembalishe Tutorial College at Gandhi Settlement at Phoenix
training students in typing, screen printing, carpentry, sewing, pottery;

Charged for second time by the State for breaking her banning order;

Organises scholarships for students to the USA and India

1981   Re-banned for five years, her banning order of 1976 having ended

1983   United Democratic Front is launched in South Africa

1984   Visiting lecturer at Swarthmore College in USA;

Researches and publishes *Factory and Family: The Divided Lives of South
Africa's Women Workers*

1985   Flees UDF memorial service for slain struggle activist Victoria Mxenge
in Umlazi with hundreds of others when the meeting is attacked by an
Inkatha impi who kill fifteen people with assegais;

Her home is petrol bombed

1986   Sets up the Natal Education Organisation to address the problem of the
low Black matric pass rate and esablishes the Phambili High School

1987   Her book *The Trial of Andrew Zondo: A Sociological Insight* is published

1988   Retires from her position as Professor of Sociology at the University of
Natal;

Continues to work from the Institute of Black Research offices at the
University and publishes a number of books in the following years;

Publishes a biography on Nelson Mandela – *Higher Than Hope*

1989   Visits Nelson Mandela in prison

1990   Mandela is released from prison;

Visiting lecturer at University of Oregon, USA

1991   Publishes *Black Women Worker*

1992   Forms the Clare Estate Environment Group in response to problems
       faced by shack dwellers in the western areas of Durban;
       Son Rashid returns from exile in London

1993   Founds the Khanyisa School Project – a bridging programme for Black
       children from informal settlements in Springfield and Clare Estate

1994   Appointed to and serves on the board of the South African Broadcasting
       Corporation;
       Member of the National Symbols Commission and the National Anthem
       Commission;
       Serves as adviser to Winnie Mandela, then Deputy Minister of Arts, Cul-
       ture, Science and Technology

1995   Undergoes heart surgery;
       Son Rashid dies in a car accident

1996   Establishes the Khanya Women's Skills Training Centre training 150 Black
       women from shack settlements in sewing, adult literacy, business
       management;
       Writes the script for a movie *The Making of a Mahatma* based on her
       book on Gandhi, directed by Indian Director Shyam Benegal

1999   Founds the Concerned Citizen's Group (CCG) with a group of activists
       challenging the anti-poor policies of the city of Durban;
       Founder member of Jubilee 2000 lobbying to cancel third world debt

2000   Husband Ismail dies in May;
       Starts work on her husband Ismail's autobiography *A Fortunate Man*;
       Starts work on her own autobiography;
       Launches an initiative to establish Resistance Park, a monument to the Pas-
       sive Resistance Campaign on the plot that the resisters occupied in 1946;
       Continues to challenge evictions and water disconnections by eThekwini
       Municipality through CCG

2001   Is a juror at the informal World Court of Women Against War, for Peace
       held in Cape Town, South Africa;
       Founder member of the Durban Social Forum (which brings together
       CCG, the Cape Town Anti-Eviction Campaign, the Anti-Privatisation
       Forum, the Landless People's Movement, Jubilee South Africa, Pales-
       tine Solidarity Committee among others);
       Leads, with Dennis Brutus, a Durban Social Forum march held alongside
       the World Anti-Racism Conference, of more than 10000 against anti-
       poor policies;
       Arranges that Mandela celebrates his birthday at the Chatsworth stadium;
       Launches her book *Prison Diary: One Hundred and Thirteen Days, 1976*

2002   Is a juror on the International Women's Tribunal Against the Blockade
          on Cuba held in Havana Cuba in March;
          Her husband's autobiography *Ismail Meer: A Fortunate Man* is published;
          Resistance Park, a monument to the Passive Resistance Campaign, is
          completed;
          Has a stroke in August which results in paralysis on her left side;
2003   Travels to India to receive the Pravasi Bharatiya Samman Award from the
          Government of India
2004   Attends the World Social Forum in Mumbai, India;
          Serves as a juror on the informal World Court on War as Crime organ-
          ised by the Asian Women's Human Rights Council, El Taller and partner
          organisations alongside the World Social Forum
2006   Resumes work on her autobiography
2007   Delivers the Harold Wolpe Memorial lecture at the University of Natal
2009   Supports stallholders and street traders from the Durban Market and
          Warwick Triangle in their struggle to prevent evictions and the closing
          of the market by the eThekwini Municipality.
2010   Dies in March

Author of numerous books including:

1969   *Portrait of Indian South Africans.* Durban: Avon House.
1970   *Apprenticeship of a Mahatma.* Durban: Phoenix Settlement Trust.
1975   *Black Women.* Durban: University of Natal Press.
1975   *The Ghetto People: A Study of the Effects of Uprooting the Indian People
          of South Africa.* London: Africa Publications Trust.
1976   *Race and Suicide in South Africa.* London: Routledge and Kegan Paul.
1980   *Documents of Indentured Labour.* Durban: Institute for Black Research.
1982   *Apartheid our Picture* (co Author M.D. Mlaba). Durban: Institute for
          Black Research.
1984   *Factory and Family: The Divided Lives of South Africa's Women Workers.*
          Durban: Institute for Black Research.
1985   *Unrest in Natal.* Durban: Institute for Black Research
1987   *The Trial of Andrew Zondo: A Sociological Insight.* Johannesburg: Skota-
          ville Publishers.
1988   *Higher Than Hope "Rolihlahla We Love You"* Nelson Mandela's Biography
          On His 70th Birthday. Johannesburg: Skotaville Publishers.
1989   *Resistance in the Townships* (edited by Fatima Meer). Durban: Madiba
          Publishers.
1989   *Treason Trial.* Durban: Madiba Publishers.
1990   *Mandela: Higher Than Hope: The Biography of Nelson Mandela.* Durban:
          Institute for Black Research.

1991   *Black Woman Worker* (With Sayo Skweyiya et al). Durban: Madiba
        Publishers.

1991   *Monty Speaks: Speeches of Dr. G.M. (Monty) Naicker, 1945-1963.* Dur-
        ban: Madiba Publishers.

1991   *Power of The Powerless: A Study of South Africa's Disenfranchised.* Dur-
        ban: Madiba Publishers.

1993   *The CODESA File: An Institute for Black Research Project.* Durban:
        Madiba Publishers.

1995   *The South African Gandhi.* Durban: Madiba Publishers

2001   *Prison Diary: One Hundred and Thirteen Days, 1976.* Cape Town: Kwela
        Books.

Among her awards received:

1975   Union of South African Journalists Award for her work

1984   Honorary Doctorate from Swarthmore College

1990   Imam Abdullah Haroon Award for the Struggle Against Oppression
        and Racial Discrimination

1994   Vishwa Gurjari Award for Contribution to Human Rights in Ahmeda-
        bad India

1994   Honorary Doctorate from Bennett College

1998   Honorary Doctorate from University of Natal

1999   Among the list of Top 100 Women Who Shook South Africa

2003   Pravasi Bharatiya Samman Award Government of India

2004   Voted 45th in the Top 100 Great South Africans

2007   Honorary Doctorate from Rhodes University

2008   The Ponnady Award from the Tamil Women's Progressive Movement

About the author

FATIMA MEER (1928-2010) is best known as a fearless campaigner against injustice who brought her political activism to her work as a sociologist and writer. She has been described as a courageous, selfless, independent-minded scholar-activist, who was never afraid to speak out.

She became involved in campaigns against apartheid in 1946, when as a seventeen-year-old high school student she co-founded the Students Passive Resistance Committee. In the 1950s she founded the Durban and District Women's League and was a founder member of the Federation of South African Women. She campaigned in the 1960s against group areas removals, and against detention without trial.

Meer taught in the Sociology Department of what was then the University of Natal in Durban for over 30 years. She authored over twenty books, and edited almost twenty others, including biographies of Mahatma Gandhi and Nelson Mandela. She was internationally renowned and taught as a visiting lecturer at Universities in India and the USA.

In 1954 Meer was one of the first South Africans, and the first woman, to be placed under a banning order. A two-year banning order confined her to Durban and prevented her from attending gatherings. She was banned again from 1976 to 1985. In 1976 she was detained without trial for six months. Soon after her release from prison she survived an assassination attempt. In the following years there were two arson attacks on her Durban home.

She continued to campaign against injustice even within the post-1994 democratic South Africa as a leading figure in the Concerned Citizen's Group and in the Durban Social Forum – advancing the rights of communities faced with evictions and disconnections of water and electricity.

Meer was married to fellow political campaigner Ismail Meer and had three children – Shamim, Shehnaz and Rashid. Her son Rashid was also detained for three months in 1976 and banned on his release from prison.

He went into exile in 1977 returning to South Africa in 1992. He died in 1995 in a car accident. Her husband Ismail Meer died in 2000. She is survived by two daughters, Shamim and Shehnaz, and five grandchildren.

Endnotes

Chapter 1

1 Travelling in a large space, like a dormitory, in the stern of the ship, near the steering gear. Conditions were cramped, food was poor and the atmosphere often bad, especially during rough weather when access to the upper deck was restricted.

2 Dada Abdulla, a successful businessman, came to Durban from Porbander, in Gujarat. In 1893 he brought Mohandas Gandhi (who became Mahatma Gandhi), to Durban, to work for his firm Dada Abdulla and Company as their lawyer.

3 The letter appears in The Collected Works of Mahatma Gandhi, Vol 13: 12 March 1913-25 December 1913, page 391 http://www.gandhiashramseva-gram.org/gandhi-literature/mahatma-gandhi-collected-works-volume-13.pdf. The Natal Indian Congress was formed in 1894.

Chapter 3

4 Grey Street is now called Dr Yusuf Dadoo Street.

5 These names have all changed – bearing the names of what could be called a different form of royalty, leaders of the anti-apartheid struggle. Victoria Street is now Bertha Mkhize Street (a former president of the ANC Women's League and long-term community activist and leader), Grey Street is Dr Yusuf Dadoo Street (a congress movement leader and former Chairperson of both the South African Indian Congress and the South African Communist Party) and Queen Street is Denis Hurley Street (a former Archbishop of Durban, chairperson of the South African Catholic Bishop's Conference and outspoken opponent of apartheid).

Chapter 4

6 Pine Street is now Monty Naicker Road.

Chapter 5

7 All white people in those days were classified as 'European' which referred to their race generally and not their origin. Everyone not classified white was called 'non-European' or non-white – defined by what they were not rather than what they were.

Chapter 6

8   Broad Street and Grey Street were an extension of each other and today are together called Dr Yusuf Dadoo Street.

9   West Street is now Dr Pixley KaSeme Street. In early Durban and through the days of apartheid the shops in West Street were predominantly white (European) owned and white run.

10 Chamberlain Nakasa's son, Nat Nakasa, was one of the more well-known journalists in South Africa, renowned for his journalistic courage and integrity.

11 A tickey was a South African three-penny piece. It was replaced by a five-cent coin in 1961 (Collins Dictionary).

12 Russell Street is now Joseph Nduli Street.

13 The Empire Exhibition was held in Johannesburg between September 1936 and January 1937 to celebrate the city's jubilee year – 50 years since gold had been found in the area.

Chapter 7

14 The Malay community in South Africa originate from present day Indonesia and Malaysia, the earliest members being slaves and political prisoners brought by the Dutch East India Company. Under apartheid Malays were a sub-category of the Coloured race.

15 A Coloured school was a school reserved only for children classified as Coloured or mixed race.

16 The first two years of school were then called class one and two. Subsequent classes were called 'standards' – ie standard one (third year at school), standard two and so on.

17 Indians were prohibited from buying properties in Durban which had anti-Asiatic clauses in their title deeds. These clauses were legal measures to exclude Indians from owning or occupying municipal property in Durban.

Chapter 8

18 Home brewing of beer was made illegal by the Native Beer Act of 1908 which gave municipalities in Natal the sole right to brew beer. Regular police raids were conducted to stamp out home brewing of beer.

19 Beatrice Street is now Charlotte Maxeke Street.

20 Now the University of KwaZulu Natal.

21 Field Street is now Joe Slovo Street.

22 Berea Road is now King Dinuzulu Road.

Chapter 7

23 The Anti-Imperial Movement for India's indepence from British rule was led by the Indian National Congress whose leaders included Mahatma Gandhi, Jawaharlal Nehru and Sarojini Naidu.

24 The focus of the Passive Resistance Campaign led by the Natal and Transvaal Indian Congresses in 1946 was the Asiatic Land Tenure and Indian Representation Bill, referred to by Indians as the "Ghetto Bill". This bill was intended to limit the land available to Indians and restrict their franchise, and came on the back of many decades of racist laws.

25 The Passive Resistance Campaign was led by Dr Yusuf Dadoo President of the Transvaal Indian Congress and Dr Monty Naicker President of the Natal Indian Congress. Dr Goonam was one of the main organisers of the Passive Resistance Campaign and one of the few women leaders in that era, campaigning among other things for the right to education for girls.

26 AI Meer, Fatima's paternal uncle Ahmed, who she called Gora Papa, was elected Joint Secretary of the Natal Indian Congress with MD Naidoo in 1945. AI Meer represented South African Indians at the UN with Ashwin Choudhree and Sorabjee Rustomjee in 1947. He was elected General Secretary of the South African Indian Congress an umbrella body of the NIC and TIC, in 1948.

27 Zainab Asvat was one of six women in the first batch of eighteen resisters in the 1946 Passive Resistance Campaign. She went on to become a medical doctor. She was arrested, banned and in the 1960s she went into exile.

28 Zainunnisa "Cissie" Gool represented Cape Town's District Six on the Cape Town City Council from 1938 to 1951. During the 1940s she was president of the Non-European Front and active in a campaign to start passive resistance.

29 Zuleikha Mayet nee Bismillah is a writer and founder of the Women's Cultural Group which publishes the popular cook book *Indian Delights*. She wrote a column for the *Indian Views* from 1956 to 1963 under the pen name Fahmida. In 1944, at the age of eighteen she submitted a letter to editor of the *Indian Views* advocating education for Muslim girls.

Chapter 10

30 Ruth First became a prominent anti-apartheid activist, journalist and scholar. She was a member of the SACP and ANC and a founder member of the South African Congress of Democrats. She was killed by a letter bomb sent by South African government agents in August 1982.

31 Dr Ahmed I Limbada became a prominent activist in the Non-European Unity Movement (NEUM). He went into exile in the 1960s.

32 Edoardo Villa became a noted sculptor.

33 The Non-European Unity Movement (NEUM) was a Trotskyist organisation formed in South Africa in 1943. It aimed to unite Blacks, Coloureds and Indians on a platform of 'non-collaboration' and the use of the boycott.

34 Seymour Papert came to be known as the pioneer of educational computing and an expert on using technology to teach mathematics. For most of his working life he was based at the Massachusetts Institute of Technology in Boston in the USA.

35 Indian South Africans were required by law at the time to obtain permits to
    move from one province of South Africa to another. When an application
    for a permit was turned down, one became a "prohibited person".

36 Flat 13, considered a landmark of the liberation struggle, features in a docu-
    mentary *Flat 13* by Zarina Maharaj and in Nelson Mandela's book *Long Walk
    to Freedom*. Mandela wrote "*(t)he centre of this tight-knit community was
    Ismail's apartment, Flat 13, Kholvad House . . . There we studied, talked . . . and
    it became a kind of headquarters for young freedom fighters. I sometimes slept
    here . . .*" (Page 105, *Long Walk to Freedom*).

37 Anton Lembede was founding president of the African National Congress
    (ANC) Youth League.

    Walter Sisulu served at times as Secretary-General and Deputy President
    of the ANC and was one of the Rivonia Trialists, charged along with Nelson
    Mandela and others, with sabotage and attempting to overthrow the govern-
    ment by violent means.

    Moses Kotane was secretary general of the South African Communist Party
    from 1939 until his death in Moscow in 1978.

    Yusuf Cachalia was a leading figure in the South African Indian Congress
    in the 1940s and 1950s, serving as its secretary.

    Maulvi Cachalia was a leading campaigner in the 1946 Passive Resistance
    Campaign and the 1952 Defiance Campaigns.

    Yusuf Dadoo was President of the Trasnvaal Indian Congress and the South
    African Indian Congress and Chairman of the South African Communist
    Party from 1972 until his death in exile in 1983.

    Ahmed Kathrada left school at age seventeen to work full-time for the
    Transvaal Passive Resistance Council. He was a Rivonia Trialist.

    Bram Fischer was a South African Communist Party leader. He went under-
    ground to support the liberation struggle. He was arrested and sentenced to
    life imprisonment. Released after seven years with failing health, he died two
    weeks later.

    Joe Slovo was a South African Communist Party and ANC leader and leader
    of the ANC's armed wing Umkhonto we Sizwe. On his return from exile in
    1990 he took part in negotiations and in 1994 he was Minister of Housing
    under Mandela's presidency.

38 For more information on this period see Fatima Meer, *Indian South Africans –
    the struggle to be South African,* 2000 available on https://www.nelsonmandela.
    org/omalley/index.php/site/q/03lv02424/04lv03275/05lv03336/06lv03344/
    07lv03346.htm

39 Chief Albert Luthuli was President of the ANC from December 1952 until 1967.
    In 1960 he was awarded the Nobel Peace Prize – becoming Africa's first laureate.

40 Phillip Tobias became a medical doctor and renowned paleoanthropologist
    best known for his work at South Africa's hominid fossil sites.

Chapter 11

41 The Congress of Democrats was a grouping of the white left (liberals and socialists). It was part of the Congress alliance together with the ANC and the South African Indian Congress.

42 Eli Weinberg was a member of the South African Communist Party, a trade unionist and a photographer. In the 1960s he served a term of imprisonment and was under house arrest.

Chapter 12

43 West Street is now Dr Pixley KaSeme Street.

44 Devi Bughwan was the first South African Indian woman to receive an MA degree in English in 1949. She became professor of Speech and Drama at the Univeristy of Durban Westville from 1975 to 1985.

Denis Bughwan was a well known photographer and owner of Crown Studios.

Debi Singh was a NIC activist, secretary of the 1946 Passive Resistance Council and among those charged for treason in 1956.

Cassim Amra was prominent in the Natal Indian Congress, served terms of imprisonment and bannings and was also a superb photographer.

Hilda Kuper was a social anthropologist, and co-founder of the Liberal Party of South Africa in 1953.

Leo Kuper was a sociologist and co-founder of the Liberal Party of South Africa in 1953.

Violaine Junod was a member of the Liberal Party. In November 1956 she and Ida Shange led a march in Pietermartizburg of 600 women against passes.

45 The municipal beer halls had the monopoly of brewing beer and selling beer to Black people. Revenue from sales of beer was used to fund the Durban System of control over the movement of Black people.

46 The notorious pass system in South Africa was designed to control the movement of Black People. In 1952 laws were made more rigid requiring all Black males to carry a "reference book" or face arrest and fines.

47 Amaboere is slang for the apartheid government or police. Literally it means 'the farmers'.

Chapter 13

48 The research Fatima Meer conducted in Newlands contributed to the book by Hilda Kuper, *Indian People in Natal,* Natal University Press, 1960.

49 The Treason Trial was a trial in which 156 people, including Nelson Mandela, were arrested and accused of treason in South Africa in 1956. The main trial lasted until 1961, when all of the defendants were found not guilty.

Chapter 14

50 Leo Kuper, *Passive Resistance in South Africa,* New Haven, Yale University Press, 1957.

Chapter 15

51 Smith Street is now Anton Lembede Street.

Chapter 16

52 This is an edited version of a chapter which first appeared in *Prison Diary: One Hundred and Thirteen Days 1976* by Fatima Meer, Kwela Books, 2001.

53 Owen Horwood was Minister of Tourism and Indian Affairs in 1972, Minister of Trade and Industry in 1974, and Minister of Finance from 1975-1984. He was the leader of the National Party in Natal from 1972–1984.

Chapter 17

54 Parts of this chapter are taken from *Prison Diary: One Hundred and Thirteen Days 1976* by Fatima Meer, Kwela Books, 2001.

55 On the morning of 16 June 1976 pupils from schools in the Soweto township outside Johannesburg began marching to protest against the enforced introduction of Afrikaans as a medium of instruction and against bantu education (inferior education for Black students). Police shot into the crowd of pupils, killing two of them on that day. This sparked a massive uprising that spread across the country over the next few months.

56 Fatima Meer was banned three times under the Suppression of Communism Act spending a total of twelve years of her life under such orders. She was first banned in 1955 for two years. In 1976 she was banned for five years and again in 1981 for another five years.

57 Fatima Meer founded the Institute for Black Research in 1972. It became the leading Black-led research institute and publishing house in South Africa.

58 Only one issue of *Africa Survey* was ever published.

59 George Sithole and David Gasa were active in the Umlazi Residents Association and were UDF activists. Jeannie Noel was active in community struggles in Sydenham and in the ANC underground.

60 Rick Turner was a philosophy lecturer best known for his book *The Eye of the Needle.* He was banned in 1973 and assassinated in 1978.

Chapter 18

61 This chapter covers Fatima Meer's activism against injustice both before and after the first democratic elections in South Africa in 1994.

62 Inkatha was established by Chief Gatsha Buthelezi as a cultural liberation

movement. In the 1980s, as opposition to the apartheid regime grew, Buthelezi tried to forcefully suppress student and community opposition. This led to open clashes with the UDF and its affiliates. The Truth and Reconciliation Commission allege that Buthelezi worked secretly with the police, security police and state-sponsored assassination squads.